Collins

Livemocha ACTIVE ITALIAN

HarperCollins Publishers
77–85 Fulham Palace Road
London W6 8JB
Great Britain

www.collinslanguage.com

First edition 2011

Reprint 10 9 8 7 6 5 4 3 2 1 0
© HarperCollins Publishers 2011

ISBN (UK edition) 978-0-00-737353-6
ISBN (export edition) 978-0-00-741980-7
ISBN (US edition) 978-0-87779-557-5

Collins® is a registered trademark of HarperCollins Publishers Limited

A catalogue record for this book is available from the British Library

Typeset by Macmillan Publishing Services

Audio material recorded and produced by Networks SRL, Milan

Printed and Bound in China by Leo Paper Products Ltd.
Series Editor: Rob Scriven

All rights reserved. No part of this publication may be reproduced, stored in a retrieval system or transmitted, in any form or by any means, electronic, mechanical, photocopying, recording or otherwise, without the prior permission of the publisher. This book is sold subject to the conditions that it shall not, by way of trade or otherwise, be lent, re-sold, hired out or otherwise circulated without the publisher's prior consent in any form of binding or cover other than that in which it is published and without a similar condition including this condition being imposed on the subsequent purchaser.

HarperCollins does not warrant that the functions contained in **www.livemocha.com** content will be interrruption- or error-free, that defects will be corrected, or that **www.livemocha.com** or the server that makes it available are free of viruses or bugs. HarperCollins is not responsible for any access difficulties that may be experienced due to problems with network, web, online or mobile phone connections.

INTRODUCTION 4

UNIT 1
Lesson 1: A chance meeting 8
Lesson 2: Having a drink together 18

UNIT 2
Lesson 1: A chance meeting at the elevator 28
Lesson 2: Ordering drinks 40

UNIT 3
Lesson 1: Where are the stores? 50
Lesson 2: Bus or subway? 60

UNIT 4
Lesson 1: Where shall we eat? 74
Lesson 2: Reserving a table 84

UNIT 5
Lesson 1: Plans for the week 94
Lesson 2: Plans for next week 103

UNIT 6
Lesson 1: Dinner at a friend's 112
Lesson 2: Finishing dinner 122

INTRODUCTION

Welcome to your Livemocha Active Italian experience! This new course goes above and beyond what a traditional book-based course can offer. With its focus on online learning, Active Italian provides the opportunity not just to study but to experience the language for yourself by interacting with native speakers online.

Why go online?
Studying a language online allows you to learn in a more natural atmosphere – watching people interact in a **video** is far more lifelike than listening to conversations on a CD. After watching a video dialog, you will be walked through an explanation of some of the **grammar** and **vocabulary** items that were introduced in the new dialog. Then, by completing a variety of **interactive quizzes**, the system will instantly be able to tell you how well you are doing. You can then **talk online** with native Italian speakers to practice what you've learned.

Who else is online?
Livemocha boasts over 7 million members and is growing every day. These members are online for the same reason as you – to learn and experience a new language. Native Italian-speaking members will be happy to read through your written and spoken submissions and to give you feedback on how you're doing. You can also connect with people who want to chat in any given language – interaction on an informal, nonacademic basis is an ideal way for you to perfect your language skills.

What do the books do?
The four accompanying books are designed to complement the online course – the dialogs for all of the videos that you can watch online are available here for you to study whenever you don't have access to the Internet. You will also find all of the Grammar and Vocabulary sections explained in the books, plus the culture notes to teach you a little about Italy.

LEVEL 1

This book is the first of four. It corresponds with Level 1 of the online course.

Level 1 is ideal for students who are newcomers to the language or for those who need to start from the basics.

What you will learn
- How to talk about yourself and what you do
- How to make plans, understand suggestions and accept invitations
- How to form and use questions, negatives, articles, adjectives, and more
- How to form the present tense and to use verbs to say what you want to do, should do, or know how to do
- Vocabulary for numbers, the alphabet, jobs, food and drink, transport, time and days of the week

 Every time you see this coffee cup symbol in these books, it indicates the presence of a pathway – a guide to exactly where you can find that particular piece of content online. Log on at www.livemocha.com and follow the path to find the online version of what you are studying in the book.

Video Dialog

As they finish their drinks, Michele and the waiter give Giulia directions to some local stores.

 Active Italian: Level 1 > Unit 3 > Lesson 1 > Video dialog

Active Italian *Level 1*

1

Lesson 1: A chance meeting

- » Different ways to say "Hello": ***Buongiorno! Salve!***
- » How to say "Excuse me!": ***Scusi!***
- » How to introduce yourself: ***Mi chiamo...***
- » How to say where you are from: ***Sono di...***
- » How to say what nationality you are: ***Sono americano/a.***

Lesson 2: Having a drink together

- » How to say what you would like: ***Vorrei...***
- » How to say what you do: ***Sono fotografo/a.***
- » Subject pronouns: ***io, tu, lui, lei,*** etc.
- » How to say where you work/study: ***Lavoro a Roma.***

Collins | **Livemocha™**

UNIT 1 › LESSON 1
A chance meeting

Culture note

As well as in Italy, Italian is also spoken by over 500,000 people in the southern part of Switzerland, mainly in the area known as Canton Ticino. According to recent figures, there are 66.5 million speakers of Italian in the world, 60 million of whom live in Italy. But there are as many as 120 million people of Italian origin throughout the world!

Unit 1 › Lesson 1: *A chance meeting*

1.1

Video Dialog

Michele and Giulia run into one another and strike up a conversation.

Watch the video dialog online at
Active Italian: Level 1 > Unit 1 > Lesson 1 > Video dialog

Michele: *Oh, mi scusi!*

Giulia: *Prego!*

Michele: *Salve, io mi chiamo Michele. E lei, come si chiama?*

Giulia: *Buongiorno, io sono Giulia.*

Michele: *Lei è italiana?*

Giulia: *No, sono svizzera. Sono di Lugano, e lei?*

Michele: *Io sono italiano. Sono di Genova. Prende un caffè?*

Giulia: *Grazie, volentieri.*

....

Michele: Oh, sorry!
Giulia: Don't mention it.
Michele: Hello, I'm Michele. And you? What's your name?
Giulia: Hello, I'm Giulia.
Michele: Are you Italian?
Giulia: No, I'm Swiss. I'm from Lugano, and you?
Michele: I'm Italian. I'm from Genoa. Would you like a coffee?
Giulia: Thanks, I'd like that.

Livemocha™ Active Italian *Level 1*

Grammar

In this section we go over some of the grammar points introduced in the dialog.

 Go to Active Italian: Level 1 > Unit 1 > Lesson 1 > Grammar to listen to these explanations and to access some interactive practice activities.

1 › | Saying hello and goodbye

Michele says *salve* and Giulia says *buongiorno*: Both mean "hello."

Buongiorno literally means "Good day" and is used in Italy for a great part of the day so it covers "good morning" and "good afternoon." *Buongiorno* is what you should use with a storekeeper, receptionist, waiter, etc.

Salve is a useful option for "hello" and can be used all day with anyone, for example someone walking towards you on a hiking path.

Another word you may be familiar with is *ciao!* This means both "hi" and "bye" and is used among friends and with children. You wouldn't use *ciao* with someone you don't know.

Unit 1 › Lesson 1: *A chance meeting*

2 › Excuse me!

If you bump into someone you can say:

> *Oh, mi scusi!*

Or simply:

> *Scusi!*

You can also use *Scusi* to get someone's attention, perhaps to ask the waiter for a coffee. Remember to add *per favore* (please).

> *Scusi! Un caffè per favore.*
> Excuse me! A coffee, please.

3 › Different types of "you"

In Italian, there are two ways of addressing someone: You should use the formal *lei* form with someone you don't know well or someone who is older than you. You should use the more familiar *tu* form when talking to a friend or a child.

Michele and Giulia have only just met so they are still using *lei* with each other.

When he invites her for a coffee, he says:

Prende un caffè?

If they knew each other better, he might use the *tu* form:

Prendi un caffè?

Note how the verb ending is the only thing indicating which form is being used.

4 ›   Not at all!

Prego is a useful word. As well as meaning "Not at all!" it also means "Don't mention it!" or "You're welcome!" It is the standard reply after *grazie* (thank you).

Grazie!
Prego!

Unit 1 › Lesson 1: *A chance meeting* **1.1**

5 › Asking someone their name

If you want to ask someone their name, you say:

> *Come si chiama?*
> What's your name?

If you were using the familiar *tu* form, you would say:

> *Come ti chiami?*

6 › Masculine and feminine endings

To say what nationality you are, you say:

Sono (I am) followed by the nationality.

Giulia says *sono svizzera* and Michele says *sono italiano*.

If it were the other way round, Giulia would say *sono italian**a*** and Michele would say *sono svizzer**o***, changing the endings to match their genders – masculine and feminine. The most common masculine ending in Italian is *-o*, and *-a* is the most common feminine ending.

Nationalities 1

Here is a selection of nationalities. First the masculine and then the feminine:

americano – americana	American
australiano – australiana	Australian
italiano – italiana	Italian
spagnolo – spagnola	Spanish
svizzero – svizzera	Swiss

Note that in Italian nationalities aren't written with a capital letter.

Nationalities 2

The *-o* and *-a* endings don't always apply. The other standard ending is *-e,* which can be either masculine or feminine, such as *ingles**e*** (English). If Michele and Giulia were both English, each would say *sono inglese*.

The following nationalities are the same for both masculine and feminine:

canadese	Canadian
francese	French
inglese	English
cinese	Chinese
giapponese	Japanese

Culture note

Italian people tend to be quite formal. When you are introduced to someone for the first time you should shake hands.

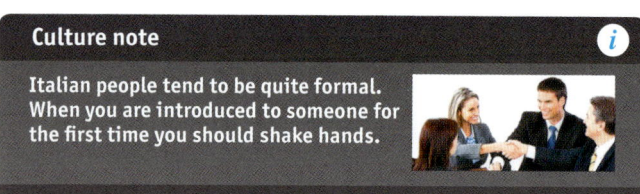

9 › Where are you from?

To say what city or town you are from, you say *Sono di...* (I'm from).

Giulia says she is from Lugano – *Sono di Lugano*, and Michele says that he is from Genoa – *Sono di Genova*.

Did you notice how Genoa is *Genova* in Italian? Most names of towns are the same – although they might be pronounced slightly differently.

> *Sono di New York.*
> *Sono di Washington.*
> *Sono di Toronto.*

Some are very similar:

Milano	Milan
Roma	Rome
Napoli	Naples

And some are very different:

Londra	London
Parigi	Paris
Firenze	Florence

Livemocha™ Active Italian *Level 1*

Vocabulary

In this section you will learn some useful words and expressions from the dialog.

Go to Active Italian: Level 1 > Unit 1 > Lesson 1 > Vocabulary to listen to each of the words being pronounced and to access some interactive practice activities.

buono/a
good, tasty

La pizza è buona in Italia.
The pizza is good in Italy.

il gelato
ice cream

Il gelato è buono in Italia.
The ice cream is good in Italy.

il formaggio
cheese

Il formaggio è buono in Francia.
The cheese is tasty in France.

bello/a
lovely, beautiful

Il Messico è bello.
Mexico is lovely.

Unit 1 › Lesson 1: *A chance meeting*

1.1

il tempo
weather

Il tempo è bello in Italia.
The weather is lovely in Italy.

in Svizzera
in Switzerland

Sara studia in Svizzera.
Sara studies in Switzerland.

negli Stati Uniti
in the United States

New York è negli Stati Uniti.
New York is in the United States.

in Inghilterra
in England

Londra è in Inghilterra.
London is in England.

del Giappone
of Japan

Tokyo è la capitale del Giappone.
Tokyo is the capital of Japan.

in Australia
in Australia

Sydney è in Australia.
Sydney is in Australia.

UNIT 1 › LESSON 2

Having a drink together

Culture note

Italians drink more coffee than tea. Espresso and cappuccino are just two of the many options. If you ask for *un caffè* in Italy, you will be served an espresso, often just a sip or two of very strong coffee.

Tea is also drunk but usually with lemon rather than milk and many people favor herbal teas for their medicinal properties. A cup of herbal tea is called *una tisane*.

Unit 1 › Lesson 2: *Having a drink together*

Video Dialog

Michele and Giulia sit down for a coffee and get to know one another a little better.

 Active Italian: Level 1 > Unit 1 > Lesson 2 > Video dialog

Waiter:	*Buongiorno, signori. Prego, dite pure.*
Michele:	*Buongiorno. Un caffè e… vuole un caffè?*
Giulia:	*No, vorrei un tè, per favore.*
Waiter:	*Un tè al latte o al limone?*
Giulia:	*Al limone, per favore. Che lavoro fa?*
Michele:	*Sono fotografo. Lavoro a Roma. E lei?*
Giulia:	*Io sono studentessa. Faccio uno stage a Roma.*
Waiter:	*Ecco. Un tè e un caffè.*

Waiter:	Good morning. What can I get you?
Michele:	Good morning. Coffee and… do you want coffee?
Giulia:	No, I'd like tea, please.
Waiter:	Tea with milk or tea with lemon?
Giulia:	With lemon, please. What do you do?
Michele:	I'm a photographer. I work in Rome. And you?
Giulia:	I'm a student. I'm doing an internship in Rome.
Waiter:	Here you are. A tea and a coffee.

Livemocha™ Active Italian *Level 1*

Grammar

 Active Italian: Level 1 > Unit 1 > Lesson 2 > Grammar

1 › **Saying what you would like**

To ask for something, use *vorrei* (I'd like). It is a polite way of asking for something.

> *Vorrei un cappuccino.*
> I'd like a cappuccino.
>
> *Vorrei una pizza.*
> I'd like a pizza.

2 › **Subject pronouns**

Subject pronouns in Italian are:

io	I
tu	familiar you
lei	formal you
lui	he
lei	she
noi	we
voi	you, when referring to more than one person
loro	they

Unit 1 › Lesson 2: *Having a drink together*

Because verb endings make it clear who is carrying out the action, subject pronouns tend not to be used much in Italian.

3 › *Lavorare* (to work): An example of an *-are* verb

Michele says *lavoro a Roma* (I work in Rome). The verb *lavorare* (to work) and many other verbs that end in *-are* follow a set pattern. Remember how we said that endings are important for understanding Italian?

*lavor**o***	I work
*lavor**i***	you (*familiar*) work
*lavor**a***	he/she/it works
*lavor**a***	you (*formal*) work
*lavor**iamo***	we work
*lavor**ate***	you (*plural*) work
*lavor**ano***	they work

Remember, subject pronouns tend not to be used in Italian unless there is some confusion about who is doing the action or for emphasis.

4 › Saying what you do (1)

When saying what you do for a living, you use *sono* (I am) followed by your profession or occupation. There is no need to add the article "a" before saying what you do.

The word describing your profession has to reflect whether you are a man or a woman.

A male photographer would say *sono fotograf**o***.

A female photographer would say *sono fotograf**a***.

Other occupations which follow this pattern are:

commesso/a	store clerk
impiegato/a	office worker
segretario/a	secretary

5 › Saying what you do (2)

Some words for jobs which end in *-e* also have feminine forms that end in *-a*. These include:

cameriere/cameriera	waiter/waitress
infermiere/infermiera	nurse
parrucchiere/parrucchiera	hairdresser

6 › Saying what you do (3)

Some occupations have a different ending altogether for females:

attore/attrice	actor/actress
direttore/direttrice	director or manager
dottore/dottoressa	doctor (both academic and medical)
studente/studentessa	student
traduttore/traduttrice	translator

7 › Saying what you do (4)

Some words for jobs are the same for men and women.

agente	agent
insegnante	teacher
rappresentante	representative

Some jobs end in *-o* but are the same for men and women:

medico	medical doctor
avvocato	lawyer

And some end in *-ista* and apply to both men and women:

artista	artist
dentista	dentist
giornalista	journalist

8 › Saying where you work or study

To say in which town, city or village you work, study or live, use *a* before the name of it.

*Lavoro **a** Roma.*	I work in Rome.
*Lavoro **a** New York.*	I work in New York.
*Studio **a** Parigi.*	I study in Paris.

Vocabulary

 Active Italian: Level 1 > Unit 1 > Lesson 2 > Vocabulary

a scuola
at a school

L'insegnante lavora a scuola.
The teacher works at a school.

in azienda
in a company

La segretaria lavora in azienda.
The secretary works in a company.

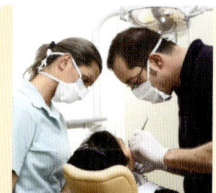

in ambulatorio
at a dental practice

Il dentista lavora in ambulatorio.
The dentist works in a dental practice.

in questura
in a police station

L'agente di polizia lavora in questura.
The police officer works in a police station.

Unit 1 › Lesson 2: *Having a drink together*

in ospedale
in a hospital

L'infermiera lavora in ospedale.
The nurse works in a hospital.

a teatro
in a theater

L'attore lavora a teatro.
The actor works in a theater.

in un ristorante
in a restaurant

Il cameriere lavora in un ristorante.
The waiter works in a restaurant.

in negozio
in a store

La commessa lavora in negozio.
The store clerk works in a store.

all'università
at the university

La studentessa studia all'università.
The student studies at the university.

Active Italian *Level 1*

2

Lesson 1: A chance meeting at the elevator

- » Further greetings: ***Buona sera***, ***Buona notte.***
- » Asking how someone feels and the reply: ***Come sta?***
- » The articles ***il***, ***la***, ***l'***, and ***lo***.
- » Typical noun endings for masculine and feminine words.
- » Adding ***-issimo*** to words.
- » How to say "Let's…": ***Andiamo!*** (Let's go!)

Lesson 2: Ordering drinks

- » How to ask for something: ***Un cappuccino***, ***un caffè***, etc.
- » About indefinite articles: ***Un***, ***una***, etc.
- » Different types of drinks.
- » Different ways of saying goodbye: ***Arrivederci, a più tardi.***
- » How to say it's for me, for you, etc: ***Per me***, ***per te***, etc.

UNIT 2 › LESSON 1
A chance meeting at the elevator

Culture note

Italians are generally more physical when they greet each other: people who know each other well, particularly women and young people, often kiss each other on both cheeks when they meet. Men tend to shake hands although you will sometimes see family members and close friends greeting one another with a kiss on both cheeks.

However, this tradition does vary, and in some regions you may find that it is customary to kiss on just one cheek, or to kiss three times on alternate cheeks.

Unit 2 › Lesson 1: *A chance meeting at the elevator*

2.1

Video Dialog

Three neighbours run into one another one morning by the elevator.

Watch the video dialog online at
Active Italian: Level 1 > *Unit 2* > *Lesson 1* > *Video dialog*

Ugo:	*Buongiorno, Lucia.*
Lucia:	*Ciao, Ugo.*
Ugo:	*Come va?*
Lucia:	*Benissimo, grazie, e tu?*
Ugo:	*Anch'io, grazie… L'ascensore è guasto.*
Lucia:	*Di nuovo? È sempre guasto… Buongiorno, signora Duranti.*
Sig.ra Duranti:	*Buongiorno, Lucia.*
Lucia:	*Come sta?*
Sig.ra Duranti:	*Bene, grazie. Buongiorno, signor Borgetti. Come sta?*
Ugo:	*Bene, grazie.*
Lucia:	*L'ascensore è guasto…*
Ugo:	*Vuoi un caffè? Offro io.*
Lucia:	*Sì, grazie, molto volentieri.*
Ugo:	*Andiamo al bar di fronte.*

Ugo:	Hello, Lucia.
Lucia	Hi, Ugo.
Ugo:	How are things?
Lucia	Very good, thanks, and you?
Ugo:	Me too, thanks... The elevator's broken.
Lucia:	Again? It's always broken... Good morning, Mrs. Duranti.
Mrs. Duranti:	Good morning, Lucia.
Lucia:	How are you?
Mrs. Duranti:	I'm well, thank you. Good morning, Mr. Borgetti. How are you?
Ugo:	Fine, thanks.
Lucia:	The elevator is broken...
Ugo:	Would you like a coffee? It's on me.
Lucia:	Yes, thanks, I'd like that.
Ugo:	Let's go to the bar across the road.

Grammar

 Active Italian: Level 1 > Unit 2 > Lesson 1 > Grammar

1 › **Good evening and goodnight!**

In the evening you use *Buona sera* (good evening). *Buona* means good. *La sera* is the evening.

> *Buona sera, signora Bianchi!*
> *Buona sera, Max!*

Later at night (after 10 p.m.) you say *Buona notte* (good night). *La notte* is the night.

Unit 2 › Lesson 1: *A chance meeting at the elevator*

2.1

Buona notte, mamma!
Buona notte, Valentina!

2 › Articles – *il* and *la*

The Italian words *il* and *la* correspond to "the" in English and are known as definite articles. They are important in Italian, as they tell you about the noun they are linked to.

All nouns (day, night, pizza, bar, Lucia) are either masculine or feminine in Italian. It's not just people!

If the ending hasn't already told you whether a word is masculine or feminine, then the article will help.

Il goes with a masculine noun: ***il** cappuccino*
La goes with a feminine noun: ***la** pizza*

If the noun ends in *-e*, then it could be either masculine or feminine:

*la nott**e***	the night
*il pan**e***	the bread

31

3 › ### Article – *l'*

When a noun starts with a vowel (*a, e, i, o* and *u*), both *il* and *la* become *l'*:

l'amico	the male friend
l'amica	the female friend

When a noun that starts with a vowel ends in *-e* as it does with *ascensore*, it's more difficult to work out whether the word is masculine or feminine.

4 › ### Article – *lo*

lo is another masculine article that also means "the." It is used when the noun it goes with starts with the following letters:

z

lo zio	the uncle
lo zoo	the zoo
lo zucchero	the sugar

s followed by a consonant such as *sc, sp, st*

lo sconto	the discount
lo sport	the sport
lo stadio	the stadium

gn

lo gnocco
the dumpling

pn

lo pneumatico
the tire

ps

lo psicologo
the psychologist

y

lo yogurt
the yogurt

5 › Noun endings – masculine

Typical masculine endings include:

-o

> *il cappuccino, l'amico*

-ore

l'attore	actor
il dottore	doctor
il colore	color
l'ascensore	elevator

Most words borrowed from other languages are masculine:

> *il bar, il computer, l'euro*

6 › Noun endings – feminine

Typical feminine endings include:

-a

| *la pizza* | the pizza |
| *l'amica* | the friend |

-trice and *-essa*

*l'att**rice***	actress
*la dotto**ressa***	doctor

-ione

*la staz**ione***	train station
*la tradiz**ione***	tradition

-tà

*la cit**tà***	city
*l'universi**tà***	university

7 › How are you?

Come va? means "How is it going?"

A more formal way of asking someone how they are is *Come sta?*

> ### *Come sta, Signor Rossi?*
> How are you, Mr. Rossi?

And if you are asking a friend how they are:

> ### *Come stai, Angela?*
> How are you, Angela?

8 › Feeling fine

The standard answer to *Come sta?* or *Come stai?* is:

> *Bene, grazie.*
> Fine, thanks.

And if you are feeling great:

> *Benissimo, grazie.*
> Very well, thanks.

9 › Adding *-issimo* to words

Adding *-issimo* to a word is like putting "very" in front of it: *Bene* is "well" but *benissimo* is "very well."

You might want to say that you are not well: *Male*. And if you really aren't well: *Malissimo*.

> *Come stai, Max? Malissimo.*
> How are you, Max? Very bad!

Unit 2 › Lesson 1: *A chance meeting at the elevator*

2.1

10 › *Andiamo* (let's go)

Ugo suggests to Lucia that they go to the bar for a coffee.

He says *andiamo al bar?*

Andiamo means "we go" but this is the form you use when you want to make a suggestion to someone or to a group of people:

Andiamo al ristorante.	Let's go to the restaurant.
Andiamo al cinema.	Let's go to the movie theater.

 ## *Vocabulary*

Active Italian: Level 1 > Unit 2 > Lesson 1 > Vocabulary

vado
I'm going

Vado al bar.
I'm going to the bar.

37

Dove?
Where?

Dove vai?
Where are you going?

Dov'è?
Where is?

Dov'è il ristorante?
Where is the restaurant?

Quando?
When?

Quando vai al cinema?
When are you going to the movies?

stasera
this evening

Stasera vado al ristorante.
This evening I am going to the restaurant.

il pomeriggio
afternoon

Oggi pomeriggio vado al cinema.
This afternoon I am going to the movies.

Unit 2 › Lesson 1: *A chance meeting at the elevator*

2.1

venire
to come

Vuoi venire?
Do you want to come?

insieme
together

Andiamo insieme?
Shall we go together?

Culture note

Signora and *Signore* are equivalent to "Madam" and "Sir." Used with a last name, they correspond to "Mr." and "Mrs." or "Ms."

Signora Duranti
Signor Duranti

Notice how the final letter e is dropped from *Signore* when used with a last name.

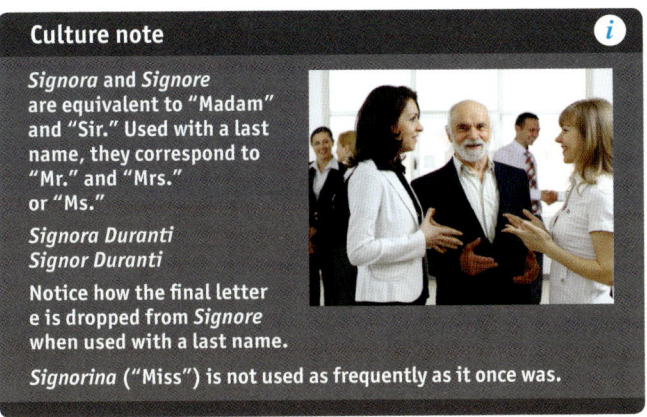

Signorina ("Miss") is not used as frequently as it once was.

UNIT 2 › LESSON 2
Ordering drinks

Culture note

In Italy, a cappuccino (*un cappuccino*, although you may also hear *un cappuccio*, an informal short form) is only ordered in the morning, whereas espresso (*un caffè*) is drunk at any time of the day. The word *macchiato* (literally "stained") means with a drop of milk. So an espresso with a drop of milk is *un caffè macchiato* or you can just say *un macchiato*.

Be aware that if you order a *latte* in an Italian bar, there's a good chance you'll get an odd look and just a glass of warm milk! If you want a milky coffee, you will have to order a *latte macchiato* (literally "stained milk"). You may also come across *un macchiatone* on the menu, which is halfway between *un caffè macchiato* and *un cappuccino*.

Unit 2 › Lesson 2: *Ordering drinks*

Video Dialog

Ugo and Lucia go for a coffee.

Active Italian: Level 1 > Unit 2 > Lesson 2 > Video dialog

Ugo:	*Buongiorno.*
Waiter:	*Buongiorno, signori. Prego, dite pure.*
Ugo:	*Per me un caffè.*
Lucia:	*E per me un cappuccino, per favore.*
Ugo:	*Ha delle brioche?*
Waiter:	*Certo.*
Ugo:	*Vuoi una brioche, Lucia?*
Lucia:	*No, grazie.*
Ugo:	*Allora un caffè, un cappuccino e una brioche.*
Waiter:	*È tutto?*
Ugo:	*Sì, grazie.*
Lucia:	*Grazie del caffè. Buona giornata!*
Ugo:	*Ciao, Lucia. A più tardi.*

Ugo:	Hello.
Waiter:	Hello. What can I get you?
Ugo:	An espresso for me.
Lucia:	And a cappuccino for me, please.
Ugo:	Have you got any croissants?
Waiter:	Of course.
Ugo:	Do you want a croissant, Lucia?

Lucia:	No, thanks.
Ugo:	So that's an espresso, a cappuccino and a croissant.
Waiter:	Is that everything?
Ugo:	Yes, thanks.
Lucia:	Thanks for the coffee. Have a good day!
Ugo:	Bye, Lucia. See you later.

Grammar

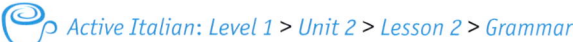

Active Italian: Level 1 > Unit 2 > Lesson 2 > Grammar

1 › **Buongiorno, signori**

It is normal for a stranger or someone you don't know very well to say *Buongiorno* or *Buongiorno, signora*. If you are in a group of people you will probably be greeted with *Buongiorno, signori*. The ending of *signori* tells you that more than one person is being greeted.

> waiter: *Buongiorno, signori.*

Unit 2 › Lesson 2: *Ordering drinks*

2 › Taking your order

> *Prego, dite pure?*
> What can I get you?

Dite pure literally means "Tell me!" The waiter is asking for your order.

Another phrase you will come across is:

> *Cosa vi porto?*
> What can I bring you?

3 › A..., please

Saying what you want is simple – just use the word *un* or *una* meaning "one" or "a" as in "a coffee," plus the item you want.

Un is the word you use with masculine things. So instead of saying *il caffè* (the coffee) you say *un caffè* (a coffee).

Una is the word you use with feminine things. So instead of saying *la pizza* you say *una pizza*.

Most coffee drinks are masculine:

> **un** *caffè*
> **un** *espresso*
> **un** *cappuccino*

Some feminine drinks include:

una birra	a beer
una cioccolata calda	a hot chocolate
un'acqua minerale	a mineral water

4 › Indefinite articles: *un, una, un', uno*

Un and *una* are known as indefinite articles. *Una* shortens to *un'* in front of words that begin with a vowel:

un'aranciata	an orange soda

Note that the indefinite article for *lo* is *uno:*

uno yogurt	a yogurt

5 › Who is the coffee for?

Per means "for."

per me	for me
per te	for you
per lei	for you (formal), for her
per lui	for him
per noi	for us
per voi	for you (plural)
per loro	for them

So if you are ordering a coffee yourself and a beer for a male friend, you would say:

Per me un espresso e per lui una birra.

6 › Saying goodbye

Arrivederci is the classic word for "goodbye" and literally means "until we see each other again."

People often use *A più tardi* or *A dopo* and both mean "See you later."

If you're planning to meet the next day, you can say:

A domani.
See you tomorrow.

7 › Have a good day!

Buona giornata means "Have a good day." You will also hear the expression *Buona serata* – "Have a good evening."

Vocabulary

 Active Italian: Level 1 > Unit 2 > Lesson 2 > Vocabulary

un caffelatte
a cafe au lait

Un espresso o un caffelatte?
An espresso or a cafe au lait?

un caffè americano
a black coffee

Vorrei un caffè americano.
I'd like a black coffee.

un latte macchiato
a latte

Prendo un latte macchiato.
I'll have a latte.

un decaffeinato
a decaf coffee

Preferisco un decaffeinato.
I prefer a decaf coffee.

due cappuccini
two cappuccinos

Vorremmo due cappuccini.
We'd like two cappuccinos.

Unit 2 › Lesson 2: *Ordering drinks* — 2.2

un succo d'arancia
an orange juice

Vorrei un succo d'arancia.
I'd like an orange juice.

un'acqua minerale
a mineral water

Una bottiglia d'acqua minerale, per favore.
A bottle of mineral water, please.

il ghiaccio
ice

Con o senza ghiaccio?
With or without ice?

Active Italian *Level 1*

3

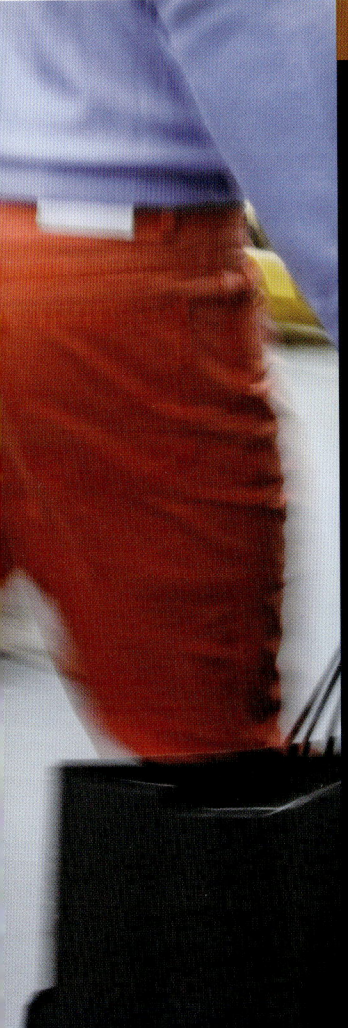

Lesson 1: Where are the stores?

- » How to ask where things are: ***Dove?***
- » How to say you have to do something: ***Dovere fare...***
- » How to say "There is" and "There are": ***C'è*** and ***Ci sono***.
- » How to make nouns plural.
- » How to ask if something is nearby or far: ***Vicino / lontano***.
- » Means of transportation: ***A piedi / in macchina***.

Lesson 2: Bus or subway?

- » How to say you don't know: ***Non lo so***.
- » How to use the verb ***prendere***.
- » How to say something is more... (fast): ***È più... (veloce)***.
- » Numbers 1–10.
- » Basic foods

Collins | **Livemocha™**

UNIT 3 › LESSON 1

Where are the stores?

Culture note

A *libreria* is a bookstore. Do not confuse it with library, which is *biblioteca* in Italian. The bookstores in Italy sell a mix of original Italian texts and foreign texts translated into Italian. In the larger towns and cities you will also find some bookstores selling books in English and other languages.

Unit 3 › Lesson 1: *Where are the stores?*

Video Dialog

As they finish their drinks, Michele and the waiter give Giulia directions to some local stores.

Active Italian: Level 1 > Unit 3 > Lesson 1 > Video dialog

Giulia: *Grazie per il tè.*

Michele: *Di nulla. Dove va?*

Giulia: *Devo andare a fare la spesa. C'è una panetteria qui vicino?*

Michele: *Sì, c'è una panetteria a due minuti da qui.*

Giulia: *E una libreria?*

Michele: *Non lo so. Ehm… Scusi, c'è una libreria qui vicino?*

Waiter: *Come?*

Michele: *C'è una libreria qui vicino?*

Waiter: *Eh… no, la libreria più vicina è in via Garibaldi.*

Giulia: *È lontano?*

Waiter: *Sì, è lontano. Bisogna prendere o l'autobus o la metro.*

....

Giulia: Thanks for the tea.
Michele: Don't mention it. Where are you going?
Giulia: I have to do some shopping. Is there a bakery near here?
Michele: Yes, there's a bakery just two minutes away.

Giulia:	And a bookstore?
Michele:	I don't know. Umm... Excuse me, is there a bookstore near here?
Waiter:	Pardon?
Michele:	Is there a bookstore near here?
Waiter:	Eh... no, the closest bookstore is in via Garibaldi.
Giulia:	Is it far?
Waiter:	Yes, it's far. You have to take a bus or the subway.

Grammar

 Active Italian: Level 1 > Unit 3 > Lesson 1 > Grammar

1 › **How to ask "where?"**

Dove? means "Where?"

Dove va?	Where are you going? (using the *lei* form)
Dove vai?	Where are you going? (using the *tu* form)

Dov'è? means "Where is?"

Dov'è la farmacia?	Where is the drugstore?
Dov'è la stazione?	Where is the train station?

2 › **Going shopping**

Fare means "to do" or "to make" and is used to talk about going shopping.

Unit 3 › Lesson 1: *Where are the stores?*

fare la spesa
to do the shopping

You also use it for getting gas:

fare benzina
to fill up with gasoline

And if you feel like a snack, you can make the suggestion:

Facciamo uno spuntino?
Shall we have a snack?

Cosa fa?	What are you doing? (using the *lei* form)
Cosa fai?	What are you doing? (using the *tu* form)
Faccio la spesa.	I am shopping.

3 › I have to...

Giulia says she has to go shopping:

Devo andare a fare la spesa.

Devo means "I have to" and is followed by the infinitive:

| *Devo andare in banca.* | I have to go to the bank. |
| *Devo andare a casa.* | I have to go home. |

4 › The verb *essere* (to be)

This is an important verb that you have already used when you described your nationality: *sono americano/a* (I am American) and that of someone else: *Max è italiano* (Max is Italian).

Here is the present tense:

sono	I am
sei	you (*familiar*) are
è	he/she/it is
è	you (*formal*) are
siamo	we are
siete	you (*plural*) are
sono	they are

Remember that as personal pronouns (I, she, we, etc.) aren't used so much in Italian, *è* can mean "it is."

Unit 3 › Lesson 1: *Where are the stores?*

5 › There is / There are

C'è means "there is" and *ci sono* means "there are."

> *C'è una panetteria qui vicino.*
> There is a bakery near here.

> *Ci sono dei negozi in via Garibaldi.*
> There are some stores on via Garibaldi

6 › Is there / Are there…?

C'è and *Ci sono* are also useful for asking questions. You just use the same expression but put a question mark in your voice.

> *C'è una libreria qui vicino?*
> Is there a bookstore near here?

If you are asking about more than one thing, for example, stores, then use *Ci sono*?

> *Ci sono dei negozi qui vicino?*
> Are there any stores near here?

The word for store is *negozio*. In the plural it is *negozi*. Notice how it is the ending of the word that changes to make it plural.

7 › Making nouns ending in -o and -a plural

Making nouns plural is quite easy. But you have to remember to change other words too. The basic rule is:

Masculine nouns ending in -o change to -i.
The article il changes to i.
The article lo changes to gli.

il giorno (day) becomes *i giorni* (days).
lo stato (state) becomes *gli stati* (states).

Feminine nouns ending in -a change to -e.
The article la changes to le.
la pizza becomes *le pizze*.

8 › Making nouns ending in -e plural

Nouns ending in -e in the singular change to -i in the plural. This applies to both masculine and feminine nouns. However the articles change depending on whether the noun is masculine or feminine.

The article il changes to i.
The article la changes to le.
The article lo changes to gli.

il mese (month) changes to *i mesi* (months).
la notte (night) changes to *le notti* (nights).
lo studente (student) changes to *gli studenti* (students).

Unit 3 › Lesson 1: *Where are the stores?*

9 › Making nouns that start with a vowel plural

Masculine nouns that begin with a vowel change the article *l'* to *gli*.

l'anno (year) changes to *gli anni* (years).
l'attore (actor) changes to *gli attori* (actors).
(Remember that *gli* is also the plural article with "*lo*" words: *lo stato*, *gli stati*.)

Feminine nouns that begin with a vowel change the article *l'* to *le*.

l'acqua (water) changes to *le acque* (waters).
l'attrice (actress) changes to *le attrici* (actresses).

10 › Near and far

Vicino means "nearby."
Lontano means "far away."
Da qui means "from here."
To ask where something is, just name it and then add *è lontano da qui?*, turning the statement into a question by raising the pitch of your voice. Remember to change the ending of *lontano* if it is something feminine you are asking about.

| *Il museo, è lontano da qui?* | The museum, is it far from here? |
| *La chiesa, è lontana da qui?* | The church, is it far from here? |

Vocabulary

 Active Italian: Level 1 > Unit 3 > Lesson 1 > Vocabulary

a piedi
on foot.

Bisogna andare a piedi.
You have to go on foot.

in macchina
by car

È meglio andare in macchina.
It's better to go by car.

la fermata dell'autobus
bus stop

Dov'è la fermata dell'autobus?
Where is the bus stop?

in battello
by boat

Può andare in battello.
You can go by boat.

Culture note

A *panificio* or *panetteria* is a bakery. Most of them bake their bread on the premises and open at about 7 a.m. so you can buy fresh bread and croissants, etc., for breakfast. Italian bread is usually white. Wholemeal bread is called *pane integrale*. In Italy fresh bread is served with most meals.

Unit 3 › Lesson 1: *Where are the stores?*

in aereo
by plane

Preferisco andare in aereo.
I prefer going by plane.

in treno
by train

Vai in treno? Bisogna cambiare.
Are you going by train? You have to change.

la stazione
train station

Dov'è la stazione centrale?
Where is the central train station?

scendere
to get off

Bisogna scendere in via Garibaldi.
You have to get off on via Garibaldi.

Culture note

Giuseppe Garibaldi (1807–1882) was an Italian military and political figure and is considered a national hero. He is credited with making the unification of Italy possible. Most towns in Italy have a road or a square named after him.

UNIT 3 > LESSON 2
Bus or subway?

Culture note

The buses in Italy are reliable and tend to be quite useful in the smaller towns or for getting across cities that don't have a streetcar or subway.

Local buses are referred to as both *autobus* and *pullman*. Buses that travel a further distance tend to be referred to more as *pullman* whereas *autobus* usually means a city bus. There is, however, no real rule to this and you may notice that this usage varies in different regions of Italy. Whichever you use you will be understood without a problem.

Unit 3 › Lesson 2: *Bus or subway*

Video Dialog

Michele begins to give Giulia some advice on public transportation but then he makes another decision.

 Active Italian: Level 1 > Unit 3 > Lesson 2 > Video dialog

Michele: *Prende l'autobus o la metro?*
Giulia: *Non lo so.*
Michele: *La metro è più veloce.*
Giulia: *Bisogna cambiare?*
Michele: *Sì, bisogna cambiare alla stazione Termini. L'autobus è più diretto.*
Giulia: *Allora prendo l'autobus.*
Michele: *È il 7. E bisogna scendere all'inizio di via Garibaldi.*
Giulia: *Dov'è la fermata dell'autobus?*
Michele: *Proprio qui di fronte. Aspetti, l'accompagno. Cameriere, il conto, per favore.*
Waiter: *Sono 4 euro e 10.*

....

Michele: Are you going to take a bus or the subway?
Giulia: I don't know.
Michele: The subway is faster.
Giulia: Do I have to change?
Michele: Yes, you have to change at Termini station. The bus is more direct.
Giulia: Then I'll take the bus.

Livemocha™ Active Italian *Level 1*

Michele:	It's bus number 7. And you need to get off at the top of via Garibaldi.
Giulia:	Where is the bus stop?
Michele:	Just across the street. Wait, I'll come with you. Waiter, the check, please.
Waiter:	That's 4 euros and 10 cents.

Grammar

 Active Italian: Level 1 > Unit 3 > Lesson 2 > Grammar

1 › I don't know

Giulia doesn't know whether she is going to take a bus or the subway:

> *Non lo so.*
> I don't know.

Unit 3 › Lesson 2: *Bus or subway?*

Non is the word you need if you want to make a negative statement. It goes in front of the verb:

Non prendo la metro.
I'm not taking the subway.

Non lavoro a Roma.
I don't work in Rome.

2 › Taking public transportation

Prendere is the verb "to take." We've already come across it when Michele and Giulia first met and he asked her if she would like to "take" a coffee.

Prende un caffè?

Prendere is also used with transportation.

Prende l'autobus?	Are you taking the bus?
Prendo la metro.	I'm taking the subway.
Prendo il treno.	I'm taking the train.

3 › The verb *prendere* (to take)

Note the verb endings for the present tense of *prendere*. They follow the simple pattern for *-ere* verbs.

prend**o**	I take
prend**i**	you (*familiar*) take
prend**e**	he/she/it takes
prend**e**	you (*formal*) take
prend**iamo**	we take
prend**ete**	you (*plural*) take
prend**ono**	they take

4 › Which is faster?

È più veloce.
It's faster.

Più means more and *veloce* means fast.

To say something is quicker you put *più* in front of *veloce* and say more fast: *più veloce*.

Unit 3 › Lesson 2: *Bus or subway?*

La metro è più veloce.
The subway is faster.

Try it with *buono* (tasty). Remember to make *buono* agree with the thing it is describing.

La pizza è più buona.
Pizza is tastier.

Il gelato è più buono.
Ice cream is tastier.

5 › **More on plurals (1)**

All Italian nouns end in *-o*, *-a*, or *-e*. Any other ending on a noun probably means it has been imported from another language. Ones we have come across already include:

bar and *autobus*.

Making these words plural is simple. They don't change!

il bar is *i bar* in the plural
l'autobus is *gli autobus* in the plural

Although *euro* sounds like an Italian word, it isn't. Therefore it remains the same in the plural:

l'euro is *gli euro* in the plural

You will also find that the majority of imported words are masculine.

6 › More on plurals (2)

A number of Italian words end with an accent. We have already come across *caffè, tè, città*.

Making these words plural is simple. They don't change!

il caffè becomes *i caffè*
il tè becomes *i tè*
la città becomes *le città*

Unit 3 › Lesson 2: *Bus or subway?*

7 › Numbers one to five

The numbers one to five are:

uno	1
due	2
tre	3
quattro	4
cinque	5

When you are referring to one specific thing, like "one cappuccino" or "one beer," then *uno* shortens to *un* for masculine "cappuccino" and becomes *una* for feminine "beer":

un *cappuccino*
una *birra*

If a feminine word starts with a vowel then *una* shortens to *un'*:

un'aranciata
an orange soda

8 › **Numbers six to ten**

The numbers six to ten are:

sei	6
sette	7
otto	8
nove	9
dieci	10

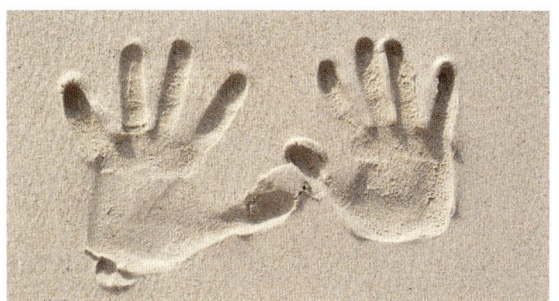

 # *Vocabulary*

Active Italian: Level 1 > Unit 3 > Lesson 2 > Vocabulary

il supermercato
supermarket

Quando apre il supermercato?
When does the supermarket open?

Unit 3 › Lesson 2: *Bus or subway?*

3.2

i panini
bread rolls

Ha dei panini?
Have you got any bread rolls?

il prosciutto cotto
cooked ham

Un etto di prosciutto cotto.
100 grams of cooked ham.

una fetta di
a slice of

Due fette di pizza, per favore.
Two slices of pizza, please.

crudo/a
cured

Prosciutto cotto o crudo?
Cooked or cured ham?

il formaggio
cheese

Ha del formaggio?
Have you got any cheese?

il burro
butter

C'è un po' di burro?
Is there some butter?

il latte
milk

Un litro di latte, per favore.
A liter of milk, please.

queste pesche
these peaches

Queste pesche sono buone.
These peaches are good.

tre pomodori
three tomatoes

Solo tre pomodori, per favore.
Just three tomatoes, please.

una mela
an apple

Vorrei mangiare una mela.
I'd like to eat an apple.

Unit 3 › Lesson 2: *Bus or subway?*

Culture note

When reading a bus schedule it's useful to pay attention to the key called *la legenda*.

Most bus schedules in Italy have separate times for different days of the week or different times of the year, for example, holidays. Be careful to look at the bottom of the schedule for a key which will explain the different letters or symbols on the schedule. Some of you may be able to guess, for example, that *L* means *lunedì* (Monday), *Ma* is *martedì* (Tuesday), *Me* stands for *mercoledì* (Wednesday) and so on. Some may be more complicated, such as *Sc* which means *Giorni Feriali Scolastici* (school vacation) or *Fe* which stands for *festivo*.

Active Italian *Level 1*

4

Lesson 1: Where shall we eat?

- » How to make suggestions using *potremmo*.
- » The verb *andare*.
- » Making adjectives agree and word order.
- » How to say "too": *È troppo caro/lontano*.
- » How to say what you like: *Mi piace/ Mi piacciono*.

Lesson 2: Reserving a table

- » How to say the numbers from 11 to 50.
- » How to tell the time.
- » How to ask "What time?": *A che ora?*
- » How to say when things happen: *Alle...*
- » The expression *Bisogna...*

C Collins | **Livemocha™**

UNIT 4 › LESSON 1
Where shall we eat?

Culture note

You will find that in Italy pizza is less densely loaded with toppings, and the base is usually thinner and crisper because it is traditionally baked in a wood-burning pizza oven.

If you order a pasta dish you might be surprised by the rather small portion. This is because in Italy pasta is served as a first course, to be followed by meat or fish, and not usually considered a meal in itself.

Italy does not offer a great variety of ethnic restaurants. You may come across some Chinese, Indian, and African restaurants, but otherwise the choice is limited.

Unit 4 › Lesson 1: *Where shall we eat?* **4.1**

Video Dialog

Michele and Giulia discuss dinner options for the evening.

Active Italian: Level 1 > Unit 4 > Lesson 1 > Video dialog

Michele:	*Salute!*
Giulia:	*Cin cin!*
Michele:	*Potremmo mangiare in albergo stasera.*
Giulia:	*No, è troppo caro.*
Michele:	*Potremmo andare in pizzeria.*
Giulia:	*Stasera è chiusa.*
Michele:	*Potremmo andare in birreria.*
Giulia:	*Oh, è troppo lontano.*
Michele:	*Che cosa preferisci, allora?*
Giulia:	*Preferisco un ristorante cinese.*
Michele:	*Buona idea, la cucina cinese mi piace tantissimo.*
Giulia:	*Piace molto anche a me.*

....

Michele:	Your health!
Giulia:	Cheers!
Michele:	We could eat at the hotel tonight.
Giulia:	No, it's too expensive.
Michele:	We could go to the pizzeria.
Giulia:	It's closed tonight.
Michele:	We could go to the bar.
Giulia:	Oh, it's too far.

75

Livemocha™ Active Italian *Level 1*

Michele:	What do you prefer, then?
Giulia:	I'd prefer a Chinese restaurant.
Michele:	Good idea. I really like Chinese food.
Giulia:	I like it a lot, too.

Grammar

Active Italian: Level 1 > Unit 4 > Lesson 1 > Grammar

1 › How to make suggestions

Potremmo means "we could." It is followed by the infinitive form of the verb.

Potremmo andare.	We could go.
Potremmo mangiare.	We could eat.
Potremmo mangiare in albergo stasera.	We could eat at the hotel tonight.

Unit 4 › Lesson 1: *Where shall we eat?* **4.1**

2 › Going somewhere to eat

To say where you are going to eat, the options include:

andare al ristorante	to go to the restaurant
andare in pizzeria	to go to the pizzeria
andare in birreria	to go to the bar

3 › The verb *andare* (to go)

Andare is an irregular verb in that it doesn't follow the simple set pattern of *lavorare*. The present tense is:

vado	I go
vai	you (*familiar*) go
va	he/she/it goes
va	you (*formal*) go
andiamo	we go
andate	you (*plural*) go
vanno	they go

4 › Open and...

Aperto means open. Remember to change it to *aper**a*** with a feminine word:

| *Il ristorante è aper**o***. | The restaurant is open. |
| *La birreria è aper**a***. | The bar is open. |

5 › ... shut

Chiuso means "shut" or "closed." Remember to change it to *chius**a*** with a feminine word.

Culture note

In addition to restaurants, called *ristorante*, there are other places that serve meals. A *trattoria* is less formal and often cheaper than a *ristorante*. It can also be more rustic and is often family-run, sometimes with no printed menus.

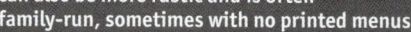

A *birreria* is more or less a bar, so even less formal, and usually has a limited menu. A *pizzeria* is a pizza parlor. You can usually get takeout food from a *pizzeria*.

Unit 4 › Lesson 1: *Where shall we eat?*

Il bar è chiuso stasera.	The bar is closed tonight.
La pizzeria è chiusa stasera.	The pizzeria is closed tonight.

6 › **Word order**

In Italian the adjective usually goes after a noun. So instead of saying a "Chinese restaurant," Italians say "a restaurant Chinese," *un ristorante cinese*.

> **Culture note**
>
> When saying how far away somewhere is, Italians often say how long it takes to get there, e.g., instead of saying 200 meters away they are more likely to say *cinque minuti* and then they might add *a piedi* (on foot) to indicate you could expect to walk there in 5 minutes. If something is very close by, they might say *è a due passi* (it's two steps away).

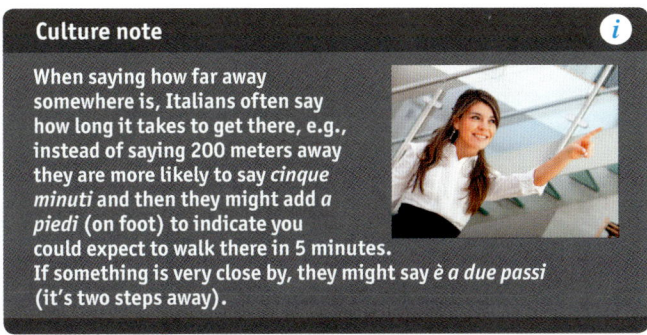

7 › *Preferire* (to prefer) – more verb patterns

Preferire means "to prefer." It follows the simple pattern of one set of *-ire* verbs.

preferisco	I prefer
preferisci	you (*familiar*) prefer
preferisce	he/she/it prefers
preferisce	you (*formal*) prefer
preferiamo	we prefer
preferite	you (*plural*) prefer
preferiscono	they prefer

8 › *Dormire* (to sleep) – the other *-ire* verb pattern

Dormire (to sleep) also ends in *-ire* but follows a slightly different pattern than *preferire*.

dorm**o**	I sleep
dorm**i**	you (familiar) sleep
dorm**e**	he/she/it sleeps
dorm**e**	you (formal) sleep
dorm**iamo**	we sleep
dorm**ite**	you (plural) sleep
dorm**ono**	they sleep

9 › I like…

Mi piace means "I like" something; for example, pizza:

Mi piace la pizza.

Mi piacciono means "I like" something, when the thing is a plural noun; for example, *spaghetti* (yes, it is plural in Italian, as is *lasagne*):

Mi piacciono gli spaghetti.
Mi piacciono le lasagne.

So if the thing that you like is singular, you use *mi piace*. If it is more than one thing and is plural, then you use *mi piacciono*.

If it is an activity such as "dancing" or "eating" then you simply use *mi piace* followed by the infinitive form of the verb: *ballare*, *mangiare*.

| *Mi piace ballare.* | I like dancing. |
| *Mi piace mangiare.* | I like eating. |

10 › **Getting the stress right**

By now you should be well on the way to a perfect Italian accent! Remember when reading Italian out loud you should in general put the stress on the second to last syllable of a word:

*Spagh**e**tti, maccher**o**ni, las**a**gne.*

If it doesn't fall there, then there is often an accent to help you:

*Caff**è**, citt**à**, dov'**è**, perch**é**.*

Occasionally you will not guess correctly. But it's all part of the learning curve:

*B**e**rgamo, N**a**poli, p**i**ccolo, G**e**nova.*

Vocabulary

Active Italian: Level 1 > Unit 4 > Lesson 1 > Vocabulary

l'albergo
hotel

Dov'è l'albergo?
Where is the hotel?

tantissimo
very much, lots

Mi piace tantissimo.
I like it very much.

caro/a
expensive

È molto caro.
It is very expensive.

una buona idea
a good idea

Che buona idea!
What a good idea!

la colazione
breakfast

Non mangio la colazione.
I don't eat breakfast.

Unit 4 › Lesson 1: *Where shall we eat?* **4.1**

il pranzo
lunch

Vieni a pranzo da me?
Will you come to lunch at my place?

la cena
dinner, evening meal

Vieni a cena da me?
Will you come to dinner at my place?

mangiare fuori
to eat out

Preferisco mangiare fuori stasera.
I prefer to eat out tonight.

aprire
to open

Quando apre il ristorante?
When does the restaurant open?

chiudere
to close

Quando chiude la pizzeria?
When does the pizzeria close?

UNIT 4 › LESSON 2
Reserving a table

Culture note

Shops in Italy usually open their doors at 9 a.m. and stay open until 1 p.m. or 2 p.m. when they close for lunch. Afternoon shopping hours are generally from about 4 p.m. until 8 p.m. Most shops are open all day Saturday, but remain closed on Sundays. They tend to be closed for a half day, either in the morning or afternoon, on one day during the week.

There is some variation in business hours in Italy between the north and the south. Generally, things tend to stay open later in the evening in the south.

Unit 4 › Lesson 2: *Reserving a table*

Video Dialog

Michele and Giulia decide to find a Chinese restaurant for dinner. They run into the waiter from the café and ask his advice on where to go.

Active Italian: Level 1 > Unit 4 > Lesson 2 > Video dialog

Michele:	*Mi scusi, c'è un ristorante cinese qui vicino?*
Waiter:	*Sì, ce n'è uno a cinque minuti da qui. Si chiama il Bambù d'oro.*
Michele:	*A che ora apre?*
Waiter:	*Ehm... Apre alle diciotto e chiude alle ventitré, credo, ma bisogna prenotare. Ecco il telefono.*
Michele:	*Grazie.*
Waiter:	*Prego.*
Michele:	*Pronto, il Bambù d'oro? Sì, c'è un tavolo per due persone stasera? A che ora? Alle otto va bene. Perfetto. A che nome? Berti, Michele Berti... Ecco fatto.*

Michele:	Excuse me, is there a Chinese restaurant near here?
Waiter:	Yes, there's one five minutes from here. It's called the Bambù d'oro.
Michele:	What time does it open?
Waiter:	Umm... It opens at 6 p.m. and shuts at 11 p.m., I think, but you need to make reservations. Here's the phone number.
Michele:	Thanks.

Livemocha™ Active Italian *Level 1*

Waiter: You're welcome.
Michele: Hello, Bambù d'oro? Yes, is there a table for two available this evening? What time? 8 p.m. is fine. Perfect. In what name? Berti, Michele Berti... That's it, done.

Grammar

Active Italian: Level 1 > Unit 4 > Lesson 2 > Grammar

1 › The time (1)

As in most of Europe, Italy uses the 24-hour clock for train schedules, movie schedules, office hours, and so on. Otherwise they use normal clock times.

Hour is *l'ora*. Hours are *le ore*.
Timetable is *l'orario*.

To say "it's one o'clock" you say *è l'una*. From then on you say *sono le due*, *sono le tre*, and so on. The *le* refers to *le ore*. To say the time with hours and minutes, *e* ("and") is used (literally the hour "and" so many minutes).

> *e due e venticinque* means "two twenty-five"
> *e un quarto* means "a quarter past"
> *e mezza* means "half past"
> *meno* (literally "minus") means "to the hour"
> *meno un quarto* means "a quarter to"

2 › **The time (2)**

È l'una.	It's 1 o'clock.
Sono le due.	It's 2 o'clock.
Sono le tre.	It's 3 o'clock.
Sono le quattro.	It's 4 o'clock.
Sono le cinque.	It's 5 o'clock.

And so on until *le dodici* (12 o'clock). People usually use words meaning noon and midnight for 12 o'clock.

È mezzogiorno.	It is noon.
È mezzanotte.	It is midnight.

3 › Numbers 11 to 24

In order to use the 24-hour clock you need to know at least the numbers from 1 to 24. You already know 1 to 10. Here are 11 to 24.

undici	11
dodici	12
tredici	13
quattordici	14
quindici	15
sedici	16
diciassette	17
diciotto	18
diciannove	19
venti	20
ventuno	21
ventidue	22
ventitré	23
ventiquattro	24

4 › Numbers 30 to 100

By now you will be able to follow the pattern. Here are the numbers 30 to 100 (going up in 10s).

trenta	30
quaranta	40
cinquanta	50
sessanta	60
settanta	70
ottanta	80
novanta	90
cento	100

Unit 4 › Lesson 2: *Reserving a table*

5 › What time? – *A che ora?*

Michele asks the waiter when the Chinese restaurant opens.

> *A che ora apre?*
> What time does it open?

We already know the word for "when?" *(quando?)*. *A che ora* is a better option for when you want a specific time.

6 › At... – *Alle...*

The waiter tells Michele the opening and closing times of the restaurant:

Apre alle diciotto.	It opens at 6 o'clock.
Chiude alle ventitré.	It closes at 11 o'clock.

All'una means "at one o'clock." For all other times it is *alle*:

alle quattro	at four o'clock
alle nove	at nine o'clock

7 › **It is necessary to...**

We have seen *bisogna* before. It literally means "it is necessary to" (but often translates as "you have to") and is followed by the infinitive form of the verb.

> *Bisogna prenotare.*
> It is necessary to reserve.

> *Bisogna andare a piedi.*
> You have to go on foot.

8 › **Hello?**

The standard greeting when someone answers the phone is *Pronto*. It literally means "Ready" (and listening!).

Vocabulary

Active Italian: Level 1 > Unit 4 > Lesson 2 > Vocabulary

prenotare
to make reservations

Ha prenotato?
Have you made reservations?

per stasera
for tonight

Un tavolo per stasera alle otto.
A table for tonight at 8 o'clock.

Unit 4 › Lesson 2: *Reserving a table*

per domani sera
for tomorrow night

Vorrei prenotare un tavolo per domani sera.
I would like to reserve a table for tomorrow night.

a nome di
in the name of

Ho prenotato a nome di Smith.
I made reservations under the name Smith.

un tavolo per due persone
a table for two people

Ho prenotato un tavolo per due persone.
I reserved a table for 2 people.

fuori
outside

Si può mangiare fuori?
Can we eat outside?

dentro
inside

Si può mangiare dentro?
Can we eat inside?

il menù
the menu

Ci porta il menù, per favore.
Can you bring us the menu, please?

Active Italian *Level 1*

5

Lesson 1: Plans for the week

- » How to use the present tense.
- » The days of the week.
- » The present tense of *avere*.
- » How to pronounce the letter *h*.
- » How to say "I'm going to..."

Lesson 2: Plans for next week

- » How to use the Italian present tense for future events.
- » How to say "on Friday," "on Saturday."
- » Asking a question back: *E tu?*
- » How to say "to the" or "at the": *Al*, *alla*, etc.
- » How to say "in the": *Nel*, *nella*, etc.

Collins | **Livemocha™**

UNIT 5 › LESSON 1
Plans for the week

Culture note

Before the unification of Italy in 1861, the Italian peninsula comprised many separate states, each of which often had its own dialects and traditions. However, once unified, an official language for the new Kingdom of Italy needed to be chosen.

Significant Florentine poets and writers of the Late Middle Ages and Renaissance periods, such as Dante Alighieri, Francesco Petrarca (Petrarch), Giovanni Boccaccio and Niccolò Machiavelli, chose to write in their native Tuscan dialect rather than in Latin, the language that had traditionally been used in literary and academic texts. Thanks to this literary movement, in subsequent centuries the Florentine dialect enjoyed perhaps the most exposure of any Italian dialect, and was therefore a natural choice as the official language of the new Kingdom of Italy.

Unit 5 › Lesson 1: *Plans for the week*

Video Dialog

Lucia asks Ugo about his plans for the coming week.

 Active Italian: Level 1 > Unit 5 > Lesson 1 > Video dialog

Lucia: *Che cosa fai la settimana prossima?*

Ugo: *Lunedì lavoro in agenzia.*

Lucia: *E martedì?*

Ugo: *Martedì ho un appuntamento con un cliente a Tivoli.*

Lucia: *Mercoledì?*

Ugo: *Mercoledì e giovedì lavoro in agenzia.*

Lucia: *Venerdì lavori tutta la giornata?*

Ugo: *No, finisco a mezzogiorno. Il pomeriggio, faccio la spesa.*

Lucia: *E che cosa fai questo fine settimana?*

Ugo: *Sabato vado a vedere una partita di calcio.*

Lucia: *E domenica?*

Ugo: *Domenica sono libero.*

Lucia: What are you doing next week?
Ugo: Monday I am working at the agency.
Lucia: And Tuesday?
Ugo: Tuesday I have a meeting with a client in Tivoli.
Lucia: Wednesday?
Ugo: Wednesday and Thursday I am working at the agency.

Lucia:	Are you working all day on Friday?
Ugo:	No, I finish at noon. In the afternoon I'm going shopping.
Lucia:	And what are you doing this weekend?
Ugo:	Saturday I'm going to watch a soccer game.
Lucia:	And Sunday?
Ugo:	Sunday I'm free.

Grammar

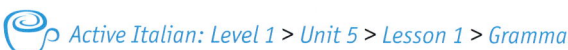

Active Italian: Level 1 > Unit 5 > Lesson 1 > Grammar

1 › The verb *fare* (to do or to make)

> *Che cosa fai la settimana prossima?*
> What are you doing next week?

Unit 5 › Lesson 1: *Plans for the week*

Fai comes from *fare*. The present tense is:

faccio	I do
fai	you (*familiar*) do
fa	he/she/it does
fa	you (*formal*) do
facciamo	we do
fate	you (*plural*) do
fanno	they do

2 › Statements and questions

Lavori means both "You work" and "You are working."

If you make it into a question it can mean "Are you working?" or "Do you work?"

3 › ## What?

Che cosa? is a way of introducing a question. Literally it means "what thing?" but usually translates simply as "what?"

Che cosa fai?	What are you doing?
Che cosa fai la settimana prossima?	What are you doing next week?
Che cosa vuoi mangiare?	What do you want to eat?

4 › ## The verb *avere* (to have)

The verb *avere* ranks alongside *essere* (to be) in importance and frequency of use. It is also an irregular verb. The present tense is:

ho	I have
hai	you (*familiar*) have
ha	he/she/it has
ha	you (*formal*) have
abbiamo	we have
avete	you (*plural*) have
hanno	they have

5 › The letter *h* (1)

The letter *h* in Italian is silent at the beginning of a word.
Ho, *hai*, and *ha* all begin with the letter *h* but it isn't pronounced.
It is the same with imported words such as *hotel* and *hamburger*.

6 › The letter *h* (2)

An *h* within an Italian word serves a purpose. And that purpose is to make the letter before it "hard."

In Italian *c* and *g* are soft before the vowels *e* and *i*. So you say: *cento*, *cinema* and *gelato*, *gita*.

If they were followed by the other vowels – *a*, *o* or *u* – then *c* and *g* would be hard, as in:
Capri, *costa* and *Cuba*
gatto, *gola* and *gusto*

7 › The letter *h* (3)

Plurals are generally made by changing the final letters to *i* or *e*. To retain the same sound of the singular ending, an *h* is often added to the plural ending:

> *parco* (park) becomes *parchi* with an h
> *lago* (lake) becomes *laghi* with an h
> *bistecca* (steak) becomes *bistecche* with an h
> *riga* (line) becomes *righe* with an h.

8 › Days of the week

lunedì	Monday
martedì	Tuesday
mercoledì	Wednesday
giovedì	Thursday
venerdì	Friday
sabato	Saturday
domenica	Sunday

The days of the week are all masculine except for *domenica* (Sunday).

Note that days of the week are not written with a capital letter in Italian.

Unit 5 › Lesson 1: *Plans for the week* **5.1**

Vocabulary

Active Italian: Level 1 > Unit 5 > Lesson 1 > Vocabulary

prossimo/a
next

Che cosa fai sabato prossimo?
What are you doing next Saturday?

scorso/a
last

Che cosa hai fatto sabato scorso?
What did you do last Saturday?

vedere
to see

Quale film vuoi vedere?
Which movie do you want to see?

la piscina
swimming pool

Andiamo in piscina?
Shall we go to the swimming pool?

la passeggiata
walk, stroll

Vorremmo fare una bella passeggiata.
We would like to go for a nice walk.

la palestra
gym

Quando vai in palestra?
When are you going to the gym?

andare a trovare
to go and visit

Domani vado a trovare mia madre.
Tomorrow I am going to visit my mother.

giocare a...
to play... (a sport)

Venerdì vado a giocare a tennis.
On Friday I am going to play tennis.

la vacanza
vacation

Questa settimana sono in vacanza.
This week I'm on vacation.

UNIT 5 › LESSON 2
Plans for next week

Cultural note

Regional dialects still exist in many regions of Italy and accents can vary greatly from place to place. Some dialects are fairly similar to the "Tuscan Italian" of Dante, Petrarch, and Boccaccio, whereas others are regarded by some as entirely different languages. As a result of this, from time to time you may encounter words or accents that don't sound familiar or are difficult to understand, but don't worry, as almost all Italians speak the official Italian language and a polite *mi dispiace, non ho capito* is usually enough to elicit a response in a more understandable form.

Video Dialog

Now it's Lucia's turn to tell Ugo what she has planned for the coming week.

Active Italian: Level 1 > Unit 5 > Lesson 2 > Video dialog

Ugo:	*E tu, che cosa fai la settimana prossima?*
Lucia:	*Lunedì e martedì lavoro in negozio.*
Ugo:	*Mercoledì?*
Lucia:	*Mercoledì e giovedì ho appuntamento con dei clienti in centro.*
Ugo:	*Venerdì io sono libero il pomeriggio. E tu?*
Lucia:	*Venerdì ho dei clienti tutta la giornata.*
Ugo:	*E questo fine settimana?*
Lucia:	*Sabato mattina lavoro in negozio ma nel pomeriggio sono libera.*
Ugo:	*Sabato pomeriggio vado a vedere una partita di calcio. Vuoi venire?*
Lucia:	*Assolutamente no!*

Ugo:	And you, what are you doing next week?
Lucia:	Monday and Tuesday I am working in the store.
Ugo:	Wednesday?
Lucia:	Wednesday and Thursday I am meeting some clients in town.
Ugo:	Friday I am free in the afternoon. And you?
Lucia:	Friday I have clients all day.
Ugo:	And this weekend?

Lucia:	Saturday morning I am working in the store, but I'm free in the afternoon.
Ugo:	Saturday afternoon I am going to watch a soccer match. Do you want to come?
Ugo:	No way!

Grammar

 Active Italian: Level 1 > Unit 5 > Lesson 2 > Grammar

1 › Using the present tense

Notice how in Italian the present tense is used for things that are going to happen in the future.

The day of the week tells us when the activity is going to happen so there is no need to use the future tense. It is the same with *Quando?* and *A che ora?*, you just use the present tense in Italian.

Quando parti?	When are you leaving?
Parto lunedì.	I am leaving on Monday.
A che ora mangi?	When are you eating?
Mangiamo alle otto.	We are eating at eight.

2 › Saying "on Saturday," "on Friday," etc

To say that you are doing something on a certain day, you just need to name the day. It is as simple as that!

Sabato vado al mercato.	On Saturday I'm going to the market.
Domenica vado a messa.	On Sunday I'm going to mass.

3 › *E tu?* Asking a question back

If someone asks you how you are in Italian, you can ask them back simply by saying "And you?" There is no need to repeat the question.

Q:	*Come stai?*	How are you?
A:	*Benissimo. E tu?*	Very well. And how are you?

If it is a more formal situation:

Q:	*Come sta?*	How are you?
A:	*Benissimo. E lei?*	Very well. And how are you?

4 › How to say "to the" or "at the" – *a + il*

Some short Italian words combine with the articles (*il, la, lo*, etc). Although confusing at first, once you know the articles thoroughly, it will all make sense and you can work out the pattern.

The word for "to" or "at" is *a*, as in *a Roma, a Milano*. In front of a masculine noun, *a* combines with *il* or *l'* to become *al* (or *all'*):

al ristorante	to the restaurant
all'aeroporto	to the airport

Unit 5 › Lesson 2: *Plans for next week*

In the plural, *a* combines with *i* to become *ai* or with *gli* to become *agli*:

ai giardini	to the gardens
ai negozi	to the stores
agli aeroporti	to the airports

5 › **How to say "to the" or "at the" – *a* + *lo***

With the article *lo*, *a* combines with *lo* to become *allo* in the singular and *agli* in the plural:

| *allo stadio* | to the stadium |
| *agli zoo* | to the zoos |

6 › **How to say "to the" or "at the" – *a* + *la***

When you use *a* in front of a feminine noun, *a* combines with *la* to become *alla* (or *all'*) in the singular and *alle* in the plural:

alla scuola	to the school
all'alba	at dawn
alle partite	to the sports matches

7 › **How to say "in the"**

The word *in* (meaning "in" or "at") also combines with the articles, following a similar pattern.

In front of a masculine noun, *in* combines with *il* to become *nel* (or *nell'*):

| *nel ristorante* | in the restaurant |
| *nell'hotel* | in the hotel |

In the plural *in* combines with *i* to become *nei*

| *nei giardini* | in the gardens |

With *lo* it's *nello* in the singular and *negli* in the plural:

| *nello stadio* | in the stadium |
| *negli Stati Uniti* | in the United States |

In front of a feminine noun *in* combines with *la* to become *nella* (or *nell'*) in the singular and *nelle* in the plural:

nell'acqua calda	in the warm water
nella casa di fronte	in the house straight across
nelle montagne	in the mountains

Vocabulary

Active Italian: Level 1 > Unit 5 > Lesson 2 > Vocabulary

noleggiare
to rent

Dove posso noleggiare una bici?
Where can I rent a bike?

Quanto costa?
How much does it cost?

Quanto costa noleggiare una macchina?
How much does it cost to rent a car?

Unit 5 › Lesson 2: *Plans for next week*

5.2

all'ora
per hour

La bici costa 10 euro all'ora.
The bike costs 10 euros per hour.

al giorno
per day

La macchina costa 30 euro al giorno.
The car costs 30 euros per day.

alla settimana
per week

Quanto costa alla settimana?
How much does it cost per week?

questo/a
this

Preferisci questo colore?
Do you prefer this color?

questo fine settimana
this weekend

Che cosa fai questo fine settimana?
What are you doing this weekend?

questa casa
this house

Chi abita in questa casa?
Who lives in this house?

Active Italian *Level 1*

6

Lesson 1: Dinner at a friend's

- » The verb "to be able": *potere*.
- » How to make a suggestion to friends.
- » How to say "some" using *di + il*, *la*, etc: *delle pizze*, *del vino*.
- » How to say "at my place": *da me*.
- » Different meanings for the verb *portare*.

Lesson 2: Finishing dinner

- » How to say something was delicious.
- » How to ask for some more of something: *Ancora un po' di...*
- » How to ask for another drink, etc: *Ancora un/una...*
- » The verb *volere*.
- » How to ask someone if they want some...
- » How to use *buono* in front of a word.

Collins | **Livemocha**™

UNIT 6 › LESSON 1
Dinner at a friend's

Culture note

Pizza is the most common takeout food in Italy. If you don't want a whole pizza, many places also sell pizza *al taglio*, which means by the slice. If you buy from a bakery, usually the price is set per kilo, and slices are sold by weight; however  from a pizzeria they are sold by the slice with prices depending upon their toppings. *Pizza margherita* (cheese and tomato) and *pizza marinara* (tomato and basil) tend to be the cheapest options, whereas *pizza farcita* are more expensive.

Unit 6 › Lesson 1: *Dinner at a friend's*

Video Dialog

Ugo and Lucia make some plans for the evening.

Active Italian: Level 1 > Unit 6 > Lesson 1 > Video dialog

Ugo:	*Potremmo cenare insieme questa stasera, che ne dici?*
Lucia:	*È mercoledì. Il ristorante è chiuso stasera.*
Ugo:	*Potresti venire da me. Posso comprare delle pizze da asporto.*
Lucia:	*D'accordo, ed io posso portare un'insalata e un po' di vino.*
Ugo:	*Potrei anche noleggiare un DVD.*
Lucia:	*OK. A stasera.*

Ugo:	We could eat together this evening, what do you say?
Lucia:	It's Wednesday. The restaurant is closed this evening.
Ugo:	You could come to my place. I can get takeout pizza.
Lucia:	Okay, and I can bring a salad and some wine.
Ugo:	I could rent a DVD too.
Lucia:	Okay, see you tonight.

Culture note

If you want to reply "yes, please" to an offer, you need to say *sì, grazie* – "yes, thank you." The equivalent of "no, thanks" is *no, grazie*.

Vuoi un caffè? Would you like a coffee?

Sì, grazie. Yes, please.

No, grazie. No, thanks.

Grammar

Active Italian: Level 1 > Unit 6 > Lesson 1 > Grammar

1 › **The verb *potere* – to be able to**

Lucia says *posso portare* (I can bring). *Posso* comes from the verb *potere* which is another useful verb to learn.

posso	I can
puoi	you (*familiar*) can
può	he/she/it can
può	you (*formal*) can
possiamo	we can
potete	you (*plural*) can
possono	they can

Unit 6 › Lesson 1: *Dinner at a friend's*

2 › More suggestions

Ugo says *potremmo cenare insieme* (we could dine together).
Potremmo is useful for making suggestions to a group of people.

Potremmo giocare a tennis.	We could play tennis.
Potremmo noleggiare una macchina.	We could rent a car.

To make a suggestion for yourself, you say *potrei* (I could).

Potrei noleggiare un DVD.	I could rent a DVD.
Potrei venire da te.	I could come over to your place.

3 › Different meals

Breakfast is *la colazione* and "to have breakfast" is *fare colazione*.
Lunch is *il pranzo* and the corresponding verb is *pranzare*.
The evening meal is *la cena* and the corresponding verb is *cenare*.
Children often have a snack (*la merenda*) when they come home
from school in the afternoon.

4 › At my place

Da me means "at my place." *Da* (meaning "at" in this context) is one of those short words like *a* and *in* which combines with the articles *il* or *la*.

dal panettiere	at the bakery
dalla mia amica	at my friend's
da te	at your place

You also use *andare da* to say you are going to a certain place. It is always linked to the person running the establishment rather than the place itself.

andare dal dottore	to go to the doctor
andare dal farmacista	to go to the pharmacist
andare dalla parruchiera	to go to the hairdresser

5 › Bringing and wearing

Portare means "to bring."

Lucia says:

> *Posso portare un'insalata*
> I can bring a salad.

Portare also means "to carry" or "to wear."

> *Porto sempre l'ombrello.*
> I always carry an umbrella.

> *Lucia porta gli occhiali.*
> Lucia wears glasses.

6 › How to say "some" (1)

"Some wine" is *del vino*. *Del* comes from *di* + the article of whatever you are referring to. *Di* (meaning "of" in this context) is another word that combines with the article.

To ask for "butter," "wine," or "bread," etc, you generally include *del* (or *della*, etc) in the question.

Ha del burro?	Do you have any butter?
Ha del vino?	Do you have any wine?
Ha del pane?	Do you have any bread?

7 › How to say "some" (2)

Del comes from the combination of *di* (of) with the article *il, la,* etc. (like *nel, al, dal*). *Di* follows a similar pattern.

In front of a masculine noun, *di* combines with *il* to become *del/dell'* :

| *del pane* | some bread, |
| *dell'olio* | some oil |

In the plural *di* combines with *i* to become *dei*:

| *dei panini* | some bread rolls |

With the *lo* article, it's *dello* in the singular and *degli* in the plural:

| *dello zucchero* | some sugar |
| *degli spaghetti* | some spaghetti |

8 › How to say "some" (3)

In front of a feminine noun *di* combines with *la* to become *della* (or *dell'*) in the singular and *delle* in the plural:

dell'acqua	some water
della birra	some beer
delle patatine	some potato chips

Unit 6 › Lesson 1: *Dinner at a friend's* **6.1**

9 › | See you...

When Lucia leaves, she says *A stasera* (See you tonight). Here are other phrases to try out:

A domani.	See you tomorrow.
A sabato.	See you on Saturday.
Alla settimana prossima.	See you next week.
All'anno prossimo.	See you next year.

 Vocabulary

 Active Italian: Level 1 > Unit 6 > Lesson 1 > Vocabulary

il pane
bread

Ci porta ancora un po' di pane?
Can you bring us some more bread?

il pesce
fish

Non mi piace il pesce.
I don't like fish.

l'insalata
salad

Devi mangiare un po' d'insalata.
You have to eat some salad.

il vino
wine

Preferisci il vino bianco o il vino rosso?
Do you prefer white wine or red wine?

il dolce
dessert

Che cosa avete come dolce?
What do you have for dessert?

un panino
a sandwich

Vuoi un panino con il salame o il prosciutto?
Do you want a sandwich with salami or ham?

Unit 6 › Lesson 1: *Dinner at a friend's* **6.1**

la minestra
soup

La minestra è buonissima.
The soup is very good.

bere
to drink

Che cosa vuoi bere?
What do you want to drink?

guardare
to watch

Potremmo guardare un film insieme.
We could watch a movie together.

uscire
to go out

Vuoi uscire stasera?
Do you want to go out tonight?

Culture note

You won't usually find creamy salad dressings in Italy. L'*insalata* (salad) can be *verde* (green) or *mista* (mixed) and is served with a simple vinaigrette of olive oil, salt, and balsamic or wine vinegar.

A well-known salad is the *insalata Caprese*, which consists of sliced buffalo mozzarella, tomatoes, and fresh basil.

UNIT 6 › LESSON 2
Finishing dinner

Culture note

At around 6 p.m. most Italian bartenders begin to place snack food on the bar for *aperitivo* (aperitif). Though an *aperitivo* is technically an alcoholic beverage usually drunk before an evening meal, the word is also synonymous with a frequent social convention. It involves buying a drink from the bar, usually priced between €5 and €10,  and then helping yourself to the food that is on offer. *Aperitivo* can range from potato chips, peanuts, and olives to a huge variety of salads, pasta dishes, pizza, focaccia, meats, and roasted vegetables. Many Italians go for an *aperitivo* before going on to a restaurant; however in the more lavishly supplied bars it is definitely possible to make an event of it and enjoy enough to call it a meal!

The Italian tradition of drinking a small amount of alcohol before an evening meal is said to originate from Turin, where vermouth (an *aperitivo*) was invented by Antonio Benedetto Carpano in the 18th century.

Unit 6 › Lesson 2: *Finishing dinner*

Video Dialog

Ugo and Lucia are finishing their pizza and settling down to watch a DVD.

Active Italian: Level 1 > Unit 6 > Lesson 2 > Video dialog

Lucia:	*Era buonissima.*
Ugo:	*Ancora un po' d'insalata?*
Lucia:	*No, grazie.*
Ugo:	*Vuoi del formaggio? Ho del buon pecorino.*
Lucia:	*No, grazie, ho mangiato abbastanza.*
Ugo:	*Un caffè?*
Lucia:	*Perché no?*
Ugo:	*Zucchero?*
Lucia:	*Hai del dolcificante?*
Ugo:	*Ecco. Adesso possiamo guardare il DVD!*

Lucia:	That was delicious.
Ugo:	A bit more salad?
Lucia:	No, thanks.
Ugo:	Do you want some cheese? I have some nice pecorino.
Lucia:	No, thanks, I've had enough to eat.
Ugo:	Coffee?
Lucia:	Why not?
Ugo:	Sugar?
Lucia:	Do you have any sweetener?
Ugo:	Here you are. Now we can watch the DVD!

Livemocha™ Active Italian *Level 1*

Grammar

Active Italian: Level 1 > Unit 6 > Lesson 2 > Grammar

1 › Describing something

When you are describing something, you say

È...	It is...
È bellissimo.	It is really nice.
È buonissimo.	It is delicious.

To say "It was really nice" or "It was delicious," you use *Era* instead of *È*.

| *Era bellissimo.* | It was really nice. |
| *Era buonissimo.* | It was delicious. |

2 › A bit more...?

Ancora un po' di... means "A bit more..." or "Some more...":

Ancora un po' di pane?	A bit more bread?
Ancora un po' di vino?	A bit more wine?
Ancora un po' d'insalata?	Some more salad?

3 › How to say "Another..."

If you want to ask for another glass of wine or another cappuccino, it is simple. Just say *Ancora un* (or *una* if it is something feminine).

| *Ancora un bicchiere di vino.* | Another glass of wine. |
| *Ancora un caffè.* | Another espresso. |

Unit 6 › Lesson 2: *Finishing dinner*

4 › Would you like some...?

If you are asking someone if they want something, remember to include the word for "some" – *del*, *della* and so on.

Vuoi del formaggio?	Do you want some cheese?
Vuoi della frutta?	Do you want some fruit?
Vuoi dell'acqua?	Do you want some water?
Vuoi dello spumante?	Do you want some sparkling wine?

5 › The verb *volere* (to want)

You've already been using this verb. Here is the present tense.

voglio	I want
vuoi	you (*familiar*) want
vuole	he/she/it wants
vuole	you (*formal*) want
vogliamo	we want
volete	you (*plural*) want
vogliono	they want

Remember, if you are asking for something in a bar or a store, you would use *vorrei* (I would like) rather than *voglio* (I want).

6 › *Buono* shortens to *buon*

Most adjectives come after the noun in Italian as in *il ristorante cinese*, *la signora americana*.

However there are a few that go in front of the noun. You have already seen one – *buono*.

Note that *buono* shortens to *buon* before most masculine nouns as in *un buon formaggio*, *del buon vino* and in that all-important phrase:

> *Buon appetito!*
> Enjoy your meal!

The standard reply to *Buon appetito!* is *Altrettanto!* Meaning "The same to you!"

Vocabulary

Active Italian: Level 1 > Unit 6 > Lesson 2 > Vocabulary At around 6 p.m. most Italian bartenders

per piacere
please

Mi può aiutare, per piacere?
Can you help me, please?

Unit 6 › Lesson 2: *Finishing dinner*

6.2

una fetta di...
a slice of...

Prendi una fetta di torta?
Will you have a slice of cake?

auguri
congratulations, best wishes

Tanti auguri per il tuo compleanno.
Best wishes for your birthday.

gentile
kind

Grazie, signora, è molto gentile.
Thank you, madam, you are very kind.

il compleanno
birthday

Quand'è il tuo compleanno?
When is your birthday?

la festa
party

Fai la festa per il compleanno di Max?
Are you having a party for Max's birthday?

Perché no?
Why not?

Mi inviti a cenare da te? Perché no?
Are you inviting me to dinner at your place? Why not?

Piacere!
Pleased to meet you!

Piacere di conoscerla, signora Rossi.
I am very pleased to meet you, Mrs. Rossi.

ottimo
excellent

Il pranzo era ottimo.
The lunch was excellent.

il regalo
gift

Dove posso comprare un regalo per Max?
Where can I buy a gift for Max?

Collins

Livemocha ACTIVE ITALIAN

HarperCollins Publishers
77–85 Fulham Palace Road
London W6 8JB
Great Britain

www.collinslanguage.com

First edition 2011

Reprint 10 9 8 7 6 5 4 3 2 1 0
© HarperCollins Publishers 2011

ISBN (UK edition) 978-0-00-737353-6
ISBN (export edition) 978-0-00-741980-7
ISBN (US edition) 978-0-87779-557-5

Collins® is a registered trademark of HarperCollins Publishers Limited

A catalogue record for this book is available from the British Library

Typeset by Macmillan Publishing Services

Audio material recorded and produced by Networks SRL, Milan

Printed and Bound in China by Leo Paper Products Ltd.
Series Editor: Rob Scriven

All rights reserved. No part of this publication may be reproduced, stored in a retrieval system or transmitted, in any form or by any means, electronic, mechanical, photocopying, recording or otherwise, without the prior permission of the publisher. This book is sold subject to the conditions that it shall not, by way of trade or otherwise, be lent, re-sold, hired out or otherwise circulated without the publisher's prior consent in any form of binding or cover other than that in which it is published and without a similar condition including this condition being imposed on the subsequent purchaser.

HarperCollins does not warrant that the functions contained in **www.livemocha.com** content will be interrruption- or error-free, that defects will be corrected, or that **www.livemocha.com** or the server that makes it available are free of viruses or bugs. HarperCollins is not responsible for any access difficulties that may be experienced due to problems with network, web, online or mobile phone connections.

INTRODUCTION	4

UNIT 1
Lesson 1: Planning a trip to the museum	8
Lesson 2: Getting directions to a museum	19

UNIT 2
Lesson 1: Asking the way to the stadium	34
Lesson 2: A quick beer before the soccer game	46

UNIT 3
Lesson 1: Where to go shopping?	58
Lesson 2: Catching the bus to the shops	70

UNIT 4
Lesson 1: In the clothes shop	84
Lesson 2: A little black dress	97

UNIT 5
Lesson 1: In need of smart clothes	112
Lesson 2: In the men's section	127

UNIT 6
Lesson 1: What are you doing tomorrow?	140
Lesson 2: Booking tickets online	151

INTRODUCTION

Welcome to your Livemocha Active Italian experience! This new course goes above and beyond what a traditional book-based course can offer. With its focus on online learning, Active Italian provides the opportunity not just to study but to experience the language for yourself by interacting with native speakers online.

Why go online?

Studying a language online allows you to learn in a more natural atmosphere – watching people interact in a **video** is far more lifelike than listening to conversations on a CD. After watching a video dialog, you will be walked through an explanation of some of the **grammar** and **vocabulary** items that were introduced in the new dialog. Then, by completing a variety of **interactive quizzes**, the system will instantly be able to tell you how well you are doing. You can then **talk online** with native Italian speakers to practice what you've learned.

Who else is online?

Livemocha boasts over 7 million members and is growing every day. These members are online for the same reason as you – to learn and experience a new language. Native Italian-speaking members will be happy to read through your written and spoken submissions and to give you feedback on how you're doing. You can also connect with people who want to chat in any given language – interaction on an informal, nonacademic basis is an ideal way for you to perfect your language skills.

What do the books do?

The four accompanying books are designed to complement the online course – the dialogs for all of the videos that you can watch online are available here for you to study whenever you don't have access to the Internet. You will also find all of the Grammar and Vocabulary sections explained in the books, plus the culture notes to teach you a little about Italy.

LEVEL 2

This book is the second of four. It corresponds with Level 2 of the online course.

Level 2 is ideal for students who can understand a simple conversation but who may still have difficulty taking part.

What you will learn
- How to buy tickets, ask for information, and understand directions
- How to make plans, understand suggestions and accept invitations
- How to form and use commands, talk about possession, and make comparisons
- How to form the perfect tense using *avere*
- Vocabulary for sports, museums, more jobs, city and town, clothes, colors, months and daily routines

 Every time you see this coffee cup symbol in these books, it indicates the presence of a pathway – a guide to exactly where you can find that particular piece of content online. Log on at www.livemocha.com and follow the path to find the online version of what you are studying in the book.

Video Dialog

As they finish their drinks, Michele and the waiter give Giulia directions to some local stores.

 Active Italian: Level 1 > Unit 3 > Lesson 1 > Video dialog

Active Italian *Level 2*

1

Lesson 1: Planning a trip to the museum

- » How to ask for help: *Mi può aiutare?*
- » How to say you are going to a place: *andare a* (or *al, alla, all'*, etc.)...
- » How to modify adjectives using adverbs: *abbastanza, molto, troppo*, etc.
- » The difference between *Bisogna...* and *Sarebbe meglio...*.
- » How to say that something happens regularly on a particular day: *il lunedì, il sabato*, etc.
- » How to make nouns and adjectives agree.

Lesson 2: Getting directions to a museum

- » Possessive adjectives "my," "your," "his," "our," etc.: *mio, tuo, suo, nostro*, etc.
- » How to say "my favorite...": *il mio... preferito.*
- » Different ways of saying "Not at all."
- » How to give directions: *Giri a sinistra/destra.*
- » The word *su* (on) and how it combines with the direct articles to become *sul, sulla, sull'*, etc.

○ Collins | Livemocha™

UNIT 1 › LESSON 1

Planning a trip to the museum

Culture note

Rome has some of the most impressive museums and archaeological sites in the world. The Vatican Museums (*Musei Vaticani*), within Vatican City, get over 4 million visitors each year. There are over 20 separate museums, palaces, galleries, and chapels, full of priceless works of art. The Sistine Chapel, with its famous ceiling painted by Michelangelo, is perhaps the most famous of these.

Unit 1 › Lesson 1: *Planning a trip to the museum*

Video Dialog

Giulia pays a visit to the tourist information office. She is looking for some information on the local sites.

 Watch the video dialog online at *Active Italian: Level 2* > *Unit 1* > *Lesson 1* > *Video dialog*

Giulia:	*Buongiorno, signora. Mi può aiutare?*
Sig.ra Duranti:	*Sì?*
Giulia:	*Vorrei andare al Museo Nazionale. È lontano da qui?*
Sig.ra Duranti:	*È abbastanza lontano, sarebbe meglio prendere la metro.*
Giulia:	*Devo cambiare?*
Sig.ra Duranti:	*Sì, deve cambiare a Termini.*
Giulia:	*Dov'è la stazione della metro?*
Sig.ra Duranti:	*C'è una stazione a due minuti da qui. Uscendo da qui, è proprio lì sulla sua sinistra. Ma il museo è chiuso oggi. È lunedì.*
Giulia:	*Come?*
Sig.ra Duranti:	*Il Museo nazionale è chiuso oggi. È chiuso il lunedì.*
Giulia:	*Oh, accidenti!*

....

Giulia:	Hello. Can you help me?

1.1 Livemocha™ Active Italian *Level 2*

Mrs. Duranti:	Yes?
Giulia:	I'd like to go to the National Museum. Is it far from here?
Mrs. Duranti:	It's quite far. It would be better to take the subway.
Giulia:	Do I need to change?
Mrs. Duranti:	Yes, you have to change at Termini.
Giulia:	Where's the subway station?
Mrs. Duranti:	There's a station two minutes away. When you walk out of here, it's just there on your left. But the museum is closed today. It's Monday.
Giulia:	Pardon?
Mrs. Duranti:	The National Museum is closed today. It's closed on Mondays.
Giulia:	Darn!

Grammar

In this section we go over some of the grammar points introduced in the dialog.

Go to Active Italian: Level 2 > Unit 1 > Lesson 1 > Grammar to listen to these explanations and to access some interactive practice activities.

1 › **Asking for help**

Mi può aiutare? (Can you help me?) is extremely useful when you need help of any kind.

You can go up to someone in the street with:
Scusi, mi può aiutare?

Then you can make your request.

Vorrei andare al duomo.	I want to go to the cathedral.
Vorrei andare alla stazione.	I want to go to the station.

Unit 1 › Lesson 1: *Planning a trip to the museum*

Potere is normally followed by the infinitive form of the verb. Italian infinitives usually end in *-are* (*parlare*), *-ere* (*prendere*) or *-ire* (*finire*).

2 › ## Going to a place

When saying where you're going, *andare* is followed by *a* and the name of the town or city: *a Roma*, *a Milano*, *a Palermo*.

If the place is introduced by *il*, *la*, *lo* or *l'*, then *a* combines with the article: *al*, *alla*, *all'* or *allo* (in the singular) and *ai*, *alle*, *agli* (in the plural).

Vado al museo.	I'm going to the museum.
Vado alla Cappella Sistina.	I'm going to the Sistine Chapel.
Vado allo stadio.	I'm going to the stadium.
Vado all'ospedale.	I'm going to the hospital.

When it is a country or continent you are going to, *andare* is followed by *in* and the name of the country or continent:

Vado in Spagna.	I am going to Spain.
Vado in Francia.	I am going to France.
Vado in Europa.	I am going to Europe.

But you say:

| *negli Stati Uniti* | to the United States |
| *nel Regno Unito* | to the United Kingdom |

3 › Quite, very, too, just

Some useful words to modify adjectives include:

| *abbastanza* | quite |
| *È abbastanza lontano.* | It's quite far. |

| *molto* | very |
| *È molto lontano.* | It's very far. |

| *troppo* | too |
| *È troppo lontano.* | It's too far. |

| *proprio* | just |
| *È proprio di fronte.* | It's just across. |

These words are called adverbs and unlike many words in Italian, adverbs always stay the same.

Unit 1 › Lesson 1: *Planning a trip to the museum*

4 › It would be better to...

Bisogna means "it is necessary" or "you have to," but if you don't want to be quite so dogmatic, you can say *Sarebbe meglio* (It would be better). It is followed by the infinitive.

| *Sarebbe meglio prendere l'autobus.* | It would be better to take the bus. |
| *Sarebbe meglio andare a piedi.* | It would be better to go by foot. |

5 › It's Monday

When saying what day it is, just use *è*.

| *È lunedì.* | It's Monday. |
| *È sabato.* | It's Saturday. |

Oggi means "today."

> *Oggi è venerdì.*
> Today is Friday.

When you want to say that something happens regularly on a certain day, you put *il* in front of the day of the week from Monday to Saturday, and *la* in front of *domenica* (Sunday).

| *È chiuso la domenica.* | It is closed on Sundays. |
| *Il martedì faccio la spesa.* | I do my shopping on Tuesdays. |

Remember, days of the week start with a small letter in Italian.

6 › Remember the gender!

As you know, Italian nouns have a gender, either masculine or feminine. Try to remember the gender of nouns when you first learn them.

Il museo is a masculine word, so when Signora Duranti refers to the museum, she says *è chius**o***.

> ### *È chiuso il lunedì.*
> It is closed on Mondays.

As you can see, you don't need a word for "it," but you must match the ending of *chiuso* to *museo*. This is known as "agreeing."

Unit 1 › Lesson 1: *Planning a trip to the museum*

But when talking about *la pizzeria* (pizzeria), which is a feminine noun, you would say *chius**a***.

> *È chiusa il lunedì.*
> It is closed on Mondays.

7 › **Agreement in the plural**

We have seen how the ending of *chiuso* has to agree with the gender of what it refers to: *il muse**o** è chius**o**, la pizzeri**a** è chius**a***. If you are referring to something plural, then it also has to be reflected:

I musei sono chiusi il lunedì.	The museums are closed on Mondays.
Le pizzerie sono chiuse il lunedì.	The pizzerias are closed on Mondays.

Listening to and reading as much Italian as you can will help you become familiar with the rules of agreement.

Livemocha™ Active Italian *Level 2*

Culture note

Many museums in Italy are closed on Mondays. Always check before you plan a visit. Most towns and cities have a well-informed and helpful tourist office (*Ufficio Turistico*) in which you can ask opening times of local museums. You can also check online, in guidebooks, or at the museums for further information.

Vocabulary

In this section you will learn some useful words and expressions from the dialog.

 Go to Active Italian: Level 2 > Unit 1 > Lesson 1 > Vocabulary to listen to each of the words being pronounced and to access some interactive practice activities.

aiutare
to help

Mi può aiutare?
Can you help me?

il museo
museum

Scusi, dov'è il Museo Nazionale?
Excuse me, where is the National Museum?

Unit 1 › Lesson 1: *Planning a trip to the museum*

qui vicino
near here

È qui vicino?
Is it near here?

da lì
from there

Da lì bisogna continuare a piedi.
From there you need to continue on foot.

cambiare
to change

Bisogna cambiare treno?
Do I need to change trains?

un minuto
a minute

C'è un albergo a cinque minuti da qui.
There's a hotel five minutes from here.

uscire
to go out

Bisogna uscire da qui.
You have to go out from here.

l'uscita
exit

Dov'è l'uscita?
Where is the exit?

entrare
to enter

Bisogna entrare da lì.
You have to go in from there.

l'ingresso
admission, entrance fee

Quanto costa l'ingresso?
How much is the admission?

Culture note

When visiting churches you should dress appropriately with shoulders covered and long pants. There are often signs before entering to remind you of this, along with other warnings advising you not to use cameras or to use them only without a flash. Remember that they are primarily places of worship.

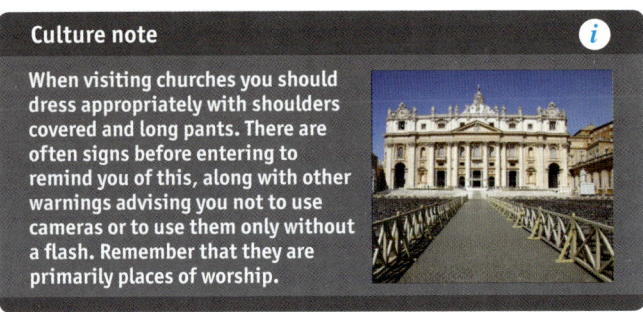

UNIT 1 › LESSON 2
Getting directions to a museum

Culture note

Italy boasts some of the greatest Renaissance artists: Titian (Tiziano), Michelangelo, and Leonardo da Vinci. Works of art by Italian Renaissance masters can be found in all major Italian cities, situated in the main squares, churches, and museums. Many towns exhibit pieces by the artists that came from the local region or worked in the area.

An example of this is the great number of Titian's work found in Venice, where the artist lived and worked.

Some of the best-known Italian masterpieces include Michelangelo's Last Judgement (*il Giudizio universale*), found in the Sistine Chapel (*la Cappella Sistina*) in St. Peter's Basilica, Rome, David (*David*), the original sculpture found in the Galleria dell'Accademia in Florence, Leonardo da Vinci's Last Supper (*L'Ultima cena*, also known as *il Cenacolo*) that is found inside Santa Maria delle Grazie, a church in Milan and the Mona Lisa (*La Gioconda*) found in the Louvre, Paris.

Video Dialog

The tourist office assistant, Signora Duranti, recommends the Civic Museum where there is an exhibition on the work of Giulia's favorite artist.

 Italian: Level 2 > Unit 1 > Lesson 2 > Video dialog

Sig.ra Duranti:	*Vada al Museo Civico, è aperto il lunedì.*
Giulia:	*Che cosa c'è in questo museo?*
Sig.ra Duranti:	*Ci sono molte opere del Rinascimento.*
Giulia:	*Adoro il Rinascimento.*
Sig.ra Duranti:	*In questo momento c'è una mostra meravigliosa su Raffaello.*
Giulia:	*Raffaello è il mio artista preferito!*
Sig.ra Duranti:	*Prenda l'autobus: se prende il 24 non deve cambiare.*
Giulia:	*Dov'è la fermata dell'autobus?*
Sig.ra Duranti:	*Continui sempre dritto per questa strada, giri a destra e la fermata dell'autobus è sulla sua sinistra.*
Giulia:	*Grazie mille, signora.*
Sig.ra Duranti:	*Non c'è di che.*

....

Mrs. Duranti:	Go to the Civic Museum, it's open on Mondays.
Giulia:	What is there in this museum?
Mrs. Duranti:	There are a lot of Renaissance works.
Giulia:	I love the Renaissance.

Mrs. Duranti:	At the moment there's a wonderful exhibition on Raphael.
Giulia:	Raphael is my favorite artist!
Mrs. Duranti:	Take the bus. If you take the number 24, you don't need to change.
Giulia:	Where's the bus stop?
Mrs. Duranti:	Continue straight along this street, turn right and the bus stop is on your left.
Giulia:	Thank you very much.
Mrs. Duranti:	Not at all.

Grammar

 Active Italian: Level 2 > Unit 1 > Lesson 2 > Grammar

8 › **My, your, his, her... (1)**

The word for "my" is *mio* as in *il mio artista preferito* (my favorite artist). It is a possessive adjective.

Possessive adjectives are:

mio	my
tuo	(*familiar*) your
suo	his/her/its
suo	(*formal*) your
nostro	our
vostro	(*plural*) your
loro	their

9 › My, your, his, her... (2)

Mio (my), *tuo* (your), *suo* (his, her, its and formal your), etc., agree with the thing they refer to (whether it is masculine, feminine, singular or plural) and not the person who owns it. The article (*il*, *la*, etc.) is also usually included.

il mio albergo	my hotel
la mia casa	my house
il tuo albergo	your hotel
la tua casa	your house
il nostro albergo	our hotel
la nostra casa	our house
il vostro albergo	your hotel
la vostra casa	your house

You need to take care with *suo* as it can mean "his, her, its" or formal "your." The situation will tell you which one it is.

Ecco, signora, il suo passaporto.	Here, madam, your passport.
Puoi dare questo a Tom? È il suo passaporto.	Can you give this to Tom? It's his passport.

"Their" is *loro*. *Loro* doesn't change.

il loro albergo	their hotel
la loro casa	their house

10 › My, your, his, her... (3)

Remember that possessive adjectives also have to agree in the plural:

i miei or *le mie*	my
i tuoi or *le tue*	(*familiar*) your
i suoi or *le sue*	his, her, its
i suoi or *le sue*	(*formal*) your
i nostri or *le nostre*	our
i vostri or *le vostre*	(*plural*) your
i loro or *le loro*	their

Dove sono le mie cose?	Where are my things?
Dove sono i nostri passaporti?	Where are our passports?
Ecco i suoi biglietti.	Here are your tickets.

11 › My favorite...

Giulia says that her favorite artist is Raphael. *Il mio artista preferito è Raffaello.*

You can use this expression for your favorite actress or singers:

| *La mia attrice preferita è Angelina Jolie.* | My favorite actress is Angelina Jolie. |
| *I miei cantanti preferiti sono...* | My favorite singers are... |

Note how you must make the words "my" and "favorite" agree with who (or what) they refer to.

Remember that Italian words ending in *-ista* can be either masculine or feminine: *il/la dentista* (dentist), *il/la ciclista* (cyclist), *l'autista* (driver), *il/la barista* (bartender), etc.

12 › Giving directions (1)

To give directions (or orders) you need a particular form of the verb.
For verbs ending in *-are* the ending is *-i*.
For verbs ending in *-ere* or *-ire* the ending is *-a*.

Continui per questa strada.	Continue down this street.
Giri a destra.	Turn right.
Prenda l'autobus.	Take the bus.

Andare (to go) has a special form:

Vada al Museo Civico.
Go to the Civic Museum.

This is the polite form that you would hear if you asked someone for directions.

13 › Giving directions (2)

If Giulia was giving the same instructions to a friend, she would use the *tu* form.

For verbs ending in *-are* the ending is *-a*.
For verbs ending in *-ere* or *-ire* the ending is *-i*.

Continua per questa strada.	Continue down this street.
Gira a destra.	Turn right.
Prendi l'autobus.	Take the bus.

The form for *andare* is:

> *Va' al Museo Civico.*
> Go to the Civic Museum.

If there were more than one of you being given directions, then the *voi* form of the verb would be used:

> *Continuate*
> *Girate*
> *Prendete*

14 › Not at all!

Non c'è di che is another way of saying *prego* ("not at all," "don't mention it" or "you're welcome").

It is slightly more formal or emphatic than *prego*.

Unit 1 › Lesson 2: *Getting directions to a museum*

15 › How to say "on the" – *su* + masculine *il*, *l'*

Another short word that combines with the article is *su* (on) and it follows the usual pattern.

In front of a masculine noun, *su* combines with *il* or *l'* to become *sul* (or *sull'*):

| *sul battello* | on the boat |
| *sull'aereo* | on the airplane |

In the plural, *su* combines with *i* to become *sui* or with *gli* to become *sugli*:

| *sui treni* | on the trains |
| *sugli aerei* | on the airplanes |

16 › How to say "on the" – *su* + *lo*

With the *lo* article, *su* combines with *lo* to become *sullo* in the singular and *sugli* in the plural:

| *sullo stoino* | on the doormat |
| *sugli stoini* | on the doormats |

17 › **How to say "on the" – *su* + *la***

When you use *su* in front of a feminine noun, *su* combines with *la* to become *sulla* (or *sull'*) in the singular and *sulle* in the plural:

sulla montagna	on the mountain
sull'erba	on the grass
sulle colline	on the hills

18 › **A thousand thanks**

A stronger alternative to *grazie* is *grazie mille* (literally "a thousand thanks").

Unit 1 › Lesson 2: *Getting directions to a museum*

Vocabulary

  Active Italian: Level 2 > Unit 1 > Lesson 2 > Vocabulary

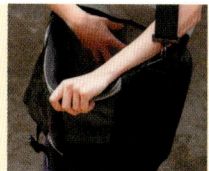

la cosa
thing

Dove sono le mie cose?
Where are my things?

aperto/a
open

La posta è aperta oggi?
Is the post office open today?

chiuso/a
closed

Il ristorante è chiuso oggi.
The restaurant is closed today.

molto/a
many/much/lots of

Ci sono molte persone qui.
There are lots of people here.

l'opera
opera, (piece of) work

Mi piacciono le opere di Michelangelo.
I like the works of Michelangelo.

il Rinascimento
the Renaissance

Adoro il Rinascimento.
I love the Renaissance.

il secolo
century

Quale secolo?
Which century?

la mostra
exhibition

Quando c'è la mostra?
When is the exhibition?

la pinacoteca
art gallery

La pinacoteca è nel centro storico.
The art gallery is in the old part of town.

Unit 1 › Lesson 2: *Getting directions to a museum*

meraviglioso/a
wonderful

Che quadro meraviglioso!
What a wonderful painting!

la statua
statue

Chi raffigura questa statua?
Who is this statue of?

a destra
to/on the right

Bisogna girare a destra.
You have to turn right.

a sinistra
to/on the left

Giri a sinistra.
Turn left.

Culture note

Once your bus or subway ticket has been date stamped, it is usually valid for a number of minutes – generally 75 minutes. If you are going to stay in a town or city for more than a couple of days, investigate the different  travel cards. A *carta turistica* allows unlimited travel. Ask at the tourist office (*Ufficio Turistico*) for further information.

Active Italian *Level 2*

2

Lesson 1: Asking the way to the stadium

- » The conditional tense and corresponding verb endings: *-ei, -esti, -ebbe, -emmo, -este, -ebbero*.
- » How to say which team you support: *Faccio il tifo per...*
- » Simple expressions: *Bisogna...* and *Basta...*
- » How to use *per* and *da*: *un treno per Roma, un aereo da Londra*.
- » Expressions with *avere: aver tempo di, aver fame, aver sete*, etc.
- » How to say "at" a time and "from" a time: *alle .../dalle...*

Lesson 2: A quick beer before the soccer game

- » How to switch from formal *lei* to friendly *tu: darsi del tu*.
- » The present tense of *dare*.
- » The expression *aver bisogno di*.
- » Different ways of saying "yes."
- » Using *che* in expressions such as *Che bella casa!*

Collins | **Livemocha™**

UNIT 2 › LESSON 1

Asking the way to the stadium

Culture note

The *Stadio Olimpico* in Rome is Italy's second biggest stadium after the San Siro in Milan and can seat over 72,000 people. It staged athletics events in the 1960 Olympic Games and continues to host international athletic meetings as well as concerts. The stadium is also shared by the soccer teams Roma and Lazio.

Unit 2 › Lesson 1: *Asking the way to the stadium*

Video Dialog

Michele asks Ugo for directions and surprises him with a generous offer.

Active Italian: Level 2 > Unit 2 > Lesson 1 > Video dialog

Michele:	*Mi scusi! Vorrei andare allo stadio Olimpico. È lontano?*
Ugo:	*Ehm... sì. Bisogna prendere la metro, la linea B. Bisogna cambiare a Termini e prendere la linea A per tre fermate. Da lì è facile, basta seguire i cartelli per lo stadio. Va alla partita di stasera?*
Michele:	*Sì, faccio il tifo per il Milan. Veramente, ho due biglietti. Il mio amico non può venire stasera. Vuole venirci lei?*
Ugo:	*Volentieri! A che ora comincia la partita?*
Michele:	*Alle diciannove e trenta.*
Ugo:	*Che ore sono adesso?*
Michele:	*Ehm, sono le sei e un quarto.*
Ugo:	*Bene, abbiamo tempo di bere qualcosa. Offro io.*

Michele:	Excuse me. I'd like to go the Olympic stadium. Is it far?
Ugo:	Er... yes. You have to take the subway, line B. You have to change at Termini and then take line A for three stops. From there it is easy, all you have to do is follow the signs to the stadium. Are you going to the game tonight?

Livemocha™ Active Italian *Level 2*

Michele:	Yes, I support Milan. Actually I have two tickets. My friend can't come this evening. Would you like to come?
Ugo:	Gladly! What time does the game begin?
Michele:	At 7:30.
Ugo:	What time is it now?
Michele:	Er... it's a quarter past six.
Ugo:	Good, we've time for a drink. It's on me.

Grammar

Active Italian: Level 2 > Unit 2 > Lesson 1 > Grammar

1 › **The conditional tense**

To ask politely for something or to express a wish, the conditional tense of *volere* (to want) is used. So *vorrei* (I would like) rather than the present tense *voglio* (I want) is used.

We have encountered it before in the expressions *sarebbe meglio* (it would be better to), *potrebbe* (you could), and *potremmo* (we could).

To make different tenses in Italian, you add different endings to the stem of the verb. For *volere*, the conditional stem is *vorr-*.

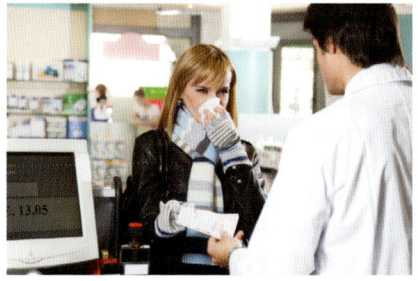

Unit 2 › Lesson 1: *Asking the way to the stadium*

Here is the conditional tense:

vorrei	I would like
vorresti	you (familiar) would like
vorrebbe	he/she/it would like
vorrebbe	you (formal) would like
vorremmo	we would like
vorreste	you (plural) would like
vorrebbero	they would like

The conditional tense endings are the same for *all* verbs.

2 › Asking a question

Remember that asking a question is simple. You don't need to change the word order of a statement, just raise the pitch of your voice in a questioning manner.

Va alla partita di stasera.	You are going to this evening's game.
Va alla partita di stasera?	Are you going to this evening's game?

3 › Simple expressions

Two useful expressions are: *Bisogna* (literally "It is necessary to") and *Basta* (literally "It is enough to"). They often translate as "We/You need to" or "All you have to do is." Both expressions are followed by the infinitive form of the verb.

| *Bisogna prendere la metropolitana.* | You need to take the subway. |
| *Basta seguire i cartelli.* | All you have to do is follow the signs. |

4 › It is easy/difficult

Other simple but useful phrases are:
È facile (It is easy) and its opposite *È difficile* (It is difficult). Again, they are followed by the infinitive form of the verb.

| *È facile parlare l'italiano.* | It is easy to speak Italian. |
| *È difficile parlare l'inglese.* | It is difficult to speak English. |

Unit 2 › Lesson 1: *Asking the way to the stadium*

5 › Making negative statements

Instead of *È difficile* (It is difficult) you could simply say *Non è facile* (It isn't easy).

To make a negative statement, put *non* in front of the verb

Il mio amico non può venire.	My friend can't come.
Il mio orologio non funziona.	My watch isn't working.
Non vorrebbe perdere la partita.	He wouldn't want to miss the game.

6 › The words *per* (for, to) and *da* (from)

Ugo tells Michele to follow the signs *per lo stadio* (to the stadium). *Per*, meaning "for," is used to indicate a destination. You use *per* when asking for a train, plane or ticket to somewhere.

Questo è il treno per Roma?	Is this the train to Rome?
L'aereo per Londra parte alle nove.	The plane to London leaves at 9.
Un biglietto per Como, per favore.	A ticket to Como, please.

When talking about where a train or plane is coming from, you use *da* (from).

> *Questo è il treno da Roma?*
> Is this the train from Rome?

> *L'aereo da Londra arriva alle venti.*
> The airplane from London arrives at 8 p.m.

Remember that *andare* (to go) is followed by *a* for places, towns, and cities, and *in* for countries and continents.

Vado a Roma.	I am going to Rome.
Andiamo in Italia.	We are going to Italy.

7 › **Avere (to have) in different expressions**

Avere (to have) is used in a number of set expressions, including:

avere tempo di	**to have time to**
Non ho tempo di mangiare.	I don't have time to eat.

avere sete	**to be thirsty**
Ho molta sete.	I am very thirsty.

Unit 2 › Lesson 1: *Asking the way to the stadium*

avere fame	to be hungry
Non ho molta fame.	I'm not very hungry.
avere... anni	to be... years old
Ho ventidue anni.	I am 22 years old.
avere caldo	to be hot
Ho molto caldo.	I am very hot.
avere freddo	to be cold
Ho molto freddo.	I am very cold.

8 › *Alle* + the time

Ugo asks Michele when the soccer game begins.

A che ora comincia la partita?

Michele replies

Alle sette e mezza.
At 7:30.

Note the use of *alle* meaning "at." It is always *alle* except when referring to one o'clock, when it is *all'una*.

Alle comes from combining *a* with the article *le* of *le ore* (the hours).

La partita comincia alle sette e mezza.	The game begins at 7:30 p.m.
Il film finisce alle dieci.	The movie finishes at 10 p.m.

Dalle + the time

We have already come across *da* meaning "from." It is also used with time and works much the same way as *alle*. To say "from" a particular time it is *dalle*, except for one o'clock, when it is *dall'una*.

dall'una e mezza	from one thirty
dalle nove	from nine o'clock

Il negozio è aperto dalle nove alle sei.
The shop is open from 9 to 6.

Vocabulary

Active Italian: Level 2 > Unit 2 > Lesson 1 > Vocabulary

fare il tifo per
to be a fan/supporter of

Per chi fai il tifo?
Who do you support?

da lì
from there

Da lì bisogna continuare a piedi.
From there you have to continue by foot.

qui
here

Vieni qui da me.
Come here to me.

là
there

Vorrei quello là.
I'd like that one there.

43

2.1 Livemocha™ Active Italian *Level 2*

cominciare
to start, to begin

A che ora comincia il film?
When does the movie start?

finire
to finish

A che ora finisce il film?
When does the movie finish?

adesso
now

Che cosa facciamo adesso?
What shall we do now?

dopo
later

Ti telefono dopo.
I'll phone you later.

Unit 2 › Lesson 1: *Asking the way to the stadium*

avere tempo di
to have time to

Non ho tempo di mangiare.
I don't have time to eat.

il biglietto
ticket

Vorrei comprare due biglietti per la partita.
I'd like to buy two tickets for the game.

Culture note

Italians are passionate about *il calcio* (soccer), which, along with food, is a topic of endless conversation. Italy has won the World Cup four times, in 1934, 1938, 1982 and 2006, and Italians are as passionate about their local teams as they are about their national representatives on the pitch.
Watching a game is often turned into an event with food, drinks, and all generations supporting their local team together.

La pallacanestro (basketball) and *la pallavolo* (volleyball) are also very popular. Other favorite sports include *il ciclismo* (bicycle racing), *l'automobilismo* (car racing) and *il motociclismo* (motorcycle racing).

UNIT 2 › LESSON 2
A quick beer before the soccer game

Culture note

When you ask for a *birra* in Italy, you will be served lager. *Una birra media* is just under a pint. *Una birra piccola* is half a pint. Italian beers are known as *birre nazionali*. If you want ale or bitter, you should ask for *birra scura* (literally "dark beer") or *birra rossa* (literally "red beer").

Unit 2 › Lesson 2: *A quick beer before the soccer game*

Video Dialog

Ugo and Michele introduce themselves properly.

Active Italian: Level 2 > Unit 2 > Lesson 2 > Video dialog

Ugo:	*Che cosa prende?*
Michele:	*Una birra alla spina, per favore. Michele. Possiamo darci del tu, no?*
Ugo:	*Certo. Io sono Ugo. Che cosa fai nella vita, Michele?*
Michele:	*Sono fotografo.*
Ugo:	*Che coincidenza! Ho giusto bisogno di un fotografo!*
Michele:	*E tu che lavoro fai?*
Ugo:	*Lavoro in un'agenzia immobiliare. Due birre medie alla spina, per favore.*
Waiter:	*Subito!*

Ugo:	What are you having?
Michele:	A draft beer, please. I'm Michele. Can we use "tu" with each other?
Ugo:	Of course. My name is Ugo. What is it you do, Michele?
Michele:	I'm a photographer.
Ugo:	What a coincidence! A photographer is just what I'm needing!
Michele:	And what do you do?
Ugo:	I work in real estate. Two pints of draft beer, please.
Waiter:	Right away!

Livemocha™ Active Italian *Level 2*

Grammar

 Active Italian: Level 2 > Unit 2 > Lesson 2 > Grammar

1 › Being less formal

The expression *darsi del tu* means to use *tu* with each other. The verb *dare* means "to give."

> *Possiamo darci del tu, no?*
> We can use *tu* with each other, can't we?

Ugo and Michele start the conversation with the more formal *lei* form but once they've introduced themselves Michele suggests that they switch to the more friendly *tu* form.

Unit 2 › Lesson 2: *A quick beer before the soccer game*

2 › The verb *dare* (to give)

The verb *dare* (to give) is another irregular verb.

Here is the present tense:

do	I give
dai	you (*familiar*) give
dà	he/she/it gives
dà	you (*formal*) give
diamo	we give
date	you (*plural*) give
danno	they give

Note how *dà* has an accent on it. This tells you not only to stress the letter but it also distinguishes it from the word *da* (from).

3 › Accents

Accents on letters indicate that the letter should be stressed. Accents also help distinguish words that are spelled the same but have different meanings.

These include:

è – e	is – and
dà – da	gives – from
tè – per te	tea – for you

4 › Saying what you do

As well as saying *Sono fotografo* you can also say *Faccio il fotografo* for "I am a photographer."

> *Sono agente immobiliare*
> or
> *Faccio l'agente immobiliare.*
> I am a real estate agent.

Note that you include the definite article *il, la* or *l'* with *Faccio*, but you don't need anything with *Sono*.

5 › *Ho bisogno di* – I need

Another expression using *avere* is *avere bisogno di*, literally "to have need of."

Ho proprio bisogno di un fotografo.	I really need a photographer.
Ho bisogno di un paio di calzini.	I need a pair of socks.
Ho bisogno di un consiglio.	I need some advice.

Unit 2 › Lesson 2: *A quick beer before the soccer game*

Bisogno is always followed by *di* (or *d'*) and a noun or the verb in the infinitive.

Ho bisogno di un taxi.	I need a taxi.
Ho bisogno di bere qualcosa.	I need something to drink.

6 › **Different ways of saying yes**

We have come across a number of ways of saying yes, without using the word *sì*.

These include:

Volentieri.	I'd love to.
Perché no?	Why not?
Certo.	Of course.

7 › What a...!

Che is used in exclamations to express "What a...!"

Che coincidenza!	What a coincidence!
Che bella vista!	What a beautiful view!
Che peccato!	What a shame!

8 › How...!

Che plus an adjective is also used to express "How...!"

Che bello!	How lovely!
Che strano!	How odd!
Che buono!	How delicious!

If you are referring to something in particular, such as *una casa* (a house), *un parco* (a park) or *dei fiori* (flowers), then you have to make the adjective agree.

> *Che bella! (casa)*
> *Che bello! (parco)*
> *Che belli! (fiori)*

Unit 2 › Lesson 2: *A quick beer before the soccer game*

9 › **What...?**

Che is also used to ask questions.

Che cosa prendi?	What are you having?
Che ore sono?	What time is it?
Che lavoro fai?	What work do you do?/What's your job?

Vocabulary

una birra media
a pint of beer

Una birra media per me, per favore.
A pint of beer for me, please.

alla spina
draft

Preferisci una birra alla spina o in bottiglia?
Do you prefer draft or bottled beer?

in lattina
in a can

Ha della birra in lattina?
Do you have beer in cans?

subito
right away

Vengo subito.
I'm coming right away.

la foto
photo

Ti mando le foto.
I will send you the photos.

la macchina fotografica
camera

Ho una macchina fotografica digitale.
I have a digital camera.

fare una foto
to take a photo

Mi può fare una foto?
Can you take a photo of me?

scaricare le foto
to download photos

Voglio scaricare le foto sul computer.
I want to download the photos onto the computer.

Unit 2 › Lesson 2: *A quick beer before the soccer game*

fare un lavoro
to do a job

Che lavoro fai?
What job do you do?

qualcosa
something

Facciamo qualcosa?
Shall we do something?

Culture note

In Italy, when drinking with a group of friends, each person tends to pay for their own drink unless someone offers to pay – *offro io* (it's on me). You might also hear the instruction *Lasci stare* (or *Lascia stare* among friends) which means "Leave it," in other words "Leave it, I'll pay."

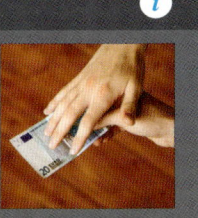

Active Italian Level 2

3

Lesson 1: Where to go shopping?

- » How word endings *-ino* and *-ina* make things small: *piantina*, *piccolino*.
- » Different types of shopping: *fare spese* and *fare la spesa*.
- » Using *fino a* with directions and time.
- » How to form past participles: *comprato*, *venduto*, *finito*.
- » Ordinal numbers: *primo*, *secondo*, etc.

Lesson 2: Catching the bus to the shops

- » Using *-iamo* ending to make suggestions: Let's…
- » How to use *tutto* and *ogni*.
- » About non-native Italian words: *sport*, *email*, etc.
- » How to tell someone not to do something.
- » How quantities are followed by *di* or *d'*.

Collins | **Livemocha™**

3.1

Livemocha™ Active Italian *Level 2*

UNIT 3 › LESSON 1

Where to go shopping?

Culture note

Mi dica pure is a formal expression you often hear in tourist offices, shops, and hotels. It means "Can I help you?" (Literally "Please tell me"). *Dica* is from the verb *dire* (to say/tell).

Unit 3 › Lesson 1: *Where to go shopping?*

Video Dialog

Giulia returns to the tourist information office – this time she needs to know how to find the shops.

 Active Italian: Level 2 > Unit 3 > Lesson 1 > Video dialog

Giulia:	*Buongiorno.*
Sig.ra Duranti:	*Buongiorno, mi dica pure.*
Giulia:	*Ha una piantina della città, per favore?*
Sig.ra Duranti:	*No, mi dispiace, sono finite. Dove vorrebbe andare?*
Giulia:	*Vorrei fare spese.*
Sig.ra Duranti:	*Allora vada in via Cavour.*
Giulia:	*Via Cavour? Dov'è?*
Sig.ra Duranti:	*Vada dritto fino al semaforo e poi giri a sinistra. Continui per il corso fino al primo incrocio…*
Giulia:	*È lontano?*
Sig.ra Duranti:	*Sì, è abbastanza lontano. È a piedi?*
Giulia:	*Sì.*

Giulia:	Good morning.
Mrs. Duranti:	Good morning. Can I help you?
Giulia:	Have you got a city map, please?
Mrs. Duranti:	No. I'm sorry. We've run out. Where would you like to go?

3.1 Livemocha™ Active Italian *Level 2*

Giulia:	I'd like to go shopping.
Mrs. Duranti:	Then go to via Cavour.
Giulia:	Via Cavour? Where is it?
Mrs. Duranti:	Go straight on as far as the traffic lights and then turn left. Carry on down the boulevard to the first intersection…
Giulia:	Is it a long way?
Mrs. Duranti:	Yes, it's quite far. Are you on foot?
Giulia:	Yes.

Grammar

  Active Italian: Level 2 > Unit 3 > Lesson 1 > Grammar

1 › **Word endings *-ino* and *-ina***

Right from the start of learning Italian, we have seen how word endings give lots of information. Endings often tell you whether a word is masculine or feminine; whether it is singular or plural; and with verbs, the endings tell you who is carrying out the verb action.

We encountered the ending *-issimo* or *-issima* that implies "very": *bello* is "beautiful" and *bellissimo* is "very beautiful."

The ending *-ino* or *-ina* means something is small. Giulia asks for a town plan or a little map, *una piantina*. *Una pianta* would be a bigger map, not quite as handy as *una piantina*.

Unit 3 › Lesson 1: *Where to go shopping?* **3.1**

You come across this ending frequently:

Piccolo means "small," *piccolino* means "tiny."

Tavolo means "table," *tavolino* means "little table" like the ones outside a bar.

Un cucchiaio means "spoon," *cucchiaino* means "teaspoon."

2 › Different types of shopping

There is a subtle difference between *fare la spesa* and *fare spese*.

Fare la spesa means "doing the shopping," as in the regular food shopping (a necessity).

Fare spese means shopping as in "going shopping," for more out-of-the-ordinary items such as clothes, etc.

Italians also say *fare shopping*. Again this implies something enjoyable rather than a chore.

Note that the article for *shopping* is *lo*, because of the rule about *lo* being used with words that begin with *s* + consonant (in this case the consonant is h).

3 › Up to or until

Fino a means "up to," "as far as," or "until."

> *Vada dritto fino al semaforo.*
> Go straight on as far as the traffic lights.

Remember that the word *a* combines with the article:

fino alla stazione	as far as the station
fino allo stadio	as far as the stadium
fino ai giardini pubblici	as far as the public gardens

Fino a is also used in expressions of time:

fino all'una	until 1 o'clock
fino alle quattro	until 4 o'clock
fino a mezzanotte	until midnight

4 › How to form past participles: finished, sold, bought.

When Giulia asks for a city map (*una piantina*), Signora Duranti replies:

> *No, mi dispiace, sono finite.*
> No, I'm sorry, they're finished.

Although she didn't actually say "The maps are finished," we know she is referring to them because of the feminine ending on *finit**e***.

Finito means "finished" and comes from the verb *finire* (to finish). It is known as a past participle. The rules for forming the past participle for regular verbs are straightforward.

With regular verbs ending in *-are*, such as *comprare* (to buy), you remove the *-are* and replace it with *-ato*:

> ***comprato***   bought

With regular verbs ending in *-ere* such as *vendere* (to sell), you remove the *-ere* and replace it with *-uto*:

> ***venduto***   sold

With regular verbs ending in *-ire* such as *finire* (to finish), you remove the *-ire* and replace it with *-ito*:

> ***finito***   finished

5 › More on past participles

When you use a past participle with *è* (is) or *sono* (are), it acts like an adjective and must agree with the word it refers to.

In *sono finite*, *finite* is agreeing with the maps (*le piantine*).

Here are some examples:

La casa è venduta.	The house is sold.
I biglietti sono venduti.	The tickets are sold.

6 › Past participles and irregular verbs

Although Italian has very regular rules for verbs, not all verbs are regular.

And not all verbs are irregular all of the time. In the present tense a verb can be regular, but in other tenses it might deviate from the rule. Fortunately good dictionaries point this out and you will always be able to check.

A couple of irregular past participles that we have been using are *chiuso* (closed) from *chiudere* (to close) and *aperto* (open) from *aprire* (to open). Another is *preso* (taken) from *prendere* (to take).

The past participle of *essere* (to be) is *stato*.
The past participle of *avere* (to have) is *avuto*.
The past participle of *andare* (to go) is *andato*.

Once you become familiar with Italian, even irregularities have their own pattern and you can often make an educated guess!

7 › | Cardinal and ordinal numbers

Il primo incrocio is "the first intersection." We have already come across the numbers *uno*, *due*, *tre*, *quattro* and so on. These are known as cardinal numbers.

First, second, third, and so on, are ordinal numbers as they put things in order.

Ordinal numbers agree with the word they are putting in order:

la prima casa	the first house
la seconda strada	the second street
i primi fiori	the first flowers

3.1 Livemocha™ Active Italian Level 2

8 ›
Ordinal numbers

The ordinal numbers from first to tenth are:

primo/a	first
secondo/a	second
terzo/a	third
quarto/a	fourth
quinto/a	fifth
sesto/a	sixth
settimo/a	seventh
ottavo/a	eighth
nono/a	ninth
decimo/a	tenth

When written with a figure, they are normally followed by a tiny superscript *o* for masculine things (1°, 2°) and a tiny superscript *a* for feminine things (1ª, 2ª).

Vocabulary

 Active Italian: Level 2 > Unit 3 > Lesson 1 > *Vocabulary*

sto cercando
I'm looking for

Sto cercando il Municipio.
I'm looking for the city hall.

Unit 3 › Lesson 1: *Where to go shopping?* **3.1**

la strada
street, road

Bisogna prendere la prima strada a sinistra.
You have to take the first road on the left.

andare dritto
to go straight

Devi andare dritto fino al duomo.
You have to go straight until the cathedral.

l'incrocio
intersection

Continua fino al secondo incrocio.
Keep going until the second intersection.

la rotonda
traffic circle

Quando arrivi alla rotonda, prendi la prima uscita.
When you get to the traffic circle, take the first exit.

il semaforo
traffic lights

Bisogna spegnere il motore al semaforo.
You need to turn your engine off at the traffic lights.

a sinistra
to/on the left

La banca è a sinistra.
The bank is on the left.

a destra
to/on the right

Per evitare la galleria prendi la strada a destra.
To avoid the tunnel, take the road on the right.

in questa zona
in this area

C'è una pizzeria in questa zona?
Is there a pizzeria in this area?

il parcheggio
parking lot

È aperto il parcheggio?
Is the parking lot open?

l'autostrada
highway

L'autostrada è chiusa a causa di un incidente.
The highway is closed because of an accident.

Unit 3 › Lesson 1: *Where to go shopping?*

l'uscita
highway exit

Per andare a Venezia, bisogna prendere la prossima uscita.
To go to Venice, you have to take the next exit.

il centro commerciale
shopping mall

Il centro commerciale è proprio di fronte all'aeroporto.
The shopping mall is right across from the airport.

Culture note

Mi dispiace means "I am sorry."

If someone approaches you in the street for directions and you are not able to help them, you can say *Mi dispiace, non lo so* (I am sorry, I don't know).

UNIT 3 › LESSON 2

Catching the bus to the shops

Culture note

A single subway ticket is generally valid for 75 minutes (from time of stamping or validation) and can often be used for one subway ride and any number of bus and tram journeys within that time limit.

There are also 10-journey tickets (*un biglietto da dieci corsi*) that need to be validated each time you make a trip. Check at the tourist office to find out about the best deals on public transportation.

It is important to remember to validate your ticket before getting on the bus or train. There are small yellow boxes at the start of train station platforms or in train stations in which you can stamp your ticket before getting on a train. For travel by bus, although you can buy tickets on some buses, it's always best to check and purchase one beforehand if possible. You can usually buy tickets in the local *tabaccheria* (tobacconist store selling stamps, postcards, candy, and tickets for local transportation). Remember to stamp your ticket when you get on the bus.

Unit 3 › Lesson 2: *Catching the bus to the shops*

Video Dialog

Signora Duranti gives Giulia some helpful directions.

Active Italian: Level 2 > Unit 3 > Lesson 2 > Video dialog

Sig.ra Duranti:	*Allora prenda l'autobus.*
Giulia:	*È frequente il servizio?*
Sig.ra Duranti:	*Ehm, vediamo... l'orario degli autobus... Ecco: prenda il 10, passa ogni dieci minuti.*
Giulia:	*Dove devo scendere?*
Sig.ra Duranti:	*L'autobus ferma proprio di fronte ai negozi.*
Giulia:	*Dove posso comprare il biglietto?*
Sig.ra Duranti:	*Può comprare un blocchetto di 10 biglietti in una tabaccheria o in un'edicola. Costa 12 euro. Altrimenti può comprare un biglietto solo, ma è più caro. E non si dimentichi di timbrare il biglietto quando sale sull'autobus.*
Giulia:	*Grazie mille, signora.*
Sig.ra Duranti:	*Di nulla, buona giornata.*

Mrs. Duranti:	Take the bus, then.
Giulia:	Is the service frequent?

Mrs. Duranti:	Er, let's see... the bus schedule... Here it is: take the number 10. It goes every 10 minutes.
Giulia:	Where do I have to get off?
Mrs. Duranti:	The bus stops right opposite the shops.
Giulia:	Where can I buy a ticket?
Mrs. Duranti:	You can get a book of 10 at a tobacconist's or at a newsstand. It costs 12 euros. Otherwise you can buy just one ticket, but it's more expensive. And don't forget to stamp your ticket when you board the bus.
Giulia:	Thanks very much.
Mrs. Duranti:	Don't mention it. Have a good day.

Grammar

....

 Active Italian: Level 2 > Unit 3 > Lesson 2 > Grammar

1 › | So... |
|---|

Allora means "so" or "then." It is often used when you are thinking about what you are going to say next.

Unit 3 › Lesson 2: *Catching the bus to the shops*

2 › Let's see...

Vediamo means "Let's see."

The *noi* form which ends in *-iamo* is what you use to make suggestions to one or more people.

Andiamo in piscina.	Let's go to the swimming pool.
Compriamo dei panini.	Let's buy some sandwiches.
Andiamo a piedi.	Let's walk.

3 › All and every...

The words *ogni* and *tutto* mean "all" or "every," depending on the context. *Ogni* is invariable and never changes. You don't use the article (*il*, *la*, *lo*, etc.) with it.

ogni giorno	every day
ogni settimana	every week
ogni dieci minuti	every ten minutes

Tutto, however, has to agree with the word it goes with and is followed by the article *il, la, lo*, etc.

tutto il pane	all the bread
tutti i negozi	all the stores
tutti i giorni	every day
tutta la gente	all the people
tutte le agenzie	all the agencies

4 › Non-native words

All Italian nouns end in *-o, -a, -i* or *-e*. Anything else you find is non-native!

The thing to remember about these words is that they don't change in the plural. Remember, though, that the article does.

l'autobus	*gli autobus*
il tram	*i tram*
lo sport	*gli sport*
il bar	*i bar*

Unit 3 › Lesson 2: *Catching the bus to the shops*

Most non-native words are masculine. A few, such as *email* and *password*, are feminine.

| *Ho ricevuto la tua email.* | I received your email. |
| *Qual è la tua password?* | What is your password? |

5 › Plural of nouns ending in *-io*

The plural of most masculine nouns ending in *-io* is *-i* and not *-ii*.

l'orario – gli orari	timetable
il negozio – i negozi	store
lo studio – gli studi	study

Occasionally a plural will end in double *i*. It happens when the stress falls on the final *i* as in *lo zio*. The plural is therefore *gli zii*.

6 › Instructions not to do something

The lady in the tourist office tells Giulia not to forget to stamp (validate) her bus ticket.

> *Non si dimentichi di timbrare il biglietto.*
> Don't forget to stamp your ticket.

To tell someone not to do something using the polite *lei* form is simple, you just place *non* in front of the verb.

Non compri questo formaggio.	Don't buy this cheese.
Non vada a piedi. È lontano.	Don't go by foot. It is far.
Non scenda qui.	Don't get off here.

If you are using the *tu* form then *non* is followed by the infinitive.

> *Non comprare questo formaggio.*
> *Non andare a piedi.*
> *Non scendere qui.*

Unit 3 › Lesson 2: *Catching the bus to the shops*

7 › Quantities followed by *di*

The lady in the tourist office advises Giulia to buy a book of 10 tickets, *un blocchetto di 10 biglietti*.

When talking about quantities such as a glass of, a bottle of, a bit of, a liter of, and so on, "of" is *di* or *d'* and not *del*, *della*, *dei* and so on.

Un bicchiere di vino.	A glass of wine.
Una bottiglia d'acqua minerale.	A bottle of mineral water.
Un po' di burro.	A bit of butter.
Un litro di latte.	A liter of milk.

Livemocha™ Active Italian *Level 2*

Vocabulary

○ *Active Italian: Level 2 > Unit 3 > Lesson 2 > Vocabulary*

fuori servizio
out of order

Il bancomat e fuori servizio.
The ATM is out of order.

Unit 3 › Lesson 2: *Catching the bus to the shops*

3.2

passare
to go by

Ogni quanto passa l'autobus?
How often do the buses go by?

l'orario
schedule

Ha l'orario dei battelli?
Do you have the boat schedule?

fermare
to stop

L'autobus ferma di fronte al museo.
The bus stops opposite the museum.

un blochetto di 10 biglietti
a book of 10 tickets

Vuole un biglietto di corsa singola o un blochetto di 10 biglietti?
Do you want a single ticket or a book of 10 tickets?

la tabaccheria
tobacco shop

Cerco una tabaccheria.
I'm looking for a tobacco shop.

un'edicola
newsstand

C'è un'edicola in Piazza Cavour.
There is a newsstand in Piazza Cavour.

la fermata
stop

Non scendere qui. Questa non è la tua fermata.
Don't get off here. This isn't your stop.

salire sull'autobus
to get on the bus

Quando sali sull'autobus devi timbrare il biglietto.
When you get on the bus you have to validate your ticket.

Unit 3 › Lesson 2: *Catching the bus to the shops*

davanti a
in front of, opposite

La fermata dell'autobus é davanti al centro commerciale.
The bus stop is opposite the shopping mall.

Culture note

City buses are generally orange. You usually enter from the rear and stamp your ticket in the machine as you enter. If the bus is very crowded, you can say either *scusi* or *permesso* to get past people. If there is no way of reaching the validating machine, hand your ticket to someone nearer the machine who will do it for you.

Active Italian *Level 2*

4

Lesson 1: In the clothes shop

- » How to ask for different items of clothing.
- » How to talk about different sizes: *piccola*, *media*, *grande*.
- » How to describe different colors.
- » How to say whether they fit or not: *mi va benissimo*.
- » How to use object pronouns: *lo, la, li, le*.
- » How to ask how much something is.

Lesson 2: A little black dress

- » How to say you are doing something using *stare: sto cercando*.
- » How to say you want something special: *qualcosa di speciale*.
- » How to make a negative construction using *non... niente.*
- » How to ask if you can pay by credit card.
- » How to form the imperfect tense: *costava*.

Collins | **Livemocha™**

UNIT 4 › LESSON 1
In the clothes shop

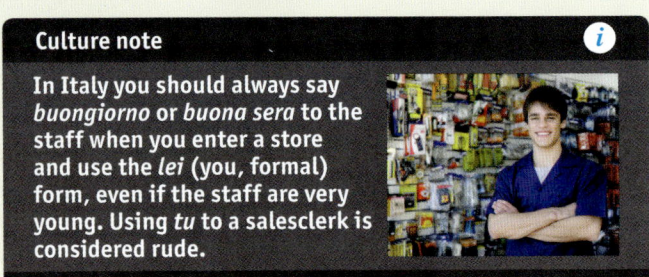

Culture note

In Italy you should always say *buongiorno* or *buona sera* to the staff when you enter a store and use the *lei* (you, formal) form, even if the staff are very young. Using *tu* to a salesclerk is considered rude.

Unit 4 › Lesson 1: *In the clothes shop*

Video Dialog

Giulia goes on the hunt for some new clothes.

 Active Italian: Level 2 > Unit 4 > Lesson 1 > Video dialog

Giulia:	*Buongiorno.*
Lucia:	*Buongiorno, desidera?*
Giulia:	*Vorrei una maglia rossa, taglia media.*
Lucia:	*Ecco, questa è una taglia 44.*
Giulia:	*Grazie, ma è troppo grande.*
Lucia:	*Provi questa.*
Giulia:	*È bella, ma è troppo piccola.*
Lucia:	*Allora provi una 42.*
Giulia:	*Ah sì, grazie. Mi va benissimo. Quanto costa?*
Lucia:	*49 euro.*
Giulia:	*Perfetto, la prendo. Posso pagare con la carta di credito?*
Lucia:	*Certo.*

Giulia:	Good morning.
Lucia:	Good morning, what would you like?
Giulia:	I would like a red sweater, medium size.
Lucia:	Here you are. This is a size 44.
Giulia:	Thank you, but it's too big.
Lucia:	Try this one.
Giulia:	It's nice but it's too small.
Lucia:	Then try a 42.

Livemocha™ Active Italian *Level 2*

Giulia:	Yes, thanks. It fits very well. How much does it cost?
Lucia:	49 euros.
Giulia:	Perfect, I'll take it. Can I pay by credit card?
Lucia:	Of course.

Grammar

Active Italian: Level 2 > Unit 4 > Lesson 1 > Grammar

1 › **Colors**

Giulia asks for a red sweater – *una maglia rossa*.
Red is *rosso*. As with most other adjectives in Italian, the color comes *after* the noun and agrees with what it is describing, in this case feminine *maglia*.

Generally a masculine adjective ending in *-o* changes to *-a* to make it feminine. In the plural, masculine adjectives end in *-i* and feminine ones in *-e*.

il cappello rosso	the red hat
la maglia rossa	the red sweater
i cappelli rossi	the red hats
le maglie rosse	the red sweaters

Normally adjectives ending in *-e* can be both masculine and feminine in the singular. In the plural, the ending (for both masculine and feminine) changes to *-i*.

il cappello verde	the green hat
la maglia verde	the green sweater
i cappelli verdi	the green hats
le maglie verdi	the green sweaters

2 › Different colors

Common colors include:

rosso	red
bianco	white
nero	black
giallo	yellow
grigio	gray
verde	green
arancio	orange
marrone (plural *marrone* or *marroni*)	brown
azzurro	blue
blu	blue
rosa	pink

Generally speaking, *azzurro* is a lighter blue than *blu*. You would use *azzurro* to describe a blue sky (*un cielo azzurro*).

3 › Colors that never change

The colors *blu* (blue), *arancio* (orange) and *rosa* (pink) are invariable, i.e. they never change. Other colours that are invariable are *beige* (beige), *viola* (purple), *bordeaux* (crimson) and *lilla* (lilac).

una camicia rosa	a pink shirt
i pantaloni rosa	pink pants
una macchina blu	a dark blue car

Unit 4 › Lesson 1: *In the clothes shop* **4.1**

4 › **Asking the color of something**

When asking the color of something, you say: *Di che colore?* (literally "Of what color?")

> *Di che colore è la macchina?*
> What color is the car?

5 › **Adjectives indicating size**

Useful words to do with size include:

piccolo/a	small
medio/a	medium
grande	large

una taglia media	a medium size
una taglia grande	a large size

You find Italians also use the English words: small, medium, large, and extra large.

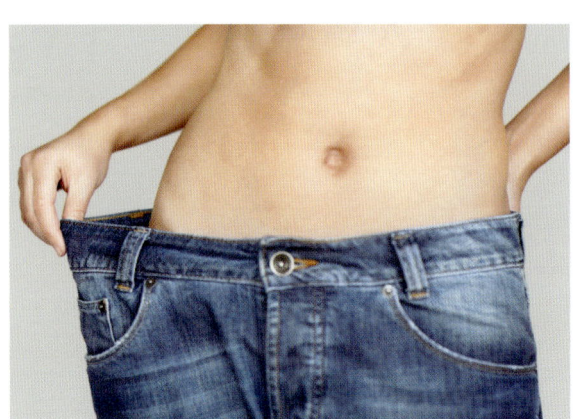

To qualify the size of an item of clothing you can use *troppo* (too) or *più* (more) and *meno* (less):

Questa giacca è troppo grande.	This jacket is too big.
Ha una taglia più piccola?	Do you have a smaller size?
Ha una gonna meno colorata?	Do you have a skirt that is less colorful?

6 › Saying something fits you

To say something fits, you use the expression *andare bene*.

Mi va benissimo.	It fits me perfectly. (literally = It goes to me very well.)
Ti va benissimo.	It fits you perfectly. (literally = It goes to you very well.)
Le va benissimo.	It fits you perfectly. (literally = It goes to you very well, using the *lei* form.)

Unit 4 › Lesson 1: *In the clothes shop* **4.1**

Questa gonna mi va benissimo.	This skirt fits me perfectly.
Che bella gonna! Ti va benissimo.	What a lovely skirt! It fits you perfectly.
Signora, le va benissimo.	Madam, it fits you perfectly.

You can use a similar expression with *stare* meaning "to suit."

Mi sta benissimo.	It really suits me.
Ti sta benissimo.	It really suits you.

7 › Object pronouns *lo* and *la*

Pronouns are words that stand in place of a noun. In the sentence "Luisa is buying a sweater" Luisa is the subject and what she is buying (a sweater) is the object. Let's replace both subject and object with pronouns. The sentence now becomes "She is buying it." *She* is the subject pronoun replacing Luisa; *it* is the object pronoun replacing the sweater.

When Giulia says *Perfetto, la prendo* (Perfect, I'll take it), the "it" refers to the sweater (*la maglia*) and that is why it is *la*.

If she were referring to a hat (*il cappello*), she would say *Perfetto, lo prendo*.

Use *lo* to replace a masculine singular word and *la* to replace a feminine singular word.

Use *li* to replace a masculine plural word and *le* to replace a feminine plural word.

> *Perfetto,* **li** *prendo* (referring to *i guanti* – gloves).
> *Perfetto,* **le** *prendo* (referring to *le scarpe* – shoes).

Unit 4 › Lesson 1: *In the clothes shop*

8 › Asking the price

There are a number of ways of asking the price of something.

Quant'è?	How much? / How much is it?
Quanto costa?	How much does it cost?
Quanto costano?	How much do they cost?

Culture note

You will notice that fur coats and jackets or fur-lined accessories such as scarves are particularly popular in Italy. Leather and fur manufacturing is an important part of the Italian fashion production industry and these materials are commonly worn in Italy, playing a crucial part in the winter wardrobe. You'll find that it is not just those living in the mountains who wear fur, in fact many women of all ages wear fur coats or at least coats with fur-lined collars, hoods or sleeves. Men also sport coats and jackets with fur-lined hoods. Such products can be found in the popular fashion stores of Italy as well as more traditional fur specialist stores and high fashion boutiques ranging in prices and styles.

Livemocha™ Active Italian *Level 2*

Vocabulary

Active Italian: Level 2 > Unit 4 > Lesson 1 > Vocabulary

il giubbotto
jacket

Ho freddo. Dov'è il mio giubbotto?
I'm cold. Where is my jacket?

la cintura
belt

È una cintura di pelle.
It is a leather belt.

Unit 4 › Lesson 1: *In the clothes shop*

4.1

un impermeabile
raincoat

Sta piovendo, metti l'impermeabile.
It's raining, put your raincoat on.

la maglietta
t-shirt

Che bella maglietta!
What a lovely t-shirt!

la cravatta
tie

Mio padre porta sempre la cravatta.
My father always wears a tie.

i guanti
gloves

Ha un paio di guanti?
Do you have a pair of gloves?

gli stivali
boots

C'è la neve. È meglio mettere gli stivali.
There's snow. It is better to wear boots.

i calzini
socks

Ho bisogno di un paio di calzini.
I need a pair of socks.

la gonna
skirt

La gonna è troppo stretta.
The skirt is too tight.

i pantaloni
pants

I pantaloni mi vanno bene.
The pants fit me.

UNIT 4 › LESSON 2
A little black dress

Culture note

The fashion industry is an important sector of the Italian economy and creates a large number of jobs in textile-producing areas such as Prato and Modena, where some of the world's best-known labels are based, as well as in retail. Many factories in these textile-industry regions have stores or outlets where spares, samples and slightly damaged items of designer clothing can be bought direct but at a fraction of the price.

4.2 Livemocha™ Active Italian Level 2

Video Dialog

Giulia continues her shopping trip and finds something nice that wasn't on her list.

Active Italian: Level 2 > Unit 4 > Lesson 2 > Video dialog

Lucia:	*Altro?*
Giulia:	*Sì, sto cercando anche un paio di pantaloni neri.*
Lucia:	*Mi dispiace, non ho niente della sua taglia. Dei jeans?*
Giulia:	*No, grazie. Vorrei qualcosa di speciale.*
Lucia:	*Ho un vestito nero della sua taglia. È molto chic.*
Giulia:	*Posso vederlo?*
Lucia:	*Eccolo.*
Giulia:	*È perfetto. Quant'è?*
Lucia:	*È in saldo. Costava 99 euro, ma adesso costa solo 57 euro.*
Giulia:	*Lo prendo!*

Lucia:	Anything else?
Giulia:	Yes, I am also looking for a pair of black pants.
Lucia:	Sorry. I don't have anything in your size. Some jeans?
Giulia:	No thanks. I want something special.
Lucia:	I have a black dress in your size. It's very chic.
Giulia:	Can I see it?

Lucia:	Here it is.
Giulia:	It's perfect. How much is it?
Lucia:	It's on sale. It was 99 euros but now it is only 57 euros.
Giulia:	I'll take it!

Grammar

 Active Italian: Level 2 > Unit 4 > Lesson 2 > Grammar

1 › *Sto cercando...* – I am looking for...

To express an ongoing activity, use the verb *stare* (to be) and a gerund: *cercando* (looking for), *mangiando* (eating).

We've come across *stare* before in the question *Come sta?* (How are you?) and the answer *Sto bene, grazie* (I'm fine, thanks).

The present tense of *stare* is:

sto	I am
stai	you (*familiar*) are
sta	he/she/it is
sta	you (*formal*) are
stiamo	we are
state	you (*plural*) are
stanno	they are

Don't confuse *stare* with *essere* which also means "to be." Think of *stare* as a more temporary state as in:

> *Quel vestito ti sta bene.*
> That dress really suits you.

2 › How to form a gerund – looking, trying, finishing

To form the gerund of regular *-are* verbs, replace *-are* with *-ando*:

> *cercare* (to look for): *cerc**ando***
> *provare* (to try on): *prov**ando***

Sto cercando un paio di pantaloni neri.	I am looking for a pair of black pants.
Sto provando una giacca nera.	I am trying on a black jacket.

To form the gerund of most *-ere* and *-ire* verbs, replace *-ere* and *-ire* with *-endo*:

> *prendere* (to take): *prend**endo***
> *finire* (to finish): *fin**endo***

Unit 4 › Lesson 2: *A little black dress*

Sto prendendo un caffè.	I am having a coffee.
Il film sta finendo.	The movie is finishing.

3 › Something special – *qualcosa di speciale*

Qualcosa means "something."
Qualcosa followed by an adjective becomes *qualcosa di*:

qualcosa di speciale	something special
qualcosa di buono	something tasty

4 › Nothing or not... anything

Non ho niente can translate "I have nothing" or "I don't have anything."

Italian has double negatives. You use both *non* and another negative word, *niente* (nothing), together.

| *Non ho niente nella sua taglia.* | I have nothing in your size. |
| *Non compro niente.* | I'm not buying anything. |

You can also use *niente* on its own:

| *Cosa vuoi comprare?* | What do you want to buy? |
| *Niente.* | Nothing. |

5 › Placing object pronouns

When Lucia tells Giulia about the dress (*il vestito*), Giulia asks if she can see it: *Posso vederlo?*

The *lo* is replacing *il vestito*.

If they were talking about the sweater (*la maglia*), then she would say: *Posso vederla?*

Note how the final -e of the infinitive is removed before adding the *lo* or *la*: *vedere – vederlo/vederla*.

Dropping the final -e from the infinitive is common in Italian and makes for a smoother flow of speech.

It is also possible to place *lo* or *la* in front of *posso*:

> *Lo posso vedere?* or *Posso vederlo?*
> *La posso provare?* or *Posso provarla?*
> Can I try it on?

6 › Imperfect tense of *-are* verbs

Lucia says that the black dress did cost 99 euros, but now it only costs 57 euros. (It is on sale.)

Costava 99 euro, ma adesso costa solo 57 euro.

Costava is the imperfect tense of *costare* (to cost). The imperfect tense is used to describe what happened in the past and is often translated by "used to."

The imperfect endings for regular *-are* verbs are:

cost**avo**	I used to cost
cost**avi**	you (*familiar*) used to cost
cost**ava**	he/she/it used to cost
cost**ava**	you (*formal*) used to cost
cost**avamo**	we used to cost
cost**avate**	you (*plural*) used to cost
cost**avano**	they used to cost

7 › Imperfect tense of -ere verbs

The imperfect tense is also used to describe actions that repeatedly took place in the past, as in *Andavo in Italia ogni anno* (I went to Italy every year).

The imperfect endings for regular -*ere* verbs are:

prend**evo**	I took
prend**evi**	you (*familiar*) took
prend**eva**	he/she/it took
prend**eva**	you (*formal*) took
prend**evamo**	we took
prend**evate**	you (*plural*) took
prend**evano**	they took

8 › ## Imperfect tense of -ire verbs

The imperfect tense is also used to describe actions that were taking place when something else happened in the past, for example "I was sleeping when he phoned." *Dormivo quando ha telefonato*.

The imperfect endings for regular *-ire* verbs are:

*dorm**ivo***	I was sleeping
*dorm**ivi***	you (*familiar*) were sleeping
*dorm**iva***	he/she/it was sleeping
*dorm**iva***	you (*formal*) were sleeping
*dorm**ivamo***	we were sleeping
*dorm**ivate***	you (*plural*) were sleeping
*dorm**ivano***	they were sleeping

Unit 4 › Lesson 2: *A little black dress*

Vocabulary

 Active Italian: Level 2 > Unit 4 > Lesson 2 > Vocabulary

la camicetta
blouse

Sara ha una camicetta rosa.
Sara has a pink blouse.

la camicia da notte
nightgown

Dov'è la tua camicia da notte?
Where is your nightgown?

il pigiama
pyjamas

Dormo nudo. Non porto pigiama.
I sleep naked. I don't wear pyjamas.

la sciarpa
scarf

Metti la sciarpa. Fa freddo.
Put your scarf on. It's cold.

le scarpe da ginnastica
sneakers

Dove hai comprato le scarpe da ginnastica?
Where did you buy your sneakers?

il costume da bagno
swimsuit

Vendono costumi da bagno al mercato.
They sell swimsuits at the market.

i calzoncini
shorts

Quando ero piccolo portavo sempre i calzoncini.
When I was little I always wore shorts.

i collant
pantyhose

Fa troppo caldo per portare i collant.
It is too hot to wear pantyhose.

Unit 4 › Lesson 2: *A little black dress*

4.2

le mutande
underpants

Si possono comprare le mutande al supermercato.
You can buy underpants at the supermarket.

le mutandine
panties

Sono molto carine quelle mutandine.
Those panties are very pretty.

Culture note

The Italian word for "size" is *la taglia* when referring to clothes and *il numero* when referring to shoes.

However, these two words are only implied when actually stating what your size is. They are represented only by the articles *la* (for *la taglia*) and *il* (for *il numero*).

Porto la quarantadue. I take clothes size 42.

Porto il trentanove. I take shoe size 39.

Active Italian *Level 2*

5

Lesson 1: In need of smart clothes

- » How to use the past tense to say what you have bought: *Ho comprato...*
- » Some common irregular past participles: *fatto*, *detto*, *preso*, etc.
- » Some irregular noun plurals: *gli uomini*, *le paia*, etc.
- » How to say "there": *ci*.
- » How to form the future tense: *costerà*.
- » The use of *da* in expressions such as *abiti da uomo*.
- » The use of *perché* to mean both "why?" and "because".

Lesson 2: In the men's section

- » How to shop for men's clothing.
- » How to address a group of male and female people.
- » How to describe a mix of masculine and feminine nouns.
- » How to use *più* and *meno*.
- » How to use *Che?* and *Quale?*
- » How to say what something is made of: *di plastica*, *di lana*, etc.
- » About the letter j in Italian.

Collins | **Livemocha™**

UNIT 5 › LESSON 1
In need of smart clothes

Culture note

Italy offers a wide range of clothes shopping for all budgets: from designer stores to supermarkets and weekly outdoor markets. Look out for sales (*saldi*) which usually take place at the end of the summer  and winter seasons. If you're in search of a bargain, try the local markets in towns and cities. They usually run on weekends and one day in the week (often Wednesdays but each city differs slightly). Bologna has a huge market that takes place every Friday and Saturday and sells a wide range of products from footwear and jewelry to fresh food and bicycles! A lot of markets have clothing that comes directly from factories where you can pick up some great deals if you shop around.

Unit 5 › Lesson 1: *In need of smart clothes*

Video Dialog

Giulia shows Michele her new clothes over a coffee. Then Michele admits that he needs some new clothes himself.

 Active Italian: Level 2 > Unit 5 > Lesson 1 > Video dialog

Michele:	*E allora, che cos'hai comprato?*
Giulia:	*Ho comprato una maglia rossa e un vestito nero.*
Michele:	*Be', anch'io dovrei comprare della roba.*
Giulia:	*Perché?*
Michele:	*Perché ho una mostra fotografica a New York e non posso mica andarci con questi jeans!*
Giulia:	*Ehm... Non è proprio il look giusto!*
Michele:	*Che cosa dovrei mettermi?*
Giulia:	*Nel negozio dove ho comprato la mia maglia vendono anche abiti da uomo.*
Michele:	*Ho l'impressione che mi costerà caro!*

....

Michele:	So, what did you buy?
Giulia:	I bought a red sweater and a black dress.
Michele:	Well, I should buy some stuff, too.
Giulia:	Why?
Michele:	Because I'm having an exhibition of my photos in New York and I can't go there in these jeans!
Giulia:	Mmm... It isn't exactly the right image!
Michele:	What should I wear?

Livemocha™ Active Italian *Level 2*

Giulia:	In the shop where I bought my sweater they also sell men's clothes.
Michele:	I get the feeling this is going to cost me dearly!

Grammar

Active Italian: Level 2 > Unit 5 > Lesson 1 > Grammar

1 › **How to form the past tense**

Michele asks Giulia *Che cos'hai comprato?* (What did you buy?) and Giulia begins her reply with *Ho comprato* (I bought).

To make the past tense, you use the present tense of *avere* (to have) and add the past participle which we've already learnt.

Here is a quick recap:

With most *-are* verbs, replace the *-are* with *-ato*:
comprare – comprato (to buy – bought).

With most *-ere* verbs, replace the *-ere* with *-uto*:
vendere – venduto (to sell – sold).

With most *-ire* verbs, replace the *-ire* with *-ito*:
finire – finito (to finish – finished).

When you use *avere* with a past participle, *avere* is known as the auxiliary verb. It helps make the past tense. Later on you will find out that some verbs take *essere* as the auxiliary verb.

Unit 5 › Lesson 1: *In need of smart clothes*

5.1

2 › | The past tense of *comprare* (to buy)

ho comprato	I have bought
hai comprato	you (*familiar*) have bought
ha comprato	he/she/it has bought
ha comprato	you (*formal*) have bought
abbiamo comprato	we have bought
avete comprato	you (*plural*) have bought
hanno comprato	they have bought

Note how it is the auxiliary *avere* verb that changes. The past participle remains the same for each person.

Culture note

The fashion industry is one of the most influential sectors of the Italian economy, and Milan is widely considered the fashion capital of the world. Avoid street vendors trying to sell designer knockoffs in the tourist areas of Italian cities. Not only is it illegal to sell them but also to buy them, and doing so can result in hefty fines for you as well.

Whereas the actual fashion production in Italy takes place in the more central textile regions, Milan is the center of the Italian fashion retail industry on an international level with a huge variety of designer boutiques, international flagship stores and one-of-a-kind store stocking smaller brands. If shopping is on your to-do list, then Milan is the place to go. However, you'll find some great stores in all Italian cities providing for all budgets.

3 › Some irregular past participles

Forming a past participle does not always follow the set pattern. Here are a number of commonly used irregular ones:

prendere	to take, to catch	*preso*
fare	to do, to make	*fatto*
dire	to say	*detto*
mettere	to put on	*messo*
cuocere	to cook	*cotto*
accendere	to light	*acceso*
rispondere	to reply	*risposto*
leggere	to read	*letto*

A good dictionary will always show you these variations.

4 › *Perché?*

Italian uses the same word for "why" and "because." It is clear from the context which meaning applies.

Unit 5 › Lesson 1: *In need of smart clothes*

Perché devi comprare della roba da vestire?	Why do you have to buy clothes?
Perché ho una mostra fotografica a New York.	Because I have an exhibition of my photos in New York.

5 › Ci meaning "there"

Michele says *non posso mica andarci con questi jeans!* This means he can hardly go to New York in these jeans. In Italian you have to indicate New York with the word *ci*.

Ci is a pronoun and it replaces the name of a place that has been referred to (or is implied). It is often attached to the end of *andare* minus the final *-e*: *andarci* (to go there).

Vado a New York.	I am going to New York.
Ci vado in aereo.	I am going there by plane.
Devo andarci domani.	I have to go there tomorrow.

By listening to as much Italian as you can, you will get a feel for these short but important words.

6 › *Abiti da uomo* – Men's clothing

Giulia uses the phrase *abiti da uomo*, meaning "men's clothes." The word for man is *uomo*. It has an irregular plural, *uomini*.

A number of Italian nouns have irregular plurals. A good dictionary will always flag these up.

Sometimes a noun is masculine in the singular but becomes feminine in the plural.
Un paio (a pair) is an example of this, changing from *un paio* in the singular to *le paia* in the plural.

Other nouns that behave like this include:

> *l'uovo* (egg) → *le uova* (eggs)
> *il dito* (finger) → *le dita* (fingers)
> *il braccio* (arm) → *le braccia* (arms)
> *il ginocchio* (knee) → *le ginocchia* (knees)
> *il lenzuolo* (sheet) → *le lenzuola* (sheets)

7 › The use of *da*

Abiti da donna is "women's clothing."

We have already come across *da* in the following contexts:
"from" as in *il treno da Roma* (the train *from* Rome)

"from" as in *dalle nove alle sei* (*from* 9:00 to 6:00)

"to someone's place" as in *vado da Tom* (I'm going *to* Tom's) or *vado dal farmacista* (I'm going *to* the pharmacist).

In *vestiti da uomo* it is being used in its other context – that of telling you what or who something is *for*. *Da uomo* tells you the clothes are for men; *da donna* tells you they are for women; *da sera* would tell you that they would be for evening wear.

You find *da* is often used to specify what something is used for.

una camera **da** letto	a bedroom
le scarpe **da** tennis	tennis shoes, sneakers
l'abito **da** sposa	wedding dress

8 › My stuff – *la mia roba*

La roba is frequently used in Italian to mean "stuff" or "things."

> *Dove hai messo la roba da ginnastica?*
> Where have you put my gym things?

> *Dovrei comprare della roba da vestire.*
> I should buy some things to wear.

9 › The future tense

When Michele says *mi costerà caro* (it will cost me dearly), he uses the future of *costare – costerà*.

The future is quite simple to form. Just add the following endings.

Unit 5 › Lesson 1: *In need of smart clothes* 5.1

With *-are* and *-ere* verbs, the endings are the same.

comprare – to buy

comp**rerò**	I will buy
comp**rerai**	you (*familiar*) will buy
comp**rerà**	he/she/it will buy
comp**rerà**	you (*formal*) will buy
comp**reremo**	we will buy
comp**rerete**	you (*plural*) will buy
comp**reranno**	they will buy

vendere – to sell

vend**erò**	I will sell
vend**erai**	you (*familiar*) will sell
vend**erà**	he/she/it will sell
vend**erà**	you (*formal*) will sell
vend**eremo**	we will sell
vend**erete**	you (*plural*) will sell
vend**eranno**	they will sell

With most *-ire* verbs the endings are as follows:

finire – to finish

fin**irò**	I will finish
fin**irai**	you (*familiar*) will finish
fin**irà**	he/she/it will finish
fin**irà**	you (*formal*) will finish
fin**iremo**	we will finish
fin**irete**	you (*plural*) will finish
fin**iranno**	they will finish

Unit 5 › Lesson 1: *In need of smart clothes* **5.1**

Vocabulary

Active Italian: Level 2 > Unit 5 > Lesson 1 > Vocabulary

accompagnare
to accompany, to go with

Ti accompagno all'ospedale.
I'll go with you to the hospital.

elegante
smart

La signora Verdi è molto elegante stasera.
Mrs. Verdi is very elegant this evening.

123

un completo
suit, outfit

Bisogna mettersi un completo per il matrimonio.
You have to wear a suit to the wedding.

un completo da donna
women's suit, ladies' suit

Dove posso comprare un completo da donna?
Where can I buy a ladies' suit?

l'abito da sposa
wedding dress

Andiamo a cercare un abito da sposa.
Let's go and look for a wedding dress.

le scarpe con i tacchi alti
high heeled shoes

Non mi piacciono le scarpe con i tacchi alti.
I don't like high heeled shoes.

Unit 5 › Lesson 1: *In need of smart clothes*

5.1

il matrimonio
wedding, marriage

Andiamo al matrimonio di Paolo e Francesca.
We are going to Paolo and Francesca's wedding.

il grande magazzino
department store

Ci sono diversi grandi magazzini a Como.
There are several department stores in Como.

il reparto
department, section

A quale piano si trova il reparto calzature?
Which floor is the shoe department?

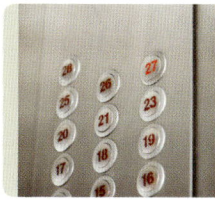

al primo piano
on the second floor

Il reparto biancheria intima è al primo piano.
The lingerie department is on the second floor.

il pianterreno
the first floor

Dove sei? Io sono al pianterreno.
Where are you? I am on the first floor.

al piano interrato
in the basement

C'è un piccolo supermercato al piano interrato.
There is a small supermarket in the basement.

UNIT 5 › LESSON 2
In the men's section

Culture note

The Italian word for cardigan is *golf* because it was worn on the golf course. It was originally said to be invented by Lord Cardigan (1797-1868). The term *cardigan* is also used in Italy but it generally means a heavy cardigan or a zip-up sweater.

Video Dialog

Now it's Michele's turn to look for a new outfit – he needs something for his upcoming exhibition.

 Active Italian: Level 2 > Unit 5 > Lesson 2 > Video dialog

Lucia:	*Buongiorno, signori.*
Michele:	*Che cosa mi consiglia? Cerco qualcosa di un po' più elegante.*
Lucia:	*Un completo con cravatta?*
Michele:	*Qualcosa di meno formale...*
Lucia:	*Dei jeans, una dolcevita e una giacca?*
Michele:	*Sì. Ha dei jeans neri e una dolcevita nera?*
Lucia:	*Vediamo... Ecco: jeans e dolcevita.*
Michele:	*Ottimo. Che tipo di giacca mi consiglia?*
Lucia:	*Una giacca di lana o una di pelle?*
Michele:	*Una giacca di pelle.*
Lucia:	*Di che colore? Marrone o nera?*
Michele:	*Marrone se ce l'ha.*
Giulia:	*Molto chic!*

Lucia:	Good afternoon.
Michele:	What do you recommend? I'm looking for something a bit smarter.
Lucia:	A suit and tie?
Michele:	Something less formal...

Lucia:	Jeans, a roll neck sweater and a jacket?
Michele:	Yes. Have you some black jeans and a black roll neck sweater?
Lucia:	Let's see... Here you are: jeans and a roll neck.
Michele:	Excellent. What sort of jacket do you recommend?
Lucia:	A wool jacket or a leather one?
Michele:	A leather jacket.
Lucia:	What color? Brown or black?
Michele:	Brown if you have it.
Giulia:	Very smart!

Grammar

....

  Active Italian: Level 2 > Unit 5 > Lesson 2 > Grammar

1 › *Buongiorno, signori!*

When Giulia and Michele enter the shop, Lucia greets them with *Buongiorno, signori!* Note that she has used the masculine *signori* even though Giulia is there. This reflects what automatically happens in Italian when there is a mixture of masculine and feminine nouns (including people). Any adjectives describing them are masculine by default.

> *Max e Luisa sono alti.*
> Max and Luisa are tall.

> *La casa e il giardino sono belli.*
> The house and garden are lovely.

5.2 Livemocha™ Active Italian *Level 2*

Unit 5 › Lesson 2: *In the men's section*

2 › More and less

Più means "more", *meno* means "less" and are useful to know when trying to explain what you would like.

| *più formale* | more formal |
| *meno formale* | less formal |

| *più caro* | more expensive |
| *meno caro* | less expensive |

Vorrei qualcosa di meno caro (I'd like something less expensive) sounds much less abrupt than *È troppo caro* (It is too expensive).

3 › What? and Which? (1)

Che? (What?) and *Quale?* (Which?) are two important question words. *Che* is easy because it never changes.

> *Che tipo di giacca vuole?*
> What kind of jacket do you want?

> *A che nome ha riservato?*
> Under what name is the reservation?

> *Che ore sono?*
> What time is it?

4 › **What? and Which? (2)**

While *Che?* never changes, *Quale?* shortens to *Qual* when it is followed by *è* (is).

> *Qual è la tua casa?*
> Which is your house?

> *Quale gonna vuoi comprare?*
> Which skirt do you want to buy?

Quale becomes *Quali* for plural things.

> *Quali pantaloni hai comprato?*
> Which pants did you buy?

> *Quali scarpe preferisci?*
> Which shoes do you prefer?

Quale is used when there is a choice of things and tends to be used for phone numbers, emails, and addresses, etc.

Qual è il tuo indirizzo?	What is your address?
Qual è il tuo numero di telefonino?	What is your cell phone number?
Qual è il tuo indirizzo email?	What is your email address?

Unit 5 › Lesson 2: *In the men's section*

5 › Made of...

To say what something is made of, use *di* (of) followed by the material (wool, leather, plastic, etc).

una maglia di lana	a wool sweater
una giacca di pelle	a leather jacket
una borsa di plastica	a plastic bag
una casa di legno	a wooden house

Other materials include: *di cotone* (cotton), *di lino* (linen), *di vetro* (glass), *di metallo* (metal), *di carta* (paper), *di seta* (silk).

6 › Single letter words

Italian is full of very short words. Here are the shortest:
e – and
è – is
o – or
a – at, to
i – the (masculine plural article)

7 › ### The letter *j*

The Italian alphabet does not contain the letter *j* (although you find it used with foreign words that have entered the language such as *jeans*, *jeep*, and *judo*). However, the sound of the letter *j* is conveyed by *gi*. We have come across it a few times.

giacca	jacket
Giappone	Japan
Giulia	Julia
giugno	June

Vocabulary

Active Italian: Level 2 > Unit 5 > Lesson 2 > Vocabulary

di moda
fashionable

Questi pantaloni sono molto di moda.
These pants are very fashionable.

Unit 5 › Lesson 2: *In the men's section*

classico/a
classic

Cerco un completo classico.
I am looking for a classic suit.

a righe
striped

Ha un paio di pantaloni a righe?
Do you have a pair of striped pants?

a quadri
checkered

Preferisci un disegno a quadri?
Do you prefer a checkered pattern?

scuro/a
dark

È un golf grigio scuro.
It is a dark gray cardigan.

chiaro/a
light

Preferirei un colore più chiaro.
I'd prefer a lighter color.

in tinta unita
plain, single color

Preferirei un maglione in tinta unita.
I'd prefer a plain sweater.

colorato/a
colored, colorful

Preferirei un vestito più colorato.
I'd prefer a more colorful dress.

corto/a
short

Questa gonna è troppo corta.
This skirt is too short.

Culture note

With leather manufacturing being such an influential part of the Italian fashion industry, Italy is a good place to go for good quality, fashionable leather shoes, belts, and other leather products. There are shoe stores in all Italian towns and cities with a wide selection of products available.

Florence is known for its specialist leather traditions and prides itself in the quality and style of its products. There are many top leather stores in Florence as well as two very good leather markets. The first can be found in **Loggia del Mercato Nuovo** (the Loggia of the new market), near **Piazza Della Republica**, selling a great selection of bags, belts, purses, and wallets for both men and women. The second is in the area surrounding the **Chiesa di San Lorenzo** (the Church of San Lorenzo) on **Via del Canto de' Nelli**, where you can find similar products.

Unit 5 › Lesson 2: *In the men's section*

con le maniche corte
with short sleeves

Ha una camicia con le maniche corte?
Do you have a shortsleeved shirt?

stretto/a
tight, narrow

Questi pantaloni sono troppo stretti.
These pants are too tight.

Active Italian *Level 2*

6

Lesson 1: What are you doing tomorrow?

- » How to say "tomorrow," "the day after tomorrow," "yesterday": *domani*, *dopodomani*, *ieri*.
- » What a reflexive verb is: to wash oneself, to enjoy oneself.
- » The present tense of reflexive verbs: *mi lavo*, *ti lavi*, *si lava*, etc.
- » How to say "going to bed" and "getting up" using reflexive verbs: *addormentarsi* and *alzarsi*.
- » The past tense of reflexive verbs: *mi sono lavato/a*.
- » How to say you are going to do something: *andare a* + infinitive.

Lesson 2: Booking tickets online

- » How to say a train is early, on time, or late: *in anticipo*, *in orario*, *in ritardo*.
- » How to use the negative with the past tense.
- » Expressions using *fare* such as *fare il biglietto*, *fare il bagno*, etc.
- » The months of the year.
- » The verb *fare* (to make or to do): present tense, gerund, past participle, and stems.

UNIT 6 › LESSON 1
What are you doing tomorrow?

Culture note

Florence is the capital city of the Italian region of Tuscany. Renowned for its art and architecture, Tuscany is considered the birthplace of the Italian Renaissance. Visitors are spoiled for choice, but nobody should miss the Basilica di Santa Maria del Fiore (the *Duomo* or cathedral), the Palazzo Vecchio, the Baptistry, the church of San Lorenzo, the Uffizi Gallery, the Boboli Gardens and the Ponte Vecchio, the bridge spanning the River Arno.

Unit 6 › Lesson 1: *What are you doing tomorrow?*

Video Dialog

Ugo and Lucia discuss their plans for the following day.

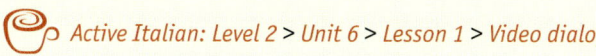

Active Italian: Level 2 > Unit 6 > Lesson 1 > Video dialog

Lucia: *Allora, che cosa facciamo stasera?*

Ugo: *Domani ho un appuntamento a Firenze. Devo alzarmi presto per prendere il treno. E tu, che cosa fai domani?*

Lucia: *Domani mattina, lavoro in negozio. Nel pomeriggio, devo andare ad una sfilata di moda.*

Ugo: *E domani sera?*

Lucia: *Vado a dormire presto, perché una sfilata è faticosa!*

Ugo: *E dopodomani?*

Lucia: *Dopodomani è mercoledì e ho appuntamento con una cliente in centro.*

Ugo: *E la sera?*

Lucia: *Tu mi inviti a cena da Cellini!*

Ugo: *Ah sì? Non lo sapevo!*

Lucia: So, what are we doing tonight?
Ugo: Tomorrow I have a meeting in Florence. I have to get up early to catch the train. What are you doing tomorrow?
Lucia: Tomorrow morning I'm working in the shop. In the afternoon, I have to go to a fashion show.

Ugo:	And tomorrow evening?
Lucia:	I'm going to bed early, because a fashion show is tiring!
Ugo:	And the day after tomorrow?
Lucia:	The day after tomorrow is Wednesday and I have a meeting with a client downtown.
Ugo:	And in the evening?
Lucia:	You're taking me out to dinner at Cellini's!
Ugo:	Oh yes? I didn't know that!

Grammar

 Active Italian: Level 2 > Unit 6 > Lesson 1 > Grammar

1 › **Talking about tomorrow, yesterday, and today**

The word for "tomorrow" is *domani* and can be used with different parts of the day.

domani mattina	tomorrow morning
domani pomeriggio	tomorrow afternoon
domani sera	tomorrow evening

Unit 6 › Lesson 1: *What are you doing tomorrow?*

The word for "yesterday" is *ieri* and can be used in much the same way.

ieri mattina	yesterday morning
ieri pomeriggio	yesterday afternoon
ieri sera	yesterday evening

The word for "today" is *oggi* and works slightly differently.

stamattina	this morning
oggi pomeriggio	this afternoon
stasera	this evening

Dopodomani is "the day after tomorrow."
L'altro ieri is "the day before yesterday."

2 › Reflexive verbs

Reflexive verbs are ones where the person doing the verb is carrying out the action on themselves. For example, washing oneself (*lavarsi*), enjoying oneself (*divertirsi*), or calling oneself (*chiamarsi*).

We use this last verb when we introduce ourselves: *Mi chiamo Max* (My name is Max), *Come ti chiami?* (What is your name?), *Come si chiama?* (What is your name? – using the polite *lei* form).

You will recognize reflexive verbs from the *si* attached to the infinitive: *preoccupar**si*** (to worry), *sentir**si*** (to feel).

3 › How reflexive verbs work

Reflexive verbs follow the same patterns as other Italian verbs, but include a pronoun (known as a reflexive pronoun) that corresponds to myself, yourself, himself, etc.

Here is the present tense of *lavarsi* (to wash oneself).

mi lavo	I wash myself
ti lavi	you (*familiar*) wash yourself
si lava	he/she/it washes himself/herself/itself
si lava	you (*formal*) wash yourself
ci laviamo	we wash ourselves
vi lavate	you (*plural*) wash yourselves
si lavano	they wash themselves

4 › Waking up and getting up – both reflexive verbs

Both waking up and getting up are reflexive in Italian.

svegliarsi	to wake up
Mi sveglio alle sei.	I wake up at 6 o'clock.
A che ora ti svegli?	What time do you wake up?

Unit 6 › Lesson 1: *What are you doing tomorrow?*

6.1

alzarsi	to get up
Luisa si alza alle sette.	Luisa gets up at 7 o'clock.
Quando vi alzate?	When do you get up?

How these verbs differ from other verbs we've seen so far is that they take *essere* as their auxiliary verb (and not *avere*).

5 › **The past tense of reflexive verbs**

Mi sono svegliato alle sei.	I woke up at 6 o'clock.
A che ora ti sei svegliato?	What time did you wake up?
Luisa si è alzata alle sette.	Luisa got up at 7 o'clock.
Quando vi siete alzati?	When did you get up?

Did you notice how the past participles (*svegliato* and *alzato*) agree with the subject of the verbs?
Luisa, being feminine, has a feminine ending: *alzat**a***.
You (*vi*) being plural, has a plural ending: *alzat**i***.

Don't worry; the past participle simply acts like an adjective. Just keep this in mind, though, when talking about yourself, particularly if you are a woman.

6 › The past tense of *divertirsi* (to enjoy oneself)

This is a chance to remind yourself of *essere* (to be).

mi sono divertito/a	I enjoyed myself
ti sei divertito/a	you (*familiar*) enjoyed yourself
si è divertito/a	he/she/it enjoyed himself/herself/itself
si è divertito/a	you (*formal*) enjoyed yourself
ci siamo divertiti(e)	we enjoyed ourselves
vi siete divertiti(e)	you (*plural*) enjoyed yourselves
si sono divertiti(e)	they enjoyed themselves

Unit 6 › Lesson 1: *What are you doing tomorrow?*

7 › A final word on reflexive verbs

Ugo tells Lucia that he has to get up early to catch a train.

Devo alzarmi presto per prendere il treno.

Note how he attaches *-mi* to the infinitive.

If he were telling Lucia to get up early, he would say:

Devi alzarti presto.

If we were suggesting we should get up early, it would be:

Dobbiamo alzarci presto.

It is quite logical, but you must remember to change the reflexive pronoun to match whoever is the subject of the verb.

8 › *Andare a* + infinitive

Ugo tells Lucia that he is going to sleep early that night.

Vado a dormire presto.
I am going to sleep early.

This is a useful way of saying what your plans are.

Vado a giocare a tennis.	I am going to play tennis.
Vado a fare la spesa.	I am going to do the shopping.
Vado a trovare Max.	I am going to visit Max.

Vocabulary

Active Italian: Level 2 > Unit 6 > Lesson 1 > Vocabulary

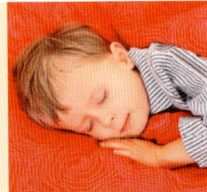

addormentarsi
to fall asleep

Mi sono addormentato sul divano.
I fell asleep on the sofa.

incontrarsi
to meet (up)

Ci incontreremo domani alle due.
We will meet tomorrow at 2 o'clock.

sposarsi
to get married

Quando ti sposerai?
When will you get married?

Unit 6 › Lesson 1: *What are you doing tomorrow?* **6.1**

cambiarsi
to get changed

Dove posso cambiarmi?
Where can I get changed?

spogliarsi
to get undressed

Non entrare! Mi sto spogliando.
Don't come in! I'm getting undressed.

arrabbiarsi
to get angry

Perché Luisa si è arrabbiata con te?
Why did Luisa get angry with you?

riposarsi
to rest

Sono stanco e vorrei riposarmi un po'.
I am tired, and I'd like to rest a little.

vestirsi
to get dressed

Dovete vestirvi. Partiamo tra venti minuti.
You need to get dressed. We are leaving in 20 minutes.

estivo/a
(in) summer

È una giacca estiva.
It is a summer jacket.

invernale
(in) winter

Mi piacciono gli sport invernali.
I like winter sports.

il paese natale
native land

L'Italia è il mio paese natale.
Italy is my native land.

Culture note

When eating out in Italy, there is normally a cover charge, *coperto*, for the table setting, bread, and *grissini* (bread sticks). It is included in the final bill and is charged per person (about 2 euros per person but it can be more). Service is always included although it is customary to leave a tip (5 per cent is fine). When Italians split the bill they generally share *alla romana* meaning the bill is divided equally.

UNIT 6 › LESSON 2
Booking tickets online

Culture note

You can't buy your ticket on the train. If you don't have a ticket you will be heavily fined. Avoid traveling during peak holiday times – during the week of August 15 (*Ferragosto* – the festival of the Madonna when most  Italian businesses and shops close for the week and most cities become deserted for the coast) or Christmas (*Natale*) when there are many foreign and Italian tourists on the move and trains can get hot and crowded.

Livemocha™ Active Italian *Level 2*

Video Dialog

Lucia gives Ugo some helpful advice.

Active Italian: Level 2 > Unit 6 > Lesson 2 > Video dialog

Lucia: *A che ora parti domani?*
Ugo: *Non lo so.*
Lucia: *Non hai ancora preso il biglietto?*
Ugo: *No, non ancora.*
Lucia: *Sarebbe meglio prenotarlo in anticipo.*
Ugo: *Perché?*
Lucia: *Perché costa meno.*
Ugo: *Be' adesso è troppo tardi.*
Lucia: *Non è mica vero. Puoi sempre fare il biglietto su internet.*
Ugo: *Ma non so come si fa.*
Lucia: *È facile. Ti faccio vedere io come si fa.*
Ugo: *D'accordo, grazie.*
Lucia: *Figurati.*

....

Lucia: What time are you leaving tomorrow?
Ugo: I don't know.
Lucia: You haven't got your ticket yet?
Ugo: No, not yet.
Lucia: But it's better to book it in advance.
Ugo: Why?

Lucia:	Because it is cheaper.	
Ugo:	Well, it's too late now.	
Lucia:	That's not true. You can always book your ticket online.	
Ugo:	But I don't know how you do it.	
Lucia:	It's easy. I'll show you how it's done.	
Ugo:	Ok, thanks.	
Lucia:	Not at all.	

Grammar

 Active Italian: Level 2 > Unit 6 > Lesson 2 > Grammar

1 › **Early, late, and on time**

Lucia says it is better to book train tickets in advance – *in anticipo*.

This is also a useful expression when talking about trains, planes, and buses:

> early is *in anticipo*
> late is *in ritardo*
> on time is *in orario*.

2 › **Using the negative with the past tense**

For negatives in the perfect tense, you put *non* before the auxiliary verb (*avere*):

> *Non hai ancora preso il biglietto?*
> You haven't got your ticket yet?

With reflexive verbs, you put *non* before the reflexive pronoun (*mi*, *ti*, *si*, etc.):

> *Non mi sono lavato.*
> I haven't washed.

3 › *Come?* How?

Questions beginning "How" are introduced by *Come* in Italian. Common questions include:

Come si chiama?	What's your name? (literally "How do you call yourself?")
Come sta?	How are you?
Come funziona?	How does it work?

You also use *Come?* if you haven't heard what someone has said, as in "Pardon?"

4 › *Si* – one, you, we, they

Ugo says *Non so come si fa*. I don't know how it is done. *Si* is an impersonal pronoun like "one".

Unit 6 › Lesson 2: *Booking tickets online*

Si mangia bene in Italia.
One eats well in Italy.

Si sta bene qui.
It is good here (literally "one feels good here").

5 › *Fare il biglietto* to buy a ticket

Fare il biglietto, literally "to make the ticket," is another idiomatic expression using *fare*.

Other expressions include:

fare la spesa	to do the shopping
fare la patente	to study for a driver's license
fare colazione	to have breakfast
fare il letto	to make the bed
fare le pulizie	to do the housework
fare i compiti	to do homework
fare benzina	to fill up with gas
fare il bagno	to go bathing/swimming

6 › Fare – an irregular verb

A quick revision of the present tense of *fare* (to make or to do):

faccio	I make
fai	you (*familiar*) make
fa	he/she/it makes
fa	you (*formal*) make
facciamo	we make
fate	you (*plural*) make
fanno	they make

facendo is the gerund (doing, making).

fatto is the past participle (made).

fac- is the stem for the imperfect (was making): *facevo*, *facevi*, *faceva*, etc.

far- is the stem for the future tense (will make): *farò*, *farai*, *farà*, etc.

7 › Months

"Month" is *il mese*. "Monthly" is *mensile*. The days of the month start with a small letter in Italian.

To say the first of a month, use *primo*: *il primo maggio* (May the first). After that, use cardinal numbers: *il due aprile* (April the second), *il sedici settembre* (September the sixteenth).
To say "in" a month, it can be either *in* or *a*: *in giugno* (in June), *a maggio* (in May).

Culture note

As with city buses and trams, you need to validate your train ticket before getting on the train. Otherwise the ticket collector can issue you with an on-the-spot penalty. This also applies to the return part of your journey. You must validate your ticket a second time.

Before boarding a train, check whether it is a fast train such as an *Intercity* or *Eurostar* and requires a supplement if you only have a normal ticket (on top of the normal price of the ticket). If you don't, the ticket collector can ask you to pay a surcharge that works out more expensive than the supplement. When buying your ticket you will be charged the correct price if you purchase a ticket for that specific train, but it's always worth checking before you get on board.

6.2 Livemocha™ Active Italian *Level 2*

Vocabulary

Active Italian: Level 2 > Unit 6 > Lesson 2 > Vocabulary

gennaio
January

Il primo mese dell'anno è gennaio.
The first month of the year is January.

febbraio
February

Carnevale di solito cade a febbraio.
Carnival usually falls in February.

marzo
March

In marzo il tempo è instabile.
The weather is unsettled in March.

aprile
April

Aprile è il mese del mio compleanno.
April is the month of my birthday.

Unit 6 › Lesson 2: *Booking tickets online*

maggio
May

Le rose fioriscono in maggio.
The roses bloom in May.

giugno
June

Le vacanze estive cominciano a metà di giugno.
The summer vacation begins halfway through June.

luglio
July

A luglio andiamo al mare.
We go to the seaside in July.

agosto
August

Agosto è afoso.
August is muggy.

settembre
September

In settembre si ritorna a scuola.
We go back to school in September.

ottobre
October

In ottobre piove spesso.
In October it often rains.

novembre
November

In novembre comincia a far freddo.
It begins to get cold in November.

dicembre
December

A dicembre ci prepariamo per il Natale.
We get ready for Christmas in December.

Collins

Livemocha ACTIVE ITALIAN

HarperCollins Publishers
77–85 Fulham Palace Road
London W6 8JB
Great Britain

www.collinslanguage.com

First edition 2011

Reprint 10 9 8 7 6 5 4 3 2 1 0
© HarperCollins Publishers 2011

ISBN (UK edition) 978-0-00-737353-6
ISBN (export edition) 978-0-00-741980-7
ISBN (US edition) 978-0-87779-557-5

Collins® is a registered trademark of HarperCollins Publishers Limited

A catalogue record for this book is available from the British Library

Typeset by Macmillan Publishing Services

Audio material recorded and produced by Networks SRL, Milan

Printed and Bound in China by Leo Paper Products Ltd.
Series Editor: Rob Scriven

All rights reserved. No part of this publication may be reproduced, stored in a retrieval system or transmitted, in any form or by any means, electronic, mechanical, photocopying, recording or otherwise, without the prior permission of the publisher. This book is sold subject to the conditions that it shall not, by way of trade or otherwise, be lent, re-sold, hired out or otherwise circulated without the publisher's prior consent in any form of binding or cover other than that in which it is published and without a similar condition including this condition being imposed on the subsequent purchaser.

HarperCollins does not warrant that the functions contained in **www.livemocha.com** content will be interrruption- or error-free, that defects will be corrected, or that **www.livemocha.com** or the server that makes it available are free of viruses or bugs. HarperCollins is not responsible for any access difficulties that may be experienced due to problems with network, web, online or mobile phone connections.

INTRODUCTION 4

UNIT 1
Lesson 1: Booking a train ticket online 8
Lesson 2: Finding out about prices 18

UNIT 2
Lesson 1: I've lost … 28
Lesson 2: Things you need to do 41

UNIT 3
Lesson 1: Found! 52
Lesson 2: Family photos 61

UNIT 4
Lesson 1: Finding out about each other 76
Lesson 2: In search of an apartment 86

UNIT 5
Lesson 1: At the restaurant 98
Lesson 2: At the table 110

UNIT 6
Lesson 1: Feeling ill 124
Lesson 2: Making a doctor's appointment 135

INTRODUCTION

Welcome to your Livemocha Active Italian experience! This new course goes above and beyond what a traditional book-based course can offer. With its focus on online learning, Active Italian provides the opportunity not just to study but to experience the language for yourself by interacting with native speakers online.

Why go online?
Studying a language online allows you to learn in a more natural atmosphere – watching people interact in a **video** is far more lifelike than listening to conversations on a CD. After watching a video dialog, you will be walked through an explanation of some of the **grammar** and **vocabulary** items that were introduced in the new dialog. Then, by completing a variety of **interactive quizzes**, the system will instantly be able to tell you how well you are doing. You can then **talk online** with native Italian speakers to practice what you've learned.

Who else is online?
Livemocha boasts over 7 million members and is growing every day. These members are online for the same reason as you – to learn and experience a new language. Native Italian-speaking members will be happy to read through your written and spoken submissions and to give you feedback on how you're doing. You can also connect with people who want to chat in any given language – interaction on an informal, nonacademic basis is an ideal way for you to perfect your language skills.

What do the books do?
The four accompanying books are designed to complement the online course – the dialogs for all of the videos that you can watch online are available here for you to study whenever you don't have access to the Internet. You will also find all of the Grammar and Vocabulary sections explained in the books, plus the culture notes to teach you a little about Italy.

LEVEL 3

This book is the third of four. It corresponds with Level 3 of the online course.

Level 3 is ideal for students who can hold a simple conversation and are looking to start to cope in slightly more complex situations.

What you will learn
- How to talk to the doctor, speak about a problem, and talk about your family, hobbies and relationships
- Phone etiquette
- How to form and use the imperfect past tense and double negatives, and some more on commands
- How to form the perfect tense using *essere*
- Vocabulary for parts of the body, ordering a meal, talking about family and giving telephone numbers

Every time you see this coffee cup symbol in these books, it indicates the presence of a pathway – a guide to exactly where you can find that particular piece of content online. Log on at www.livemocha.com and follow the path to find the online version of what you are studying in the book.

Video Dialog

As they finish their drinks, Michele and the waiter give Giulia directions to some local stores.

 Active Italian: Level 1 > Unit 3 > Lesson 1 > Video dialog

Active Italian *Level 3*

1

Lesson 1: Booking a train ticket online

- » How to talk about computers.
- » Different ways of saying "great!"
- » How to say "the same...": *lo stesso*/*la stessa*.
- » Verbs that take *essere* as an auxiliary verb: *il treno è partito*.
- » How to say "how much?" or "how many?": *quanto? quanti?*, etc.
- » How to say dates: *il 22 marzo 2011 (il 22 marzo duemilaundici)*.

Lesson 2: Finding out about prices

- » How to say how much something costs.
- » How to follow online instructions to buy train tickets.
- » How to use the command form of the verb.

○ Collins | Livemocha™

UNIT 1 › LESSON 1

Booking a train ticket online

Culture note

Railway travel is efficient, comfortable, and relatively cheap in Italy. In the last few years, the new High Speed network (TAV, *Treno ad Alta Velocità*), with trains traveling at over 300 km/h has greatly reduced journey times. The new *Frecciarossa* (Red Arrow) travels from Milan to Rome in less than 3 hours and from Bologna to Florence in just 37 minutes and is far more comfortable than the slower trains. Of course, this speed and comfort comes at a higher price!

Unit 1 › Lesson 1: *Booking a train ticket online*

Video Dialog

Lucia helps Ugo to book his train tickets online.

Watch the video dialog online at
Active Italian: Level 3 > Unit 1 > Lesson 1 > Video dialog

Lucia:	*Guarda:... ecco...trenitalia punto com, sezione "Biglietti." Da dove vuoi partire?*
Ugo:	*Roma.*
Lucia:	*Dove vuoi arrivare?*
Ugo:	*Firenze.*
Lucia:	*Quando vuoi partire?*
Ugo:	*Domani... è il 22 marzo.*
Lucia:	*A che ora?*
Ugo:	*Verso le otto.*
Lucia:	*Quando vuoi tornare?*
Ugo:	*Lo stesso giorno... ehm... alle 19 circa.*
Lucia:	*Allora, c'è un treno diretto la mattina alle 7.45.*
Ugo:	*Quanto dura il viaggio?*
Lucia:	*Un ora e trentacinque minuti.*
Ugo:	*È perfetto.*

....

Lucia:	Look... there you are: trenitalia dot com, "Tickets" section. Where do you want to leave from?
Ugo:	Rome.
Lucia:	Where do you want to arrive?

Ugo:	Florence.
Lucia:	When do you want to leave?
Ugo:	Tomorrow, it's March 22nd.
Lucia:	At what time?
Ugo:	About 8.
Lucia:	When do you want to return?
Ugo:	The same day... um... at about 7 p.m.
Lucia:	Well, there's a direct train in the morning at 7:45.
Ugo:	How long does the trip take?
Lucia:	One hour and 35 minutes.
Ugo:	That's perfect.

Grammar

In this section we go over some of the grammar points introduced in the dialog.

Go to Active Italian: Level 3 > Unit 1 > Lesson 1 > Grammar to listen to these explanations and to access some interactive practice activities.

1 > **On and off**

> *Il tuo computer... è acceso?*
> Your computer... is it on?

Computer, like most foreign words in Italian, is masculine.

Acceso/a (on) is the past participle of *accendere* (to light or to switch on).

The opposite is *spento/a* (off) from *spegnere* (to switch off, to turn off, or to put out, depending on what you are referring to).

Il computer è acceso.	The computer is on.
Spegni la luce.	Turn the light off.
Bisogna accendere il riscaldamento.	You have to turn the heating on.
Hai spento il gas?	Have you switched the gas off?

2 › Internet talk

When reading out web addresses, use the following terms:

vu vu vu	www
punto	dot
chiocciola	at @
barra	slash

Most Italian websites end in *punto it* (dot it). "it" stands for Italy.

3 › Just the same!

Lo stesso means "the same."

Like all Italian adjectives, it agrees with the noun it describes:

lo stesso	for masculine singular words
la stessa	for feminine singular words
gli stessi	for masculine plural words
le stesse	for feminine plural words

Note the word for "the" is *lo* rather than *il*, and *gli* rather than *i*. This is because *stesso* begins with **st** and the rule is that masculine words beginning with s+consonant take the article *lo* in the singular and *gli* in the plural.

lo stesso giorno	the same day
gli stessi giorni	the same days
la stessa settimana	the same week
le stesse settimane	the same weeks

A common expression with *stesso* is:

> *È lo stesso* or *Fa lo stesso.*
> It's all the same / It makes no difference.

4 › Different ways of saying "great"

There are a number of ways of saying "great." Take your pick!

ottimo	excellent
eccellente	excellent
perfetto	perfect
fantastico	fantastic

Unit 1 › Lesson 1: *Booking a train ticket online*

5 › Verbs to do with motion

A number of verbs having to do with motion and traveling use *essere* in the past tense rather than *avere*. This means that the past participle acts like an adjective and agrees with the subject of the verb.

These verbs include:

arrivare	to arrive
I treni **sono** arriva**ti** in ritardo.	The trains arrived late.

partire	to leave, to depart
La nave **è** parti**ta** alle sette.	The ship left at 7:00.

ritornare	to return
Siamo ritorna**ti** molto tardi.	We got back very late.

andare	to go
Giulia **è** anda**ta** al teatro.	Giulia went to the theater.

venire	to come
Perché non **siete** venu**ti** alla festa?	Why didn't you come to the party?

Note that *essere* (to be) also takes *essere* as its auxiliary verb.

> **Siamo** *stati a Roma l'anno scorso.*
> We were in Rome last year.

How much? How many?

To ask "How much?" or "How many?" use *Quanto?* or *Quanti?*

Quanto costa?	How much does it cost?
Quant'è?	How much is it?
Quanti sono?	How many are they?

When *quanto* is followed by a noun, it needs to agree with it.

Quanto tempo?	How much time?
Quanta panna?	How much cream?
Quanti biglietti?	How many tickets?
Quante birre?	How many beers?

Dates

In the video dialog, Ugo says that tomorrow is *il ventidue marzo*. Apart from the first (*il primo*), cardinal numbers (2, 3, 4 and so on) are used with dates in Italian.

il primo gennaio 2010	(January 1st 2010)
il diciassette giugno 2011	(June 17th 2011)
il venti agosto 2012	(August 20th 2012)

Unit 1 › Lesson 1: *Booking a train ticket online*

To say the names of years, you just string the numbers together!

2010	*duemiladieci*
2011	*duemilaundici*
2012	*duemiladodici*

Culture note

Termini is the main railway station in Rome. The station has regular train services to all major Italian cities as well as daily international services to the main European capital cities. With its 29 platforms and over 150 million passengers each year, *Roma Termini* is one of the largest train stations in Europe.

Termini is also the main hub for public transportation within Rome. Both current subway lines (A and B) intersect at *Termini*, and there are many bus stops in front of it.

Live**mocha**™ Active Italian *Level 3*

Vocabulary

In this section you will learn some useful words and expressions from the dialog.

 Go to *Active Italian: Level 3 > Unit 1 > Lesson 1 > Vocabulary* to listen to each of the words being pronounced and to access some interactive practice activities.

caricare
to upload

Non riesco a caricare l'immagine.
I am unable to upload the picture.

scaricare
to download

Come si fa a scaricare una canzone?
How do you download a song?

la stampante
printer

La stampante non funziona.
The printer isn't working.

il portatile
laptop

Ho lasciato il portatile a casa.
I left my laptop at home.

Unit 1 › Lesson 1: *Booking a train ticket online*

lo schermo
screen

Che cosa vedi sullo schermo?
What do you see on the screen?

la tastiera
keyboard

Ha bisogno di una tastiera.
He needs a keyboard.

la chiavetta USB
flash drive, memory stick

Non trovo una chiavetta USB.
I can't find find a flash drive.

il sito web
website

Il sito web dell'Ambasciata d'Italia a New York è stato trasferito.
The website of the Italian Embassy in New York has been moved.

l'indirizzo
address

Qual è l'indirizzo del sito web?
What is the website address?

UNIT 1 › LESSON 2
Finding out about prices

Culture note

Trenitalia is the primary operator of trains within Italy. Their website is www.ferroviedellostato.it. It has extensive information on trains, schedules, and special offers. It allows you to purchase tickets online.

Unit 1 › Lesson 2: *Finding out about prices*

Video Dialog

Just before reserving his tickets Ugo suggests a last-minute change of plan.

 Active Italian: Level 3 > Unit 1 > Lesson 2 > Video dialog

Ugo:	*Quanto costa?*
Lucia:	*Costa... ehm... 43.50 euro perché prenoti all'ultimo momento.*
Ugo:	*È caro!*
Lucia:	*Per il ritorno, puoi prendere... un biglietto per il treno delle 17.10.*
Ugo:	*D'accordo, va bene, seleziona quello...*
Lucia:	*Intestazione biglietti... Bene, inserisci tu i tuoi particolari ed il numero della carta.*
Ugo:	*Ti piacerebbe venire con me?*
Lucia:	*Sì, molto volentieri.*
Ugo:	*E la sfilata di moda...?*
Lucia:	*Ci posso andare un altro giorno*
Ugo:	*Allora, ricominciamo...*

Ugo:	How much does it cost?
Lucia:	It costs... er... 43 euros 50 cents because you're booking at the last minute.
Ugo:	That's expensive!

Lucia:	For the return trip you can get... a ticket on the 17:10.
Ugo:	OK, that's fine, choose that one.
Lucia:	Passenger's details... OK, you put your details and your card number in...
Ugo:	Would you like to come with me?
Lucia:	Yes, I'd love to.
Ugo:	And the fashion show...?
Lucia:	I can go another day.
Ugo:	Well then, let's start again...

Grammar

 Active Italian: Level 3 > Unit 1 > Lesson 2 > Grammar

1 › **Giving instructions**

When telling someone what to do, the verb ending is *-i* for *-ere* and *-ire* verbs.

> *Leggi questo libro.*
> Read this book.

> *Finisci di mangiare.*
> Finish eating.

With *-are* verbs, the ending is *-a*.

> *Seleziona la quantità.*
> Select the quantity.

Unit 1 › Lesson 2: *Finding out about prices*

Telling someone not to do something is even simpler. Just place *non* before the infinitive.

Non leggere.	Don't read.
Non dormire.	Don't sleep.
Non parlare.	Don't talk.

2 › **Sit down, Stand up, Take a seat**

These verbs are reflexive in Italian, which means that they include a reflexive pronoun. With instructions, the pronoun *ti* (for one person you know well) or *vi* (for more than one person) is attached to the end of the verb.

Siediti / Sedetevi	Sit down!
Alzati / Alzatevi	Get up!
Accomodati / Accomodatevi	Take a seat!

When telling someone not to sit down, etc., the pronoun can come before the verb or be attached to it:

Non alzarti! or Non ti alzare!
Don't get up!

3 › Using a computer

Everyday computer terms include:

collegare la stampante	to connect the printer
fare clic su	to click on
stampare il biglietto	to print the ticket
inserire i propri dati	to enter your details
scegliere una password	to choose a password
effettuare il pagamento/ l'acquisto	to complete the payment/ purchase
autorizzare	to authorize

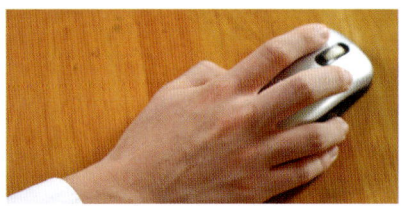

4 › How much is it?

To say how much something costs, use the verb *costare*:

Costa 30 euro.	It costs 30 euros.
Costano 60 euro.	They cost 60 euros.
Un biglietto di andata e ritorno costa 40 euro.	A round-trip ticket costs 40 euros.

5 › The 5:10 train

The 24-hour clock is used for official time, but in everyday speech the 12-hour clock is used.

Unit 1 › Lesson 2: *Finding out about prices*

To specify a particular train, you need to use *di* (of). *Di* is one of those short words that combines with the definite article (*il*, *la*, etc). When talking about time *di* combines with *le* and becomes *delle*.

il treno delle 17:10 (cinque e dieci)

il treno delle 20:00 (otto)

6 › **The first and the last**

The opposite of *primo* (first) is *ultimo* (last).

all'ultimo momento	at the last moment
il primo treno	the first train
l'ultimo treno	the last train

Vocabulary

 Active Italian: Level 3 > Unit 1 > Lesson 2 > Vocabulary

il biglietto
ticket

Un biglietto per Torino, per favore.
A ticket to Turin, please.

lo sportello
ticket counter

I biglietti si acquistano allo sportello.
Tickets can be bought at the ticket counter.

la biglietteria
ticket office

La biglietteria è sempre aperta un'ora prima dello spettacolo.
The ticket office is always open an hour before the show.

il passeggero
passenger

I passeggeri sono in attesa all'uscita numero 3.
The passengers are waiting at gate number 3.

il viaggio
trip, journey

Quanto dura il viaggio?
How long is the trip?

il finestrino
window (in train, car)

Preferisco un posto vicino al finestrino.
I prefer a seat by the window.

il corridoio
aisle (in train, plane)

Vorrei un posto sul corridoio.
I would like an aisle seat.

Unit 1 › Lesson 2: *Finding out about prices*

il supplemento
supplement

Ecco il biglietto e il supplemento.
Here is the ticket and the supplement.

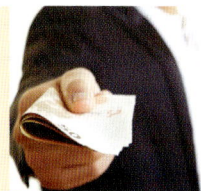

pagare
to pay

Che seccatura! Non posso pagare con questa carta di credito!
What a drag! I can't pay with this credit card!

di seconda classe
second class

Un biglietto di seconda classe, per favore.
A second class ticket, please.

Culture note

If you plan to travel by train, it is worth becoming familiar with the following words:

binario	platform, track
orario	schedule
arrivi	arrivals
partenze	departures
proveniente da	coming from
in testa	at the front of the train
in coda	at the rear of the train
ritardo	delay
solo 2ª classe	2nd class only (*2ª* is written *seconda*)
1ª classe	first class (*1ª* is written *prima*)

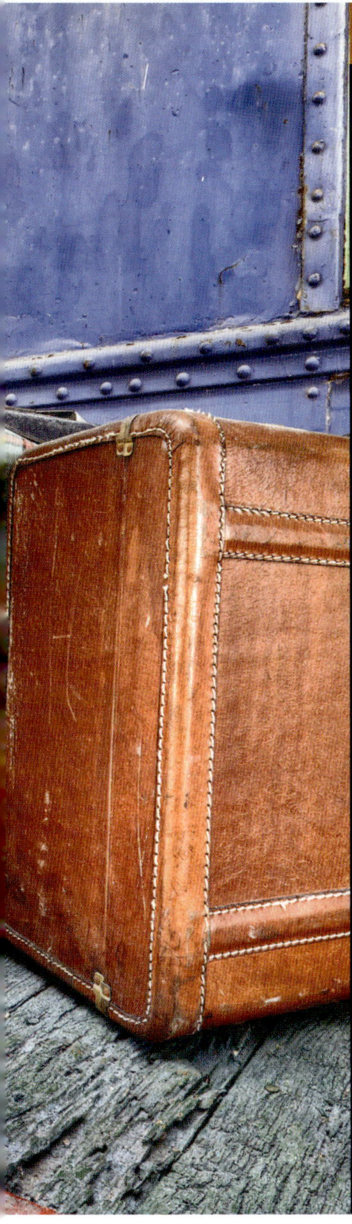

Active Italian *Level 3*

2

Lesson 1: I've lost...

- How to say you have lost something: ***Ho dimenticato la borsa.***
- How to give personal details: ***nome, cognome***
- The imperfect tense of ***essere*** (to be)
- The Italian alphabet
- How to give instructions using reflexive verbs: ***Non si preoccupi*** (Don't worry)

Lesson 2: Things you need to do

- What to do when you have lost something: ***Bisogna chiamare...***
- Past participles of irregular verbs: ***perso*** (lost), ***successo*** (happened), etc.
- How to use ***per*** to mean "for," "in order to": ***per annullare la carta***
- How to form adverbs by adding ***-mente***
- How to use object pronouns with the past tense: ***Dove l'hai lasciata?*** (Where did you leave it?)

Collins | Livemocha™

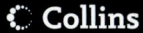

UNIT 2 › LESSON 1
I've lost ...

Culture note

In Italy ID cards (*la carta d'identità*) are compulsory, and Italians are required to carry a form of identification with them at all times. An ID card is the most important document for an Italian citizen, as it can be used to open a bank account, to vote, and to check in for all flights to EU destinations.

When traveling in Italy be sure to remember to take a form of identification with you everywhere you go, as it is illegal to travel without it and you may well be fined if a policeman decides to do a random check.

Unit 2 › Lesson 1: *I've lost...*

Video Dialog

Giulia has to report some bad news at the tourist information office.

 Active Italian: Level 3 > Unit 2 > Lesson 1 > Video dialog

Giulia: *Buongiorno, mi può aiutare, per favore?*

Sig.ra Duranti: *Sì, che cosa c'è?*

Giulia: *Ho dimenticato la borsa sull'autobus.*

Sig.ra Duranti: *Quale autobus?*

Giulia: *Il 24.*

Sig.ra Duranti: *Allora, bisogna telefonare al capolinea dell'autobus. Come si chiama?*

Giulia: *Ramozzino.*

Sig.ra Duranti: *Come si scrive, per favore?*

Giulia: *R A M O Z Z I N O*

Sig.ra Duranti: *E di nome?*

Giulia: *Giulia.*

Sig.ra Duranti: *Qual è il suo indirizzo?*

Giulia: *Sono all'albergo Continente, in via Dante.*

Sig.ra Duranti: *Che cosa c'era nella borsa?*

Giulia: *Il portafogli, il passaporto.*

Sig.ra Duranti: *La carta di credito?*

Giulia:	*Oh accidenti! Sì, era dentro il portafogli.*
Sig.ra Duranti:	*Altro?*
Giulia:	*Le chiavi e l'astuccio del trucco, la spazzola, gli occhiali da sole, delle foto della mia famiglia... praticamente tutto!*
Sig.ra Duranti:	*Non si preoccupi. Ora telefono al capolinea.*

Giulia:	Good morning. Can you help me, please?
Mrs. Duranti:	Yes, what's wrong?
Giulia:	I have left my purse on the bus.
Mrs. Duranti:	Which bus?
Giulia:	The number 24.
Mrs. Duranti:	OK, we'll have to telephone the bus terminal. What is your name?
Giulia:	Ramozzino.
Mrs. Duranti:	How do you spell it, please?
Giulia:	R A M O Z Z I N O
Mrs. Duranti:	And your first name?
Giulia:	Giulia.
Mrs. Duranti:	What is your address?
Giulia:	I'm at the Hotel Continente, in via Dante.
Mrs. Duranti:	What was in your purse?
Giulia:	My wallet, my passport.
Mrs. Duranti:	Your credit card?
Giulia:	Oh darn it! Yes, it was in my wallet.
Mrs. Duranti:	Anything else?
Giulia:	My keys and my makeup bag, my hairbrush, my sunglasses, some photos of my family... practically everything.
Mrs. Duranti:	Don't worry. I will call the terminal right now.

Unit 2 › Lesson 1: *I've lost...*

Grammar

 Active Italian: Level 3 > Unit 2 > Lesson 1 > Grammar

1 › Leaving out "my," "your," etc.

Giulia tells Michele:

> *Ho dimenticato la borsa sull'autobus.*
> I have left my purse on the bus.

Note how Giulia doesn't say *la **mia** borsa*. In Italian it is understood that it is her purse so just the definite article (*la*) is required.

This is particularly true of personal items such as clothing:

> *Ho lasciato la maglia a casa.*
> I left my sweater at home.

> *Non uscire senza mettere l'impermeabile.*
> Don't go out without putting on your raincoat.

The past of *C'è* and *Ci sono*

The expression *c'è* (there is) becomes *c'era* (there was) in the past. *Ci sono* (there are) becomes *c'erano* (there were).

> *Che cosa c'era nella borsa?*
> What was in your purse?

> *Nella borsa c'erano le chiavi e il passaporto.*
> In my purse there were my keys and my passport.

Imperfect tense of *essere*

When describing things in the past, you normally use the imperfect of *essere* (to be).

Here is the imperfect tense.

ero	I was
eri	you (*familiar*) were
era	he/she/it was
era	you (*formal*) were
eravamo	we were
eravate	you (*plural*) were
erano	they were

Unit 2 › Lesson 1: *I've lost ...*

2.1

Le scarpe erano bianche.
The shoes were white.

La macchina era grigia.
The car was gray.

Giulia era molto contenta.
Giulia was very pleased.

4 › *Telefonare a* (to phone...)

Signora Duranti says *Bisogna telefonare **al** capolinea* (We need to phone the bus terminal).

Telefonare is followed by *a* and then the person or place you are phoning. Remember to combine *a* with the definite article when necessary:

*telefonare **al** consolato*	to phone the consulate
*telefonare **alla** polizia*	to phone the police
*telefonare **all'**albergo*	to phone the hotel
*telefonare **allo** stadio*	to phone the stadium
telefonare ai cugini	to phone the cousins
telefonare alle ragazze	to phone the girls
telefonare agli studenti	to phone the students

Livemocha™ Active Italian *Level 3*

When it is a person you are phoning, *a* is followed by their name:

telefonare a Roberto
to phone Roberto

5 › Verbs followed by *a* + a noun or pronoun

Other verbs followed by *a* and a noun or pronoun include:

assomigliare ***a***	to look like.
Assomiglia a sua nonna.	She looks like her grandmother.
piacere ***a***	to please
Piace a me.	It pleases me.
rispondere ***a***	to reply to
Rispondo al telefono.	Answer the phone.
pensare ***a***	to think of
Penso a Jessica.	I'm thinking of Jessica.
insegnare ***a***	to teach (someone)
Insegno l'italiano a mia figlia.	I'm teaching Italian to my daughter.

6 › Verbs followed by *di* + infinitive

A number of verbs are followed by *di* and the infinitive. These include:

decidere **di**	to decide
Abbiamo deciso di partire.	We decided to leave.
pensare **di**	to think of
Penso di ritornare l'anno prossimo.	I am thinking of returning next year.
tentare **di**	to try
Ho tentato di telefonare.	I tried to phone.
vietare **di**	to forbid
Mi hanno vietato di uscire.	They forbade me from going out.

2.1 Livemocha™ Active Italian *Level 3*

7 › The alphabet

The Italian alphabet has only 21 letters. The other five (j, k, w, x, and y) are only used in foreign words.

A	*a*	B	*bi*	C	*ci*
D	*di*	E	*e*	F	*effe*
G	*gi*	H	*acca*	I	*i*
L	*elle*	M	*emme*	N	*enne*
O	*o*	P	*pi*	Q	*cu*
R	*erre*	S	*esse*	T	*ti*
U	*u*	V	*vi*	Z	*zeta*

And the foreign letters are:

| J *i lunga* | K *kappa* | W *vu doppia* | X *ics* | Y *i greca* |

8 › *Come si scrive?* – How do you spell it?

Scrivere means "to write" so *Come si scrive?* means "How do you write it?" using the impersonal *si* form.

Come si dice?	How do you say it?
Come si pronuncia?	How do you pronounce it?
Come si fa?	How do you do it?

Memorize the letters of your name and then say them out loud starting off with:

Si scrive...

9 › Polite and friendly instructions

Signora Duranti tells Giulia not to worry: *Non si preoccupi!*

Unit 2 › Lesson 1: *I've lost...*

Worrying is something you do to yourself and the verb is reflexive in Italian: *preoccuparsi*. The *si* here is the reflexive pronoun.

Signora Duranti uses the polite *lei* form with Giulia. If you were telling your friend not to worry then you would say:

| *Non preoccuparti!* | Don't worry! |
| *Non si dimentichi di prenotare l'albergo.* | Don't forget to book the hotel. |

And if you were saying it to a friend:

Non dimenticarti di prenotare l'albergo.

Culture note

If you lose your passport in Italy you should notify the police (*la polizia*) and your consulate (*il consolato*) as quickly as possible. The consulates can be found in the major cities including Rome, Florence, and Milan, while you can also find contact details for your nearest consulate online.

Livemocha™ Active Italian *Level 3*

Vocabulary

Active Italian: Level 3 > Unit 2 > Lesson 1 > Vocabulary

un astuccio
case (for makeup, glasses, etc.)

Dov'è il mio astuccio per gli occhiali?
Where is my glasses case?

il trucco
makeup

Non uso trucco.
I don't wear makeup.

la spazzola
brush, hairbrush

Ho bisogno di una spazzola per i capelli.
I need a hairbrush.

gli occhiali da sole
sunglasses

Quanto costano quegli occhiali da sole?
How much are those sunglasses?

Unit 2 › Lesson 1: *I've lost ...*

2.1

le chiavi
keys

Non so dove ho lasciato le chiavi.
I don't know where I left the keys.

la cartella
briefcase

Di che colore è la cartella?
What color is the briefcase?

un paio d'orecchini
a pair of earrings

Cerco un paio d'orecchini d'oro.
I am looking for a pair of gold earrings.

il telefonino
cell phone

Ce l'hai il telefonino?
Do you have a cell phone?

il modulo
form

Bisogna riempire questo modulo.
You have to fill out this form.

il cognome
family name, last name

Bisogna scrivere il proprio nome, il cognome, e la cittadinanza.
You need to write your first name, family name, and nationality.

la data di nascita
date of birth

Qual è la sua data di nascita?
What is your date of birth?

UNIT 2 › LESSON 2
Things you need to do

Culture note

The national bus lines provide another cost-effective way of traveling from city to city in Italy. The website www.sena.it is useful for finding low-cost tickets for travel as far north as Milan and all the way down to Calabria.

Video Dialog

Giulia tells Michele her bad news.

Active Italian: Level 3 > Unit 2 > Lesson 2 > Video dialog

Michele:	*Che cosa è successo?*
Giulia:	*Ho perso il passaporto, i soldi, e la chiave dell'albergo.*
Michele:	*E il telefonino?*
Giulia:	*Per fortuna l'avevo in tasca.*
Michele:	*Hai bisogno di tirarti su. Ti offro qualcosa?*
Giulia:	*Mi basta un caffè.*
Michele:	*Dove l'hai persa?*
Giulia:	*Sull'autobus, l'ho dimenticata sull'autobus.*
Michele:	*E hai chiamato l'ufficio oggetti smarriti?*
Giulia:	*Sì.*
Michele:	*Hai telefonato alla banca per annullare la carta?*
Giulia:	*No.*
Michele:	*Bisogna farlo immediatamente. E al consolato per il passaporto?*
Giulia:	*Accidenti!*

....

Michele:	What's happened?
Giulia:	I've lost my passport, my money, and my hotel key.

Michele:	And your cell phone?
Giulia:	Luckily it was in my pocket.
Michele:	You need a pick-me-up. A drink?
Giulia:	Just a coffee.
Michele:	Where did you lose it?
Giulia:	On the bus. I left it on the bus.
Michele:	And have you called the lost-and-found office?
Giulia:	Yes.
Michele:	Have you called the bank to cancel your card?
Giulia:	No.
Michele:	You've got to do it right away. And the consulate about your passport?
Giulia:	Darn!

Culture note

When traveling across Italy, be sure to try the local cuisine at every opportunity. Italy is well-known for its great food and this is for a good reason. You may find a tasty dish in the most tourist-filled café in the center of a town; however, if you can hunt out a hidden away family-run restaurant and ask the proprietor what they recommend, you won't regret it.

Each region has its own specialties and even though you'll find them done well in other parts of Italy, they will always taste best in their most traditional surroundings, using the secret family traditions and fresh, locally grown ingredients.

Livemocha™ Active Italian *Level 3*

Grammar

Active Italian: Level 3 > Unit 2 > Lesson 2 > Grammar

1 › Irregular past participles

The past participle of *perdere* is *perso*. Here are a few other past participles that don't follow the regular pattern of *-ato* (*-are* verbs), *-uto* (*-ere* verbs), and *-ito* (*-ire* verbs).

accendere – acceso	to light – lit
vedere – visto	to see – seen
mettere – messo	to put – put
scendere – sceso	to go down – gone down
rispondere – risposto	to reply – replied
succedere – successo	to happen – happened
bere – bevuto	to drink – drunk
chiudere – chiuso	to close – closed
nascere – nato	to be born – born
chiedere – chiesto	to ask – asked

2 › *Succedere* – to happen

Michele asks Giulia *Che cosa è successo?* (What has happened?)

If Michele arrived in the midst of something happening, he would say *Che cosa succede?* or *Che cosa sta succedendo?* (What's happening?)

Unit 2 › Lesson 2: *Things you need to do*

3 › *Per* meaning "in order to"

You have already met *per* meaning "for" as in *un caffè **per** me* (a coffee for me) or to indicate a destination – *un treno per Roma* (a train to Rome).

Per also means "in order to" and is followed by the infinitive:

> *Hai telefonato alla banca **per** annullare la carta?*
> Have you phoned the bank to cancel the card?

> *Bisogna telefonare al ristorante **per** prenotare un tavolo.*
> You need to phone the restaurant to reserve a table.

4 › Italian adverbs ending in -*mente*

Adverbs are words that describe verbs (to run **quickly**), or adjectives (**very** small) or other adverbs (**very** quickly).

In Italian many adverbs end in -*mente* (*immediatamente*). To form an adverb, add -*mente* to the singular feminine form of the adjective.
So *immediata* becomes ***immediata**mente* (immediately)
lenta becomes ***lenta**mente* (slowly)
sfortunata becomes ***sfortunata**mente* (unfortunately)

5 › Object pronouns with the past tense

We have already met object pronouns (*lo*, *la*, *li*, and *le*) when buying clothes.

Mi piace **il vestito**, **lo** prendo.	I like the dress, I'll take it.
Mi piace **la gonna**, **la** compro.	I like the skirt, I'll buy it.
Mi piacciono **i pantaloni**, **li** prendo.	I like the pants, I'll take them.
Mi piacciono **le scarpe**, **le** compro.	I like the shoes, I'll buy them.
Mi piacciono **gli stivali**, **li** compro.	I like the boots, I'll buy them.

When using the object pronouns *lo*, *la*, *li* or *le* in the past tense, the past participle should agree with whatever the object pronoun has replaced.

> *Ho perso **la** borsa. Dove l'hai pers**a**?*
> I lost my purse. Where did you lose it?

> *Non ho perso **il** telefonino. Per fortuna, l'avev**o** in tasca.*
> I didn't lose my cell phone. Luckily, I had it in my pocket.

Vocabulary

 Active Italian: Level 3 > Unit 2 > Lesson 2 > Vocabulary

la volta
time

C'era una volta...
Once upon a time...

per caso
by any chance

Avete per caso una maglia viola?
Do you by any chance have a purple sweater?

i soldi
money

Mi hanno rubato i soldi.
They've stolen my money.

la tasca
pocket

Avevo i soldi in tasca.
I had the money in my pocket.

annullare
to cancel

Ho dovuto annullare la prenotazione.
I had to cancel my reservation.

perdere
to lose

Ho perso le chiavi di casa.
I have lost my house keys.

rispondere
to answer/to reply

Il consolato non risponde.
The consulate isn't answering.

la risposta
reply

Ho bisogno di una risposta entro due giorni.
I need a reply within two days.

aspettare
to wait for

Aspetto una mail.
I am waiting for an email.

ritirare
to fetch, to pick up

Bisogna ritirarlo domani mattina.
You have to fetch it tomorrow morning.

Unit 2 › Lesson 2: *Things you need to do*

Active Italian *Level 3*

3

Lesson 1: Found!

- » How to use "it's been..." and "they have...": ***è stato..., hanno...***
- » The negative form of ***esserci***: ***non c'era*** (there was no), ***non c'erano*** (there were no).
- » How to say "with" and "without": ***con*** and ***senza***.
- » Different tenses for ***andare*** (to go).
- » The irregular verb ***venire*** (to come).

Lesson 2: Family photos

- » How to use subject pronouns to describe people: ***lui, lei, loro***.
- » How to say your age.
- » About the pronoun ***ne*** meaning "of it," "of them."
- » How to say "oldest" and "youngest": ***maggiore, minore***.
- » How to use demonstrative pronouns and adjectives: ***questo, quello***.
- » The use of possessive adjectives with family members: ***mia madre*** (my mother), ***mio padre*** (my father)
- » How articles work with family members.

۞ Collins | **Livemocha™**

UNIT 3 › LESSON 1
Found!

Culture note

Pronto (literally "ready") is normally used when answering the telephone, although it may sound strange and rather unfriendly to foreign ears.

The country code for Italy is +39 (for Switzerland it is +41), and a full area code is used for landlines (so to call a landline in Rome from another country, you would dial +39 06 12345678).

Unit 3 › Lesson 1: *Found!*

Video Dialog

Giulia receives some good news and some bad news.

Active Italian: Level 3 > Unit 3 > Lesson 1 > Video dialog

Giulia:	*Pronto, sì, sono Giulia Ramozzino.*
Sig.ra Duranti:	*La sua borsa è stata ritrovata ma il portafogli non c'era.*
Giulia:	*E il passaporto?*
Sig.ra Duranti:	*Mi dispiace, non c'erano documenti oltre alla patente di guida.*
Giulia:	*Grazie. Posso venire a prenderla?*
Sig.ra Duranti:	*Certo, deve andare all'ufficio oggetti smarriti.*
Giulia:	*Grazie, ci vado subito.*
Sig.ra Duranti:	*Deve annullare la carta di credito e fare denuncia di smarrimento di un documento d'identità presso un commissariato di polizia.*
Giulia:	*Grazie.*
Michele:	*E allora?*
Giulia:	*Hanno trovato la mia borsa, ma senza portafogli, senza carta di credito, e senza passaporto.*
Michele:	*Va bene, stasera offro io.*

Giulia:	Hello, yes, it's Giulia Ramozzino speaking.
Mrs. Duranti:	Your purse has been found, but your wallet wasn't in it.
Giulia:	And my passport?
Mrs. Duranti:	Sorry, there were no documents except your driver's license.
Giulia:	Thanks. Can I come and get it?
Mrs. Duranti:	Certainly, you have to go to the lost-and-found office.
Giulia:	Thanks, I'll go right away.
Mrs. Duranti:	You must cancel your credit card and report the loss of your ID at the police station.
Giulia:	Thanks.
Michele:	So?
Giulia:	They have found my purse but without my wallet, my credit card, and my passport.
Michele:	OK. Tonight it's on me.

Grammar

 Active Italian: Level 3 > Unit 3 > Lesson 1 > Grammar

1 › ... has been found

When you don't know who has carried out an action, you can say:

*La sua borsa **è stata** ritrovata.*	Your bag has been found.
*La macchina **è stata** danneggiata.*	The car has been damaged.
*Il passaporto di Max **è stato** rubato.*	Max's passport has been stolen.
*Anche le chiavi **sono state** rubate.*	Even the keys have been stolen.

Unit 3 › Lesson 1: *Found!*

Stato is the past participle of *essere*, which also takes *essere* as its auxiliary verb. Therefore *stato* agrees with whatever has been damaged or stolen: *la macchina*, *il passaporto*, *le chiavi*.

2 › | They have...

You can also use the "they" form of the verb to say that something has happened when you don't know who has done it:

> ***Hanno trovato*** *la sua borsa.*
> **They've found** her bag.

This means that her bag has been found, but "they" doesn't refer to anyone in particular.

| ***Hanno trovato*** *il passaporto.* | **They've found** his passport. |
| ***Hanno rubato*** *le chiavi.* | **They've stolen** the keys. |

Because *avere* is the auxiliary verb here, there is no agreement of the past participle.

3 › With and without

The word for "with" is *con*.

con ghiaccio	with ice.
con il limone	with lemon
con piacere	with pleasure

"Without" is *senza*.

| *senza ghiaccio* | without ice |
| *senza zucchero* | without sugar |

When it is followed by a verb, the verb must be in the infinitive in Italian:

senza pensare
without thinking

4 › How to say "There was no..." and "There were no..."

You have already encountered *c'è* (there is) and *ci sono* (there are), and *c'era* (there was) and *c'erano* (there were).

To say "there was no..." or "there were no...", you place *non* first.

| *Il passaporto **non** c'era.* | There was no passport. |
| ***Non** c'erano documenti oltre alla patente di guida.* | There were no documents except the driver's license. |

5 › Andare – to go

Andare is an irregular verb you have already seen. Here is a quick review.

vado	I go
vai	you (*familiar*) go
va	he/she/it goes
va	you (*formal*) go
andiamo	we go
andate	you (*plural*) go
vanno	they go

andando is the gerund (going).
andato is the past participle (gone). Note that *andare* takes *essere* as its auxiliary verb and therefore *andato* agrees with whoever is carrying out the action.
and- is the stem for the imperfect (was going): **and**avo, **and**avi, **and**ava, etc.
andr- is the stem for the future tense (will go): **andr**ò, **andr**ai, **andr**à, etc.

6 › *Venire* – to come

Venire is another important irregular verb.

The present tense is:

vengo	I come
vieni	you (*familiar*) come
viene	he/she/it comes
viene	you (*formal*) come
veniamo	we come
venite	you (*plural*) come
vengono	they come

venendo is the gerund (coming).
venuto is the past participle (come). Note that *venire* takes *essere* as its auxiliary verb, therefore *venuto* agrees with whoever is carrying out the action.
ven- is the stem for the imperfect (was coming): **ven**ivo, **ven**ivi, **ven**iva, etc.
verr- is the stem for the future tense (will come): **verr**ò, **verr**ai, **verr**à, etc.

Culture note

There are many different types of police in Italy, and in any given city you may see the following varieties: the *Polizia Statale*, who concern themselves with crime; the *Carabinieri*, part of the Italian Armed Forces; the *Polizia Municipale*, who deal with traffic; the *Guardia di Finanza*, the financial police; and the *Polizia Penitenziaria*, who operate the Italian prison system.

If you happen to lose your passport, the loss may be reported to either the *Polizia Municipale* or the *Carabinieri*.

Unit 3 › Lesson 1: *Found!*

3.1

Vocabulary

 Active Italian: Level 3 > Unit 3 > Lesson 1 > Vocabulary

mancare
to be missing

Che cosa manca?
What is missing?

la descrizione
description

Mi dà una descrizione della borsa?
Can you give me a description of the purse?

la valigia
suitcase

Ho fatto la valigia ieri.
I packed the suitcase yesterday.

disfare la valigia
to unpack the suitcase

Hai finito di disfare la valigia?
Have you finished unpacking the suitcase?

59

lo zaino
backpack

Portavo lo zaino in spalla.
I was carrying the backpack on my back.

il portafogli
wallet

Sono uscita senza portafogli.
I came out without my wallet.

il braccialetto
bracelet

Che bel braccialetto!
What a lovely bracelet!

la collana
necklace

Che bella collana! Dove l'hai presa?
What a lovely necklace! Where did you get it?

un anello
ring

Era l'anello di mia nonna.
It was my grandmother's ring.

la fede
wedding ring

Mio marito non porta la fede.
My husband doesn't wear a wedding ring.

il valore
value

Qual è il valore dell'anello?
What is the value of the ring?

UNIT 3 › LESSON 2
Family photos

Culture note

Family bonds in Italy are traditionally very strong. It is not uncommon for children to live at home with their parents until they are well into their twenties. Students, too, often opt to stay at home throughout their studies both as a money saving measure and because it is much more common for Italians to study at a university close to their home towns.

Livemocha™ Active Italian *Level 3*

Video Dialog

Giulia, reunited with her lost belongings, shows Michele some photos.

Active Italian: Level 3 > Unit 3 > Lesson 2 > Video dialog

Giulia: *Finalmente, la mia borsa.*

Michele: *Chi sono questi?*

Giulia: *Sono i miei genitori.*

Michele: *Abitano in montagna?*

Giulia: *No, questa è la casa di mia nonna. Loro abitano in città, a Chiasso.*

Michele: *E questa?*

Giulia: *Questa è la mia sorellina quando aveva cinque anni. Adesso, ne ha diciannove.*

Michele: *Che lavoro fa?*

Giulia: *Lavora in una banca.*

Michele: *Questo è tuo fratello. Ti assomiglia!*

Giulia: *Sì, è Ludovico.*

Michele: *E quello?*

Giulia: *Quello è il mio cane!*

....

Giulia:	At last, my purse!
Michele:	Who are these people?
Giulia:	They are my parents.
Michele:	They live in the mountains?

Giulia:	No, this is my grandmother's house. They live in town, in Chiasso.
Michele:	And this one?
Giulia:	This is my little sister when she was 5. Now she's 19.
Michele:	What does she do?
Giulia:	She works in a bank.
Michele:	This is your brother. He looks like you!
Giulia:	Yes, it's Ludovico.
Michele:	And that one?
Giulia:	That's my dog!

Grammar

Active Italian: Level 3 > Unit 3 > Lesson 2 > Grammar

1 › **Referring to other people**

When you are talking about other people you use the following pronouns:

lui	he
lei	she
loro	they

In Italian they are generally left out because the verb ending is enough to tell you who is "doing" the verb (the subject).

Subject pronouns are mostly used to add emphasis or to avoid any confusion.

> *Chi vuole gelato al limone? Lo voglio **io**.*
> Who wants lemon ice cream? **I** want it.

> *Sara e Francesco lavorano in banca. **Lui** è impiegato e **lei** è direttrice.*
> Sara and Francesco work in the bank. He is a clerk and she is a manager.

2 › Giving your age

In Italian you use *avere* to indicate your age: you say "I have (so many) years."

Ho vent'anni.	I am 20.
Michele ha 28 anni.	Michele is 28.
Elena ha 22 anni.	Elena is 22.
I miei genitori hanno 50 anni.	My parents are 50.
Quanti anni hai?	How old are you?

3 › ### The pronoun *ne* (of it, of them)

In Italian you cannot leave out *anni* but you can replace it with a pronoun *ne* meaning "of it" or "of them."

> *Quanti anni hai?*
> How old are you?

If you are 34, for example, you have 3 possible replies. Either you simply state the number:

| *Trentaquattro.* | 34 |

or:

| *Ho trentaquattro anni.* | I am 34 years old. |

or:

| *Ne ho trentaquattro.* | I am 34. (Literally "I have 34 of them.") |

Like the other pronoun *ci* (to there, there), *ne* is a pronoun that should be included to avoid repeating what it replaces, which is *anni* (years) in the previous example.

> *Quanti panini vuole?*
> How many rolls do you want?

You can simply state the number:

| *Sei.* | Six |

Or, if you use *voglio* or another verb, you include *ne*.

| *Ne voglio sei.* | I want six (of them). |

4 › **Talking about oldest and youngest.**

We have already come across *-ino* or *-ina* as endings that indicate that something is small. Giulia refers to her little sister as *la mia sorellina* (my little sister). You can do the same with a brother *un fratellino* (a little brother).

When talking about age you use *maggiore* (older, oldest) and *minore* (younger, youngest).

| *La maggiore delle tre sorelle è Anna.* | The oldest of the three sisters is Anna. |
| *Harry è il fratello minore.* | Harry is the younger brother. |

5 › *Questo* and *quello* as pronouns

The words *questo* (this) and *quello* (that) can be used on their own or with a noun.

On their own, they are technically pronouns because they are replacing something. Usually it is something you are pointing out. If it is something near to you, then you use *questo*. If it is further away, then you use *quello*.

If they are replacing a noun or person, then *questo* and *quello* have to agree with what they replace.

Unit 3 › Lesson 2: *Family photos*

Quale vino? Questo o quello?	Which wine? This one or that one?
Quale casa? Questa o quella?	Which house? This one or that one?
Quali ragazzi? Questi o quelli?	Which kids? These (ones) or those (ones)?
Quali bambine? Queste o quelle?	Which little girls? These (ones) or those (ones)?

6 › ## *Questo* as an adjective

If you use *questo* and *quello* with a noun, then they behave like adjectives but ones that introduce the noun rather than come after it. *Questo* is straightforward:

questo bambino	this little boy
questa bambina	this little girl
quest'amico	this boyfriend
quest'amica	this girlfriend
questi libri	these books
queste riviste	these magazines

Note how both *questo* and *questa* shorten to *quest'* before a word beginning with a vowel.

7 › Quello as an adjective

Quello is slightly more complicated than *questo* as it follows a similar pattern to that of the combining articles *al, alla, del, della, sul, sulla, sugli* etc.

quello shortens to *quel* in front of most masculine nouns:

> *quel giorno, quel parco, quel ristorante*

With words that take *lo* as the article *quello* stays as it is:

> *quello stadio, quello sport, quello yogurt*

With a feminine noun it is *quella*:

> *quella casa, quella macchina, quella notte*

With a masculine or feminine word beginning with a vowel, *quello* shortens to *quell'*:

> *quell'albergo, quell'università*

8 › Quello as an adjective

In the plural *quello* becomes *quei* with most masculine nouns:

> *quei giorni, quei parchi, quei ristoranti*

quelle with all feminine nouns:

> *quelle case, quelle macchine, quelle università*

Unit 3 › Lesson 2: *Family photos*

And *quegli* with masculine nouns that begin with a vowel or take *lo* as the article in the singular:

> *quegli uomini, quegli studenti, quegli yogurt.*

9 › Using *mio*, *tuo*, etc., with single family members

We are already familiar with the possessive adjectives such as *mio* (my), *tuo*, *suo*, or *vostro* (your).

In Italian the article is included as in *il mio nome* (my name), *la mia casa* (my house), *i nostri vestiti* (our clothes).

However, the article is dropped when referring to a single close family member: *mio padre* (my father), *tua madre* (your mother), *nostro fratello* (our brother), *mia zia* (my aunt).

Mio padre è alto.	My father is tall.
Mia madre è bella.	My mother is beautiful.
Nostro fratello ha vent'anni.	Our brother is 20 years old.

10 › When the articles are used with family members

Just when you think you have learned a rule, you find exceptions!

Although the *il* or *la* isn't included with a close family member, it is with *mamma* (mom) and *papà* (dad).

la mia mamma	my mom
il tuo papà	your dad

It is included if you add an ending to the word.

> *mio fratello* but *il mio fratellino* my little brother
> *mia sorella* but *la mia sorellina* my little sister

And it is included if you add more description:

mio nonno my grandfather
but
il mio nonno italiano my Italian grandfather

mio fratello my brother
but
il mio fratello maggiore my older brother

11 › The article with more than one family member

With more than one family member (for instance brothers and sisters) then the article is included.

i miei fratelli	our brothers
le nostre sorelle	our sisters
i nostri nonni	our grandparents

And *loro* (their) always has an article. The word *loro* is invariable and never changes.

il loro padre	their father
la loro madre	their mother
i loro nonni	their grandparents.

Don't worry if you make the odd mistake – it's bound to happen!

Unit 3 › Lesson 2: *Family photos*

3.2

Vocabulary

 Active Italian: Level 3 > Unit 3 > Lesson 2 > Vocabulary

il fratello
brother

Il mio fratello maggiore abita a Milano.
My older brother lives in Milan.

la sorella
sister

Mia sorella è sposata e vive a Londra.
My sister is married and lives in London.

i genitori
parents

I miei genitori sono morti.
My parents are dead.

il padre
father

Suo padre è divorziato da due anni.
His father has been divorced for 2 years.

la madre
mother

La madre di Anna è spagnola.
Anna's mother is Spanish.

il nonno
grandfather

Mio nonno ha più di novant'anni.
My grandfather is more than ninety.

la nonna
grandmother

La nonna di Mario è vedova.
Mario's grandmother is a widow.

gli amici
friends

Usciamo con gli amici stasera.
We're going out with friends this evening.

lo zio
uncle

Mio zio non si è mai sposato.
My uncle never got married.

la zia
aunt

Mia zia è una brava cuoca.
My aunt is a good cook.

Unit 3 › Lesson 2: *Family photos*

il cugino/la cugina
cousin

I miei cugini sono simpaticissimi.
My cousins are very nice.

i gemelli/le gemelle
twins

Sono gemelle: una è simpatica mentre l'altra è antipatica.
They are twins: one is nice while the other is not nice.

lasciarsi
to split up

Ci siamo lasciati due anni fa.
We split up two years ago.

Culture note

Families in Italy are generally quite small. For many years Italy was one of the only Western European countries with a steadily declining population, and a recent study showed that one in five Italians were senior citizens. However, a wave of immigration throughout the 1980s and 1990s has led to population growth for the first time since the 1970s.

Active Italian *Level 3*

4

Lesson 1: Finding out about each other

- » How to talk about whether you are single, married, divorced: *single*, *sposato/a*, *divorziato/a*.
- » How to say you have a boyfriend or girlfriend: *avere un ragazzo/una ragazza*.
- » Sporting activities using *fare* and *giocare*.
- » How to say you have never done something: *non... mai*.
- » How to talk about the seasons.
- » The difference between *sapere* and *conoscere*.

Lesson 2: In search of an apartment

- » How to say how long you have lived somewhere: *da 2 mesi*.
- » How to use *avere intenzione di* to express future plans.
- » How to talk about mixed couples: *i genitori*, *i nonni*.
- » How to say where you were born or grew up: *sono nato/a a*, *sono cresciuto/a a*.
- » How to say "to be right" (*avere ragione*) and "to be wrong" (*avere torto*).

UNIT 4 › LESSON 1
Finding out about each other

Culture note

Sports are very popular throughout the year in Italy. The country's favorite sport is definitely soccer, with many Italians being passionate supporters of their local teams. Winter sports (*sport invernali*) include  skiing, sledding, snowboarding, and ice-skating. Resorts like Courmayeur and Cortina d'Ampezzo are well known for first-class skiing.

Unit 4 › Lesson 1: *Finding out about each other*

4.1

Video Dialog

Giulia and Michele get to know one another a little better.

 Active Italian: Level 3 > Unit 4 > Lesson 1 > Video dialog

Giulia:	*E tu?... Sei sposato?*
Michele:	*Sono divorziato, e tu?*
Giulia:	*Io sono single.*
Michele:	*Non hai il ragazzo?*
Giulia:	*Ce l'avevo ma è finita.*
Michele:	*Hai sempre abitato in Svizzera?*
Giulia:	*Sì, sono nata vicino a Chiasso.*
Michele:	*Vai a sciare?*
Giulia:	*Sì, d'inverno vado a sciare e faccio snowboard.*
Michele:	*Allora sei molto sportiva...*
Giulia:	*Sì, lo sport mi piace molto. E tu?*
Michele:	*Anche a me piace lo sport. Mi piace giocare a calcio.*
Giulia:	*Sai sciare?*
Michele:	*No, non ho mai provato.*
Giulia:	*Dovresti provarci, è fantastico. Dovresti venire a trovarmi d'inverno.*
Michele:	*Con piacere!*

Giulia:	And you...? Are you married?
Michele:	I'm divorced. And you?
Giulia:	I'm single.
Michele:	Haven't you got a boyfriend?
Giulia:	No, I had one but it's over.
Michele:	Have you always lived in Switzerland?
Giulia:	Yes, I was born near Chiasso.
Michele:	Do you go skiing?
Giulia:	Yes in winter I go skiing and I snowboard.
Michele:	You're very sporty, then...
Giulia:	Yes, I like sports very much. And you?
Michele:	I like sports, too. I like playing soccer.
Giulia:	Can you ski?
Michele:	No, I've never tried it.
Giulia:	You should try it; it's great. You should come and visit me in winter.
Michele:	I would love to!

Grammar

Active Italian: Level 3 > Unit 4 > Lesson 1 > Grammar

1 › **How to talk about yourself**

In Italian, the English word *single* is used in conversation. On official documents, however, the terms *celibe* (for a man) and *nubile* (for a woman) are used to indicate that you are unmarried.

Other terms to describe your marital status include:

sposato/a	married
divorziato/a	divorced
vedovo/a	widowed

Unit 4 › Lesson 1: *Finding out about each other* **4.1**

2 › Having a boyfriend or girlfriend

Michele asks Giulia

> *Hai il ragazzo?*
> Do you have a boyfiend?

If she were asking Michele if he had a girlfriend she would say

> *Hai la ragazza?*
> Do you have a girlfriend?

Avere il ragazzo or *avere la ragazza* is to have a boyfriend or girlfriend.

3 › Saying you have never done something

The word for never is *mai*. As with other negatives in Italian it pairs up with *non*. *Non* comes before the verb and *mai* after.

| *Non esco mai.* | I never go out. |
| *Non vado mai a nuotare.* | I never go swimming. |

In the past tense, *non* and *mai* go around the auxiliary verb.

| *Non sono mai stato in Italia.* | I have never been to Italy. |
| *Non ho mai provato a sciare.* | I have never tried skiing. |

You can also use *mai* on its own.

> *Hai provato a sciare? Mai.*
> Have you tried skiing? Never.

4 › **Fare and giocare with sporting activities**

Fare (to do) is often used with sporting activities.

D'inverno faccio snowboard.	In winter I go snowboarding.
Faccio anche equitazione.	I also go horseback riding.
Mio fratello fa molto ciclismo.	My brother does a lot of cycling.

Giocare a (to play) is also used for playing games and team sports.

| *Giulia gioca a tennis.* | Giulia is playing tennis. |
| *Mi piace giocare a calcio.* | I like playing soccer. |

5 › The seasons

Winter is *l'inverno*. "In winter" is *d'inverno*. *Invernale* is the adjective, as in *l'orario invernale* (the winter schedule).

Summer is *l'estate*. "In summer" is *d'estate*. *Estivo* is the adjective, as in *l'orario estivo* (the summer schedule).

Spring is *la primavera*. "In spring" is *in primavera*.

Fall is *l'autunno*. "In the fall" is *in autunno*.

Season is *la stagione*. "In season" (when talking about fruit and vegetables, for example) is *di stagione*. Seasonal is *stagionale*.

6 › I was born in...

Giulia says *sono nata in Svizzera* (I was born in Switzerland).

Nascere is the verb "to be born" and *morire* means "to die." Verbs to do with living and dying take *essere* as the auxiliary verb.

> *Paola è nata in Italia.*
> Paola was born in Italy.

> *Sua madre è morta due giorni fa.*
> Her mother died two days ago.

7 › Knowing how to do something

There are two verbs "to know" in Italian: *sapere* and *consoscere*.

Sapere is used for knowing facts (like where something is or how much something costs) and for knowing how to do something (such as ski or swim).

Sai dov'è l'albergo?	Do you know where the hotel is?
Sai quanto costa il biglietto?	Do you know how much the ticket is?
Sai sciare?	Do you know how to ski?, Can you ski?
Sai nuotare?	Do you know how to swim?, Can you swim?

The other verb, *conoscere*, is for knowing people, places, and being familiar with something (such as a book or music).

Non conosce mio fratello.	He doesn't know my brother.
Conosci Firenze?	Do you know Florence?
Non conosco questo romanzo.	I am not familiar with this novel.

Culture note

In Florence, a 500-year-old game that vaguely resembles soccer is played three times a year in *Piazza Santa Croce*. *Calcio Storico*, as it is called (literally "historical soccer"), is a very violent affair in which fistfights are an almost certain occurrence between the 54 (27 per team) authentically dressed players on the pitch.

Unit 4 › Lesson 1: *Finding out about each other*

8 › **The verb *sapere* (to know)**

Sapere is another irregular verb.

This is the present tense:

so	I know
sai	you (*familiar*) know
sa	he/she/it knows
sa	you (*formal*) know
sappiamo	we know
sapete	you (*plural*) know
sanno	they know

sapendo is the gerund (knowing).

saputo is the past participle (known).

sap- is the stem for the imperfect (was knowing): **sap**evo, **sap**evi, **sap**eva, etc.

sapr- is the stem for the future tense (will know): **sapr**ò, **sapr**ai, **sapr**à, etc.

Culture note

As with many aspects of contemporary Italian culture, there is also a strong link to the past for sports. Various cities around the country celebrate historical horse races every year, with the *Palio* of Siena being the most famous and extravagant. Seventeen different areas, or *contrada*, of the city compete in two bareback horse races yearly around the central *Piazza del Campo*.

Livemocha™ Active Italian *Level 3*

 # *Vocabulary*

....

🌀 Active Italian: Level 3 > Unit 4 > Lesson 1 > Vocabulary

fare sport
to do sports

Che sport fai?
What sport do you do?

essere bravo/a a
to be good at

Luca è molto bravo a calcio.
Luca is very good at soccer.

sciare
to ski

D'inverno andiamo a sciare.
In winter we go skiing.

nuotare
to swim

Suo figlio sa nuotare?
Can your son swim?

passare l'estate
to spend the summer

Passiamo l'estate sul Lago di Garda.
We spend the summer on Lake Garda.

Unit 4 › Lesson 1: *Finding out about each other*

4.1

giocare a calcio
to play soccer

I ragazzi giocano a calcio tutte le sere.
The boys play soccer every evening.

la pallavolo
volleyball

Vuoi giocare a pallavolo con noi?
Do you want to play volleyball with us?

fare equitazione
to go horseback riding

Sara è molto fortunata. Ha un cavallo e fa equitazione.
Sara is very lucky. She has a horse and she rides.

la squadra
team

Per che squadra tieni?
What team do you support?

sul lago
on the lake

Tremezzo è un paese bellissimo sul Lago di Como.
Tremezzo is a beautiful village on Lake Como.

UNIT 4 › LESSON 2
In search of an apartment

Culture note

If you are looking to rent or buy an apartment or house in Italy, here is some of the vocabulary that you may come across:

cerco	I am looking for
in affitto	to let
in vendita	for sale
monolocale	a studio apartment
bilocale	a two-room apartment
apartamento	apartment
casa	house
ingresso	hallway
salone/soggiorno	living room
riscaldimento	central heating
ristrutturato	redecorated/restored
stanza	room
camera da letto	bedroom
cucina	kitchen
giardino	garden
terrazza	balcony
bagno	bathroom
piano	floor
arredato	furnished

Unit 4 › Lesson 2: *In search of an apartment*

4.2

Video Dialog

Giulia asks Michele more about his plans and makes a very useful suggestion.

 Active Italian: Level 3 > Unit 4 > Lesson 2 > Video dialog

Giulia: *E tu? Dimmi un po',...dove abitano i tuoi genitori?*

Michele: *I miei genitori abitano a Torino, in periferia.*

Giulia: *Sei cresciuto a Torino?*

Michele: *Nelle vicinanze. I miei nonni hanno una vigna in Piemonte.*

Giulia: *Da quanto tempo abiti a Roma?*

Michele: *Sono qui da due mesi.*

Giulia: *Hai intenzione di fermarti qui?*

Michele: *Sì, sto cercando un appartamento.*

Giulia: *Il tipo con cui sei andato alla partita di calcio, non lavora in un'agenzia immobiliare?*

Michele: *Ugo? Sì, hai ragione.*

Giulia: *Ti potrebbe aiutare lui.*

Michele: *Ottima idea!*

....

Giulia: And you? Tell me... where do your parents live?
Michele: My parents live in Turin, in the suburbs.

Giulia:	Did you grow up in Turin?
Michele:	In the area. My grandparents have a vineyard in Piedmont.
Giulia:	How long have you been living in Rome?
Michele:	I have been here for 2 months.
Giulia:	Are you going to stay here?
Michele:	Yes, I'm looking for an apartment.
Giulia:	The guy you went to the soccer match with, doesn't he work in real estate?
Michele:	Ugo? Yes, you're right.
Giulia:	He could help you.
Michele:	Excellent idea!

Grammar

 Active Italian: Level 3 > Unit 4 > Lesson 2 > Grammar

1 › **How long have you been here?**

> *Da quanto tempo abiti a Roma?*
> How long have you been living in Rome?

Da means "from" so the question literally means *From how much time are you living in Rome?*

In Italian the present tense is used because Michele is still living in Rome. So, when saying that you have been somewhere for a length of time the present tense is used.

> *Sono qui da due mesi.*
> I've been here for two months.

Unit 4 › Lesson 2: *In search of an apartment*

2 › Using *avere intenzione di* to express future plans

To express the near future (something you "are going" to do, such as "I am going to go shopping," "I am going to study this evening"), in Italian *avere intenzione di* (to intend to) is used and is followed by the infinitive.

> *Ho intenzione di restare a Roma.*
> I'm going to stay in Rome.

> *Ho intenzione di studiare medicina.*
> I'm going to study medicine.

3 › Parents and grandparents

Giulia asks Michele about his parents (*i genitori*) and grandparents (*i nonni*). Note how the masculine ending is used even though they include a mother and a grandmother.

When there is a mixed group of things (people or objects), the masculine noun ending is automatically applied. Any adjectives used to describe them are also masculine.

> *I suoi genitori sono molto bravi.*
> His parents are very good.

When talking about parents, Italians often just refer to them as *i miei*, *i tuoi*, *i suoi*, etc. and leave off the word *genitori*.

> *I miei abitano a Milano.*
> My parents live in Milan.

4 › To grow up

The verb *crescere* means to grow up. Like the verbs *nascere* (to be born) and *morire* (to die), it takes *essere* as its auxiliary.

Giulia asks Michele if he grew up in Turin.

> *Sei cresciuto a Torino?*

To say you grew up in a town or city, use ***a***.
To say you grew up in a country, use ***in***.

And remember that *cresciuto* becomes *cresciuta* if it refers to a female.

> *Sono cresciuto a New York.*
>
> I grew up in New York.

> *Sally è cresciuta in Australia.*
>
> Sally grew up in Australia.

5 › **To be right and wrong**

When Giulia asks whether Ugo works in real estate, Michele replies *Sì, hai ragione.* (Yes, you're right.)

In Italian "to be right" is *avere ragione*.
And "to be wrong" is *avere torto*.

> *Mi dispiace, ma ha torto.*
>
> I'm sorry, but you're wrong.

Culture note

Much like in other cities around the world, residents of cities in Italy often feel a sense of patriotism for their hometowns. This is often manifested as rivalry between soccer teams of respective cities, but its root can be traced back well before the advent of modern sports.

The word *campanilismo* comes from the word *campanile*, or bell tower, is used to describe the loyalty that residents owe to their town (the bell tower being a symbol of the city). *Campanilismo* in the past led to fierce rivalries between neighboring towns, often resulting in violent battles.

In Siena and Florence, these battles are still remembered to this day, and often victories in the distant past are alluded to during modern-day soccer games in order to put the opponent down.

Vocabulary

Active Italian: Level 3 > Unit 4 > Lesson 2 > Vocabulary

un accento
an accent

Max ha un accento molto forte.
Max has a very strong accent.

in periferia
in the suburbs

Abito in periferia.
I live in the suburbs.

nelle vicinanze
in the vicinity

Abita nelle vicinanze della stazione.
He lives in the vicinity of the train station.

una volta all'anno
once a year

Ci vediamo una volta all'anno.
We see each other once a year.

così
so

È così simpatica.
She is so nice.

Unit 4 › Lesson 2: *In search of an apartment*

in campagna
in the country

Hanno una casa in campagna.
They have a house in the country.

la gallina
hen

Quella gallina si chiama Tina.
That hen is called Tina.

oltre
over, beyond

Non vedo Tom da oltre tre mesi.
I haven't seen Tom for over 3 months.

frequentare
to go to

Frequento un corso d'inglese.
I go to English classes.

il tipo
guy

È un tipo molto strano.
He is a really strange guy.

il marito
husband

Mio marito è morto.
My husband is dead.

la moglie
wife

Mia moglie è italiana.
My wife is Italian.

uscire con
to go out with

Voglio uscire con te.
I want to go out with you.

Unit 4 › Lesson 2: *In search of an apartment* 4.2

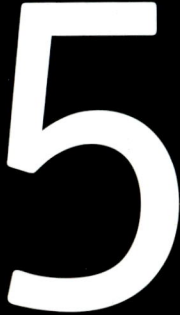

Active Italian *Level 3*

5

Lesson 1: At the restaurant

» How to say something went well: ***è andato bene***.
» The difference between a subject and an object in a sentence.
» The difference between direct and indirect object pronouns.
» Different cooking terms: ***al forno***, ***allo spiedo***, etc.
» Different flavors of ice cream: ***alla vaniglia***, ***al limone***, etc.

Lesson 2: At the table

» How to talk about food, cheese, and desserts
» How to say "some" or "any": ***di***, ***del***, ***della***, etc.
» How to say "a little …": ***un po' di***.
» How to use the pronoun ***ne***.
» How to say "Enjoy your meal": ***buon appetito***.

Collins | Livemocha™

UNIT 5 › LESSON 1
At the restaurant

Culture note

The structure of a classic Italian meal is usually as follows: *antipasto* (appetizer), *primo piatto* (first course), *secondo piatto* (main course) of meat or fish (usually with a side dish – *contorno*), and finally *dolce* (dessert).

This may be followed by coffee (usually an *espresso*) and a *digestivo*, usually a liqueur such as *amaretto* or *limoncello* to aid digestion. Typically an *aperitivo* (an aperitif) precedes an evening meal.

Unit 5 › Lesson 1: *At the restaurant*

Video Dialog

Ugo and Lucia eat out together in a local restaurant.

Active Italian: Level 3 > Unit 5 > Lesson 1 > Video dialog

Lucia: *È andato bene l'incontro?*

Ugo: *Sì, benissimo. Il cliente vuole vendere la sua casa a Roma.*

Lucia: *Bene, ecco il cameriere.*

Waiter: *Che cosa vi porto da bere?*

Ugo: *Una birra piccola, per favore.*

Lucia: *E per me una bottiglia d'acqua minerale.*

Waiter: *Naturale o frizzante?*

Lucia: *Frizzante.*

Waiter: *Benissimo, le porto subito.*

Ugo: *Qual è il menu del giorno?*

Waiter: *Risotto ai quattro formaggi e cotoletta alla milanese con patatine.*

Ugo: *Perfetto!*

Lucia: *Io preferisco il pesce. Ne avete oggi?*

Waiter: *Certo. C'è il filetto di sogliola, alla griglia o al vapore.*

Lucia: *Al vapore, grazie.*

5.1 Livemocha™ Active Italian *Level 3*

Lucia:	Did your meeting go well?
Ugo:	Yes, very well. The client wants to sell his house in Rome.
Lucia:	Good, here's the waiter.
Waiter:	What can I get you to drink?
Ugo:	A small beer, please.
Lucia:	And a bottle of mineral water for me.
Waiter:	Plain or sparkling?
Lucia:	Sparkling.
Waiter:	Very well, I'll get them straight away.
Ugo:	What's the meal of the day?
Waiter:	Four-cheese risotto followed by veal cutlet in breadcrumbs, Milanese style, with french fries.
Ugo:	Great!
Lucia:	I prefer fish. Do you have any today?
Waiter:	Of course. There's fillet of sole, grilled or steamed.
Lucia:	Steamed, please.

Grammar

  Active Italian: Level 3 > Unit 5 > Lesson 1 > Grammar

1 › **Did it go well? *È andato bene?***

This useful phrase can be used in a number of different contexts.

È andato bene l'incontro?	Did the meeting go well?
È andato bene il viaggio?	Did you have a good trip?
È andata bene la partita?	Did the game go well?

Unit 5 › Lesson 1: *At the restaurant*

2 › Understanding pronouns

The waiter asks *Che cosa vi porto da bere?* (What can I bring you to drink?)

Italian is full of short words and *vi* is one of them. It means "to you", and is an indirect object pronoun.

We have already met direct object pronouns when we were asking to try on a dress (*un vestito*). Rather than repeat *il vestito*, we replaced it with the pronoun *lo: Posso provarlo?* (Can I try it on?). If you wanted to try on a t-shirt (*una maglietta*) then you would say: *Posso provarla?*

3 › Subject and object pronouns explained

The person performing the action of the verb is the subject. The object has the action done to it (or to him, her or them).

In *Julie legge un libro* (Julie reads a book), Julie is the subject of the verb *legge* and *libro* is the object. If you were to replace *un libro* with a pronoun, then it would be *Julie lo legge* (Julie reads it).

If the object were a person rather than a book, you might have *David ama sua madre* (David loves his mother). David is the subject of the verb and *sua madre* is the object. Replacing *sua madre* with a pronoun gives *David l'ama* (David loves her).

4 >
Object pronouns in Italian (1)

Remember that subject pronouns aren't as important in Italian because the verb ending tells you who is doing the verb. However it is important to recognize object pronouns:

mi	me
ti	you
lo	him/it (as in *il vestito*)
la	her/it (as in *la maglietta*)
la	you (when replacing formal *lei*)
ci	us
vi	you
li	them (when they are masculine)
le	them (when they are feminine)

Here are a few examples using object pronouns:

Mi *ama.*	He loves me.
Ci *odiano.*	They hate us.
*Spero di veder***la** *presto.*	I hope to see you soon.

Unit 5 › Lesson 1: *At the restaurant*

5 › **Object pronouns in Italian (2)**

There are two kinds of object pronouns: direct and indirect. You have just seen the direct ones. Now look at indirect pronouns.

If we lengthen the sentence "Julie reads a book" to "Julie reads a book **to David**," then we now have two objects of the verb: "the book" and "David." The book is the direct object and David is the indirect object.

When the waiter says *Che cosa vi porto? Che cosa* (What thing) is the direct object and *vi* (to you) is the indirect object.

Indirect object pronouns in Italian are pretty similar to the direct object pronouns.

mi	to me
ti	to you
gli	to him/it
le	to her/it
le	to you (when replacing formal *a lei*)
ci	to us
vi	to you
gli/loro	to them

Here are a few examples using them:

Ti faccio un regalo.	I give you a present, I give a present to you.
Ci hanno mandato un sms.	They sent us a text, They sent a text to us.
Che cosa posso portarle?	What can I bring (to) you?

6 › Cooking in the manner of ...

Many dishes include *al, all', alla* and so on. This means that they have been cooked in a certain way or style.

We have already come across:

risotto ai quattro formaggi	four-cheese risotto
cotoletta alla milanese	veal cutlet in breadcrumbs, Milanese style
filetto di sogliola al vapore	steamed fillet of sole

7 › Different cooking terms

Common cooking terms include:

al forno	cooked in the oven, baked
al vapore	steamed
alla griglia	grilled
allo spiedo	spit-roasted, on a skewer
in brodo	in bouillon
in umido	braised

Culture note

Gelato (ice cream) is a staple of most Italian diets. Bought from a *gelateria*, it is nearly always handmade, and there is normally an incredible amount of choice available, ranging from common flavors such as *cioccolato* (chocolate) and *vaniglia* (vanilla), to more obscure varieties such as *puffo*, literally "smurf," colored bright blue!

8 › Different flavors of ice cream

You also use *a*, *al*, *all'*, and *alla* with flavors of *gelato* (ice cream). Popular flavors include:

Un gelato ...

al limone	lemon
alla fragola	strawberry
al cioccolato	chocolate
alla vaniglia	vanilla
alla nocciola	hazelnut
al fior di latte	milk-flavored
al pistacchio	pistachio
ai frutti di bosco	fruits of the forest
al lampone	raspberry
all'albicocca	apricot

The word for "flavor" is *gusto*.

Unit 5 › Lesson 1: *At the restaurant*

5.1

Vocabulary

 Active Italian: Level 3 > Unit 5 > Lesson 1 > Vocabulary

gli stuzzichini
snacks, nibbles

Il Bar Roma fa degli stuzzichini favolosi.
Bar Roma does wonderful snacks.

l'antipasto
appetizer

Salto l'antipasto.
I'll skip the appetizer.

il primo
first course

Per primo prendo gli spaghetti.
I'll have spaghetti as a first course.

il secondo
main course

Che cosa avete come secondo?
What main courses do you have?

il dolce
dessert

Non prendo il dolce.
I'm not having a dessert.

il formaggio
cheese

Avete del formaggio locale?
Do you have any local cheese?

il contorno
side dish

Come contorno abbiamo insalata o patate arrosto.
For a side dish we have salad or roast potatoes.

la carne
meat

Sono vegetariano. Non mangio carne.
I'm vegetarian. I don't eat meat.

Unit 5 › Lesson 1: *At the restaurant* 5.1

il pesce
fish

Vorrei assaggiare un pesce di lago.
I'd like to try a fish from the lake.

i frutti di mare
shellfish

Purtroppo sono allergico ai frutti di mare.
Unfortunately I am allergic to shellfish.

l'insalata
salad

Volete insalata verde o mista?
Do you want green salad or mixed salad?

le patatine fritte
french fries

Basta mangiare patatine fritte!
Stop eating french fries!

UNIT 5 › LESSON 2
At the table

Culture note

Many restaurants in popular locations offer a tourist menu, the *menù turistico*, in which you will find typical Italian dishes along with local specialities at a set price for *primo piatto*, *secondo piatto*, *contorno* and *dolce*, often including a drink. If the full menu proves more difficult to understand due to the range of exotic dishes, then the *menù turistico* is always a safe bet.

Video Dialog

In the restaurant: Ugo and Lucia enjoy their meal.

Active Italian: Level 3 > Unit 5 > Lesson 2 > Video dialog

Waiter:	*Ecco. Cotoletta … e sogliola. Buon appetito!*
Ugo:	*Scusi, mi porta ancora un po' di pane, per favore?*
Waiter:	*Subito.*
Lucia:	*La sogliola è buonissima.*
Ugo:	*Anche la cotoletta.*
Lucia:	*E come dolce c'è il tiramisù!*
Ugo:	*Dov'è il mio cucchiaio?*
Lucia:	*È caduto per terra?*
Ugo:	*Scusi, mi porta un altro cucchiaio, per favore?*
Waiter:	*Certo. Formaggio e frutta? Porto del formaggio?*
Ugo:	*Io prendo del taleggio e del pecorino*
Lucia:	*Ed io del parmigiano e un po' d'uva.*
Ugo:	*Vuoi del tiramisù?*
Lucia:	*No, grazie, ho mangiato abbastanza!*

Waiter:	Here you are: cutlet ... and sole. Enjoy your meal.
Ugo:	Excuse me, can you bring me some more bread, please?

Waiter:	Right away.
Lucia:	The sole is delicious.
Ugo:	So is the cutlet.
Lucia:	And for dessert there's tiramisù!
Ugo:	Where is my spoon?
Lucia:	Did it fall on the floor?
Ugo:	Excuse me, can you bring me another spoon, please?
Waiter:	Of course. Cheese and fruit? Shall I bring some cheese?
Ugo:	I'll have some taleggio and some pecorino.
Lucia:	And I'll have some parmesan and some grapes.
Ugo:	Do you want some tiramisù?
Lucia:	No thanks, I've had enough to eat!

Grammar

 Active Italian: Level 3 > Unit 5 > Lesson 2 > Grammar

1 › **Asking for some bread**

In Italian, when you ask for something, you usually introduce the thing you ask for with *di* to mean "of," "some" or "any."

Here is a quick reminder of how *di* combines with the articles.

> *di + il = del*
> *di + la = della*
> *di + l' = dell'*
> *di + lo = dello*
> *di + i = dei*
> *di + gli = degli*
> *di + le = delle*

Unit 5 › Lesson 2: *At the table*

Vuole del vino?
Do you want some wine?

Mi porta del pane?
Can you bring me some bread?

Vorrei del formaggio locale.
I'd like some local cheese.

Culture note

Wine is a point of pride for most Italians, and, indeed, wine production is a thriving industry in Italy. Much like traditional foods, every region has its own specialty, and wherever you go, there will be good quality wine available.
One of the best ways to experience this aspect of Italian culture is to take part in a wine tour, during which visitors are shown the winemaking process from the vine to the bottle, and are given an opportunity to sample some of the local varieties.

Do you have any?

When Lucia was deciding what to eat, she said *Io preferisco il pesce* (I prefer fish). She then went on to ask *Ne avete oggi?* (Do you have any today?)

Instead of repeating fish, Lucia has used the pronoun *ne* (meaning "of it," "of them," "some," or "any"). Italians try to avoid repeating a word wherever possible and substitute it with a shorter, handier pronoun.

Ne is used to replace things that are introduced by *di* (or *del*, *della*, etc.) and they are often quantities or numbers of things (as in *anni* years).

C'è ancora del pane?	Is there any more bread?
Sì, ce n'è.	Yes there is.
Quanti anni hai?	How old are you?
Ne ho venti.	I am 20.
Quanti panini vuole?	How many bread rolls do you want?
Ne voglio 4.	I want 4.

Unit 5 › Lesson 2: *At the table*

3 › Not having any

If there weren't any bread or you didn't want any rolls, you would say:

No, non ce n'è.	No there isn't any.
No, non ne voglio.	No I don't want any.

4 › *Buon appetito!*

Buon appetito! means "Enjoy your meal!"

If you say it to someone else who is also eating, then the standard reply is *Altrettanto!* (The same to you!)

We have already come across a couple of ways of saying cheers:

> *Cin Cin!* or *Alla salute!*
> To your health!

Livemocha™ Active Italian *Level 3*

5 › **A little more …**

To ask for more of something you can use:

> *Ancora un po' di …*
> Some more …

Un po' is a shortened form of *un poco* (a little).

Here are a few possibilities:

Ancora un po' di formaggio.	A little more cheese.
Ancora un po' di vino.	A little more wine.
Ancora un po' d'insalata.	A little more salad.
Ancora un po' di dolce.	A little more dessert.

Culture note

An increasingly popular vacation option is to stay at an *agriturismo*, usually a farm or villa with extensive grounds that has been converted into holiday apartments. Depending on the region, *agriturismi* often have their own olive groves and vineyards that can be explored, and they frequently sell their own in-house products.

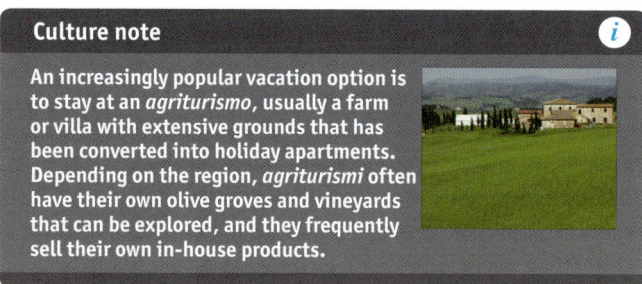

Unit 5 › Lesson 2: *At the table*

5.2

6 › **A little more about *di***

Un po' is normally followed by *di* or *d'* as happens with quantities:

un litro di	a liter of
un bicchiere di	a glass of
un chilo di	a kilo of
Un pezzo di torta.	A piece of cake.
Un litro d'acqua.	A liter of water.
Un chilo d'arance.	A kilo of oranges.

 ## *Vocabulary*

Active Italian: Level 3 > Unit 5 > Lesson 2 > Vocabulary

il piatto
plate, dish

Chi ha rotto il piatto?
Who has broken the plate?

la forchetta
fork

Mancano le forchette.
The forks are missing.

il cucchiaio
spoon

Quanti cucchiai ci vogliono?
How many spoons are needed?

il cucchiaino
teaspoon

Volele dei cucchiani?
Do you want teaspoons?

il coltello
knife

Mi è caduto il coltello.
I dropped my knife.

il tovagliolo
napkin

Ho bisogno di un tovagliolo.
I need a napkin.

Unit 5 › Lesson 2: *At the table*

5.2

la tazza
cup

Berrei una bella tazza di tè.
I could drink a nice cup of tea.

il bicchiere
glass

Bisogna lavare il bicchiere, è sporco.
You have to wash the glass; it's dirty.

il sale
salt

Manca sale.
It needs salt.

il pepe
pepper

Mi passa il pepe, per favore?
Can you pass the pepper, please?

l'olio
oil

Deve condirlo con olio d'oliva.
You have to dress it with olive oil.

l'aceto
vinegar

Non c'è abbastanza aceto.
There's not enough vinegar on it.

avere una fame da lupo
to be famished (literally as hungry as a wolf)

Ho una fame da lupo.
I'm famished.

Unit 5 › Lesson 2: *At the table* **5.2**

Active Italian Level 3

6

Lesson 1: Feeling ill

- » How to say you are not well: ***sentirsi male.***
- » How to say what is wrong with you: ***ho mal di...***
- » About the verb ***sentirsi*** (to feel).
- » About different parts of the body: ***la bocca, la schiena***, etc.
- » Common expressions such as ***in farmacia, in banca***, etc.

Lesson 2: Making a doctor's appointment

- » How to make an appointment with the doctor.
- » The numbers 20 and above: ***venti, trenta, quaranta***, etc.
- » How to say dates in years: 2010, 2011.
- » How to give phone numbers in Italian.
- » The difference between ***Chi?*** and ***Che?***.
- » About ***qualcuno***.

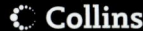

UNIT 6 › LESSON 1
Feeling ill

Culture note

Over-the-counter medicine in Italy is available from either a pharmacy (*farmacia*) or from larger supermarkets. A pharmacy is easily identifiable by the green cross sign, often illuminated. Pharmacies operate a rotation system so that at least one in every town will be open late for emergencies.

Unit 6 › Lesson 1: *Feeling ill*

6.1

Video Dialog

Lucia finds Ugo feeling a little off color – he needs to see a doctor.

 Active Italian: Level 3 > Unit 6 > Lesson 1 > Video dialog

Lucia: *Ciao, come stai?*

Ugo: *Non troppo bene... Ho il raffreddore e sono stanco.*

Lucia: *Poverino! Hai tempo di prendere un caffè?*

Ugo: *Sì, certo.*

Lucia: *Ma dovresti andare dal medico.*

Ugo: *Vado in farmacia a comprare delle pastiglie per la gola.*

Lucia: *Hai mal di gola?*

Ugo: *Un po'.*

Lucia: *Mal di testa?*

Ugo: *Un po'.*

Lucia: *Hai la febbre?*

Ugo: *Non penso.*

Lucia: *Sì, hai un po' di febbre. Probabilmente hai l'influenza o un po' di bronchite. Sarebbe meglio andare dal medico.*

Lucia:	Hi! How are you?
Ugo:	Not too good. I've got a cold, and I'm tired.
Lucia:	Poor thing. Have you time for a coffee?
Ugo:	Yes, of course.
Lucia:	But you should to go to the doctor.
Ugo:	I'll go to the pharmacy and get some throat lozenges.
Lucia:	Have you got a sore throat?
Ugo:	A bit.
Lucia:	Headache?
Ugo:	A bit.
Lucia:	Do you have a temperature?
Ugo:	I don't think so.
Lucia:	Yes, you have a bit of a temperature. You've probably got flu or a chest infection. It would be better to go to the doctor.

Grammar

 Active Italian: Level 3 > Unit 6 > Lesson 1 > Grammar

1 › **How to say something hurts**

To say you have a pain somewhere, you can say *Ho mal di...* and then name the part of the body which hurts.

Ho mal di testa.	I have a headache.
Ho mal di gola.	I have a sore throat.
Ho mal di stomaco.	I have a stomachache.
Ho mal di denti.	I have a toothache.

ammalarsi means "to get ill."
malato/a means "ill" or "sick."

Unit 6 › Lesson 1: *Feeling ill*

2 › To have a cold – *avere il raffreddore*

Avere is used with a number of ailments, including a cold:

avere il raffreddore	to have a cold
avere l'influenza	to have the flu
avere la febbre	to have a fever
avere la tosse	to have a cough

Note how the definite article (*il, la*) is used in Italian.

Other useful expressions include:

stare male	to be unwell
stare meglio	to feel better
guarire	to get better

3 › **To feel (*sentirsi*)**

Sentirsi meaning "to feel" is a reflexive verb. *Sentirsi male* is "to feel unwell." Here is the present tense:

mi sento male	I feel unwell
ti senti male	you (*familiar*) feel unwell
si sente male	he/she feels unwell
si sente male	you (*formal*) feel unwell
ci sentiamo male	we feel unwell
vi sentite male	you (*plural*) feel unwell
si sentono male	they feel unwell

sentendo is the gerund (feeling).

sentito is the past participle (felt). Note that *sentire* takes *essere* as its auxiliary verb and therefore *sentito* agrees with the subject of the verb.

> *Sara si è sentita male.*
> Sara didn't feel well.

sent- is the stem for the imperfect (was feeling): *mi **sent**ivo, ti **sent**ivi, si **sent**iva*, etc.

sentir- is the stem for the future tense (will feel): *mi **sentir**ò, ti **sentir**ai, si **sentir**à,* etc.

Unit 6 › Lesson 1: *Feeling ill*

4 ›
My... hurts

To say a certain part of you hurts, your head (*la testa*), for example, you say *Mi fa male la testa* (literally the head is hurting me).

Note that in Italian the possessive adjective (*mia*) is not used with *testa* as the prounoun *mi* makes it clear whose head is hurting. Instead the definite article (*il* or *la*) is used.

> *Gli fa male il ginocchio.*
> His knee is hurting.

> *Le fa male la pancia.*
> Her tummy is hurting.

5 ›
Parts of the body

A number of body parts have slightly irregular plurals that are worth learning.

The following become feminine in the plural

il ginocchio – le ginocchia	knees
il braccio – le braccia	arms
il dito – le dita	fingers, toes

And note that "hand" is *la man**o** – le mani*.

6 › Going somewhere (andare da/in)

Lucia says *Dovresti andare **dal** medico* (you should go to the doctor) and Ugo says *Vado **in** farmacia* (I'll go to the pharmacy).

Da is used with people (in this case the doctor) and Ugo could have said *Vado **dal** farmacista* (I'll go to the pharmacist).

7 › *Andare in farmacia* (to go to/into the pharmacy)

With familiar everyday places, you often use *in* to say "to" or "into" or "in."

in farmacia	to/into/in the pharmacy
in città	to/into/in town
in cucina	to/into/in the kitchen
in acqua	to/into/in the water
in banca	to/into/in the bank
in posta	to/into/in the post office
in chiesa	to/into/in the church

Try to listen to as much Italian as possible to get a feel for how the language works.

Unit 6 › Lesson 1: *Feeling ill*

Vocabulary

Active Italian: Level 3 > Unit 6 > Lesson 1 > Vocabulary

la testa
head

Avevo mal di testa ieri.
I had a headache yesterday.

il braccio
arm

Nino si è rotto il braccio.
Nino broke his arm.

l'occhio
eye

Sara ha gli occhi e i capelli castani.
Sara has brown eyes and brown hair.

Culture note

Like much of Europe during the Middle Ages and the Renaissance, Italy was ravaged by the Black Death on numerous occasions and the populations of many large cities were decimated. During these outbreaks, medicine men depicted as wearing primitive gasmasks with long beaks (as the plague was believed to be airborne), wide-brimmed hats and heavy dark overcoats would provide all manner of concoctions and procedures to treat or prevent the plague, including grisly regular bleedings.

il piede
foot

Devi lavarti i piedi.
You have to wash your feet.

la mano
hand

Mi puoi dare una mano?
Can you give me a hand?

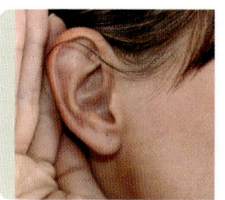

l'orecchio
ear

Ho un orecchio tappato.
I have a blocked ear.

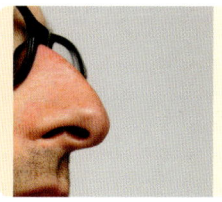

il naso
nose

Si è soffiato il naso.
He blew his nose.

Unit 6 › Lesson 1: *Feeling ill*

6.1

la bocca
mouth

Harry non ha aperto bocca tutto il giorno.
Harry hasn't opened his mouth all day.

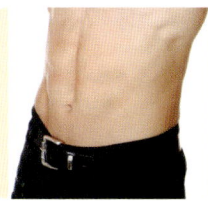

lo stomaco
stomach

Ha qualcosa per il mal di stomaco?
Have you got something for a stomachache?

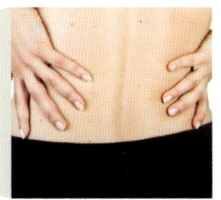

la schiena
back

Mi fa male la schiena.
I have backache.

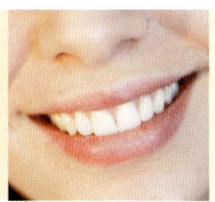

i denti
teeth

Vai a lavarti i denti!
Go and brush your teeth!

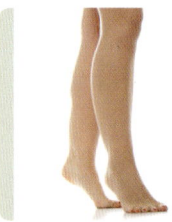

la gamba
leg

La gamba non mi è ancora guarita.
My leg hasn't gotten better yet.

tossire
to cough

Tossisco in continuazione.
I keep coughing.

6.2 Unit 6 › Lesson 2: *Making a doctor's appointment*

UNIT 6 › LESSON 2
Making a doctor's appointment

Culture note

Modern Italy's National Health System, the *Servizio Sanitario Nazionale*, provides high quality and inexpensive treatment to all European citizens. Italy adopted a tax-funded universal healthcare system in the late 1970s, based upon the system in Britain. Doctors are passionate and well-trained, and facilities are generally comparable to those of other Northern European countries. Nonetheless, medical insurance is recommended when traveling in Italy, especially if you are not a European citizen.

Video Dialog

Ugo follows Lucia's advice and calls the doctor's office to make an appointment.

 Active Italian: Level 3 > Unit 6 > Lesson 2 > Video dialog

Receptionist:	*Studio Garelli, buongiorno.*
Ugo:	*Pronto, buongiorno. Vorrei un appuntamento con il medico, per favore.*
Receptionist:	*Sì, chi parla?*
Ugo:	*Sono il signor Borgetti*
Receptionist:	*Come si scrive?*
Ugo:	*B O R G H E T T I.*
Receptionist:	*Numero di telefono?*
Ugo:	*06.*
Receptionist:	*06.*
Ugo:	*82.*
Receptionist:	*82.*
Ugo:	*43.*
Receptionist:	*43.*
Ugo:	*79.*
Receptionist:	*79.*
Ugo:	*04.*
Receptionist:	*04. Resti in linea... Oh, è fortunato. Qualcuno ha disdetto l'appuntamento oggi pomeriggio alle 14.30. Le va bene?*

Ugo:	*È perfetto, mille grazie.*

Receptionist:	Dr. Garelli's office, good morning.
Ugo:	Hello, good morning. I would like an appointment with the doctor, please.
Receptionist:	Yes, who's calling?
Ugo:	It's Mr. Borghetti.
Receptionist:	How do you spell that?
Ugo:	B O R G H E T T I.
Receptionist:	Your phone number?
Ugo:	06.
Receptionist:	06.
Ugo:	82.
Receptionist:	82.
Ugo:	43.
Receptionist:	43.
Ugo:	79.
Receptionist:	79.
Ugo:	04.
Receptionist:	04. Hold on... Oh, you're lucky. Someone has canceled their appointment this afternoon at 2:30. Does that suit you?
Ugo:	It's perfect. Many thanks.

Grammar

 Active Italian: Level 3 > Unit 6 > Lesson 2 > Grammar

1 › **The numbers from 20 to 100**

Once numbers get above 20 they follow a regular pattern.

20 *venti*	27 *venti**sette***
21 *vent**uno***	28 *vent**otto***
22 *venti**due***	29 *venti**nove***
23 *venti**tré***	30 *trenta*
24 *venti**quattro***	31 *trent**uno***
25 *venti**cinque***	32 *trenta**due***
26 *venti**sei***	33 *trenta**tré*** and so on.

40 is *quaranta*	70 is *settanta*
50 is *cinquanta*	80 is *ottanta*
60 is *sessanta*	90 is *novanta*

Note the accent on numbers finishing in *tré*: *ventitré*, *trentatré*, and so on.

2 › Numbers above 100

After 101 *centouno*, the sequence carries on as normal.
102 is *centodue*.
103 is *centotré* and so on.

200 is *duecento*.
300 is *trecento* and so on.

1,000 is *mille*
1,001 is *milleuno*.

Note that 2,000 is *due**mila***, 3,000 is *tre**mila*** and so on.

2011 is *duemilaundici*. There is no gap between numbers nor any connecting word such as "and."

3 › Who's speaking?

The receptionist asks *Chi parla?* (Who's speaking?)

Unit 6 › Lesson 2: *Making a doctor's appointment*

Chi? means Who?
Che? means What?

4 › It's...

In Italian when you say who you are on the phone, you say

> *Sono **il** signor Borghetti*
> (literally "I am the Mr. Borghetti.")

If you were female, you would say

> *Sono **la** signora Borghetti.*

If you are using first names, then you would say.

> *Sono Paolo.*
> *Sono Carla.*

5 › **Someone – *Qualcuno***

We have already met *qualcosa* (something); *qualcuno* is the equivalent word for a person and means "someone" or "somebody" or "anyone" or "anybody."

> *Qualcuno mi ha telefonato. Sai chi era?*
> Somebody phoned me. Do you know who it was?

> *È arrivato qualcuno?*
> Has anyone arrived?

Vocabulary

il cuore
heart

Mia madre soffriva di cuore.
My mother had problems with her heart.

Unit 6 › Lesson 2: *Making a doctor's appointment*

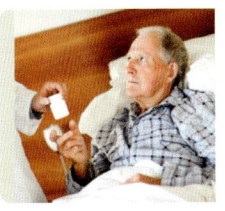

un infarto
a heart attack

Il padre di Giuseppe ha avuto un infarto.
Giuseppe's father has had a heart attack.

un colpo di sole
sunstroke

Fa' attenzione a non prendere un colpo di sole.
Be careful not to get sunstroke.

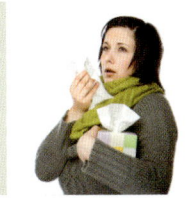

un raffreddore
a cold

Non brontolare: è solo un raffreddore, non un'influenza.
Don't moan; it's a cold, not flu.

la tosse
cough

Ho la tosse.
I have a cough.

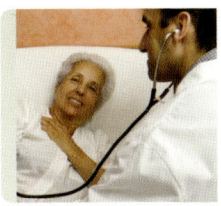

la pressione (alta)
high blood pressure

Prendo una medicina per la pressione.
I take medicine for high blood pressure.

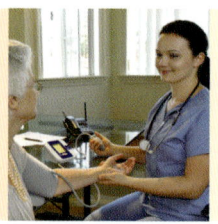

la pressione bassa
low blood pressure

Deve stare attenta in sauna perché ha la pressione bassa.
She has to be careful in the sauna because she suffers from low blood pressure.

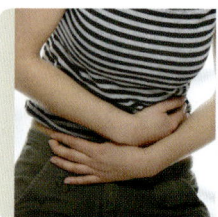

il bruciore di stomaco
heartburn

Ha qualcosa contro il bruciore di stomaco?
Do you have anything for heartburn?

allergico/a a
allergic to

Il figlio di Teresa è allergico ai gatti.
Teresa's son is allergic to cats.

incinta
pregnant

Sono incinta di quattro mesi.
I am four months pregnant.

Unit 6 › Lesson 2: *Making a doctor's appointment*

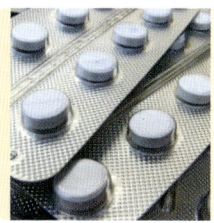

l'antidolorifico
painkiller

Ho bisogno di un'antidolorifico contro il mal di schiena.
I need a painkiller for my backache.

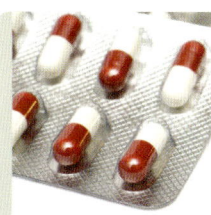

gli antibiotici
antibiotics

Se stai prendendo antibiotici non puoi bere whisky.
If you are taking antibiotics you can't drink whiskey.

Culture note

The *Ospedale degli Innocenti* is a famous hospital in Piazza Santissima Annunziata in Florence. Literally "Hospital of the Innocents," the hospital was an orphanage for abandoned children until its closure in 1875. There was once a wheellike mechanism installed outside the hospital to allow people to abandon their children in anonymity. Designed in the fifteenth century by Filippo Brunelleschi, the architect responsible for the incredible dome of Florence's cathedral, the hospital's loggia is one of the first examples of a revived style of classical architecture.

Collins

Livemocha ACTIVE ITALIAN

HarperCollins Publishers
77–85 Fulham Palace Road
London W6 8JB
Great Britain

www.collinslanguage.com

First edition 2011

Reprint 10 9 8 7 6 5 4 3 2 1 0
© HarperCollins Publishers 2011

ISBN (UK edition) 978-0-00-737353-6
ISBN (export edition) 978-0-00-741980-7
ISBN (US edition) 978-0-87779-557-5

Collins® is a registered trademark of HarperCollins Publishers Limited

A catalogue record for this book is available from the British Library

Typeset by Macmillan Publishing Services

Audio material recorded and produced by Networks SRL, Milan

Printed and Bound in China by Leo Paper Products Ltd.
Series Editor: Rob Scriven

All rights reserved. No part of this publication may be reproduced, stored in a retrieval system or transmitted, in any form or by any means, electronic, mechanical, photocopying, recording or otherwise, without the prior permission of the publisher. This book is sold subject to the conditions that it shall not, by way of trade or otherwise, be lent, re-sold, hired out or otherwise circulated without the publisher's prior consent in any form of binding or cover other than that in which it is published and without a similar condition including this condition being imposed on the subsequent purchaser.

HarperCollins does not warrant that the functions contained in **www.livemocha.com** content will be interrruption- or error-free, that defects will be corrected, or that **www.livemocha.com** or the server that makes it available are free of viruses or bugs. HarperCollins is not responsible for any access difficulties that may be experienced due to problems with network, web, online or mobile phone connections.

INTRODUCTION 4

UNIT 1
Lesson 1: Looking for an apartment 8
Lesson 2: Looking around the apartment 19

UNIT 2
Lesson 1: What will the weather be like? 32
Lesson 2: Making plans 42

UNIT 3
Lesson 1: How do you like living here? 54
Lesson 2: Making new friends 66

UNIT 4
Lesson 1: At the tourist office 78
Lesson 2: Sorting out travel documents 88

UNIT 5
Lesson 1: Booking a hotel in Rome 102
Lesson 2: Getting a hotel room in New York 112

UNIT 6
Lesson 1: Saying farewell 124
Lesson 2: Have a good trip, Michele! 133

INTRODUCTION

Welcome to your Livemocha Active Italian experience! This new course goes above and beyond what a traditional book-based course can offer. With its focus on online learning, Active Italian provides the opportunity not just to study but to experience the language for yourself by interacting with native speakers online.

Why go online?
Studying a language online allows you to learn in a more natural atmosphere – watching people interact in a **video** is far more lifelike than listening to conversations on a CD. After watching a video dialog, you will be walked through an explanation of some of the **grammar** and **vocabulary** items that were introduced in the new dialog. Then, by completing a variety of **interactive quizzes**, the system will instantly be able to tell you how well you are doing. You can then **talk online** with native Italian speakers to practice what you've learned.

Who else is online?
Livemocha boasts over 7 million members and is growing every day. These members are online for the same reason as you – to learn and experience a new language. Native Italian-speaking members will be happy to read through your written and spoken submissions and to give you feedback on how you're doing. You can also connect with people who want to chat in any given language – interaction on an informal, nonacademic basis is an ideal way for you to perfect your language skills.

What do the books do?
The four accompanying books are designed to complement the online course – the dialogs for all of the videos that you can watch online are available here for you to study whenever you don't have access to the Internet. You will also find all of the Grammar and Vocabulary sections explained in the books, plus the culture notes to teach you a little about Italy.

LEVEL 4

This book is the fourth of four. It corresponds with Level 4 of the online course.

Level 4 is ideal for those who feel at ease making general conversation in Italian and who are looking for further practice of more complex topics and grammar.

What you will learn
- How to exchange contact information, understand "text speak" Italian, and cope in the airport, hotel and bank
- How to use *piacere* to talk about likes and dislikes, and *ci vuole/vogliono* to talk about needs
- The different "you" forms and uses
- How to form the future and conditional tenses
- Vocabulary for ordinal numbers, the weather, rooms of the house, the airport, hotel and bank

Every time you see this coffee cup symbol in these books, it indicates the presence of a pathway – a guide to exactly where you can find that particular piece of content online. Log on at www.livemocha.com and follow the path to find the online version of what you are studying in the book.

Video Dialog

As they finish their drinks, Michele and the waiter give Giulia directions to some local stores.

 Active Italian: Level 1 > Unit 3 > Lesson 1 > Video dialog

Active Italian *Level 4*

1

Lesson 1: Looking for an apartment

- » How to say something is on the first floor: *al primo piano*.
- » How to form ordinal numbers from 11th onwards.
- » How to use words that change their meaning: *vecchio/a*, *grande*, *caro/a*.
- » The names of different rooms in a house.

Lesson 2: Looking around the apartment

- » How to say "per month," "per week," etc: *al mese*, *alla settimana*.
- » How to talk about the euro and prices.
- » Different expressions using *avere*: *avere paura di*, etc.
- » How to recognize the gender of Italian words.

Collins | **Livemocha**™

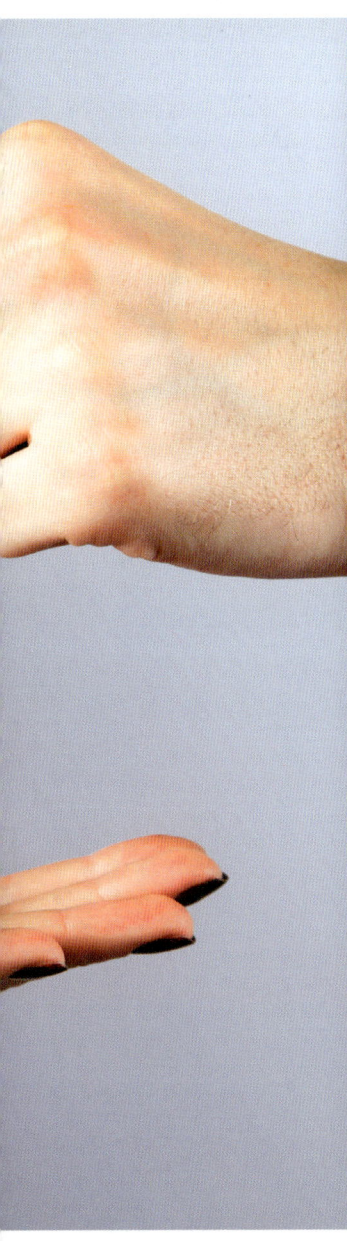

UNIT 1 › LESSON 1
Looking for an apartment

Culture note

Most Italians live in apartments and in towns. Only the wealthiest can afford a *villa*, a single-family house, although the majority of Italians live in a *palazzo*, as that is the word for a building divided into apartments. In suburban areas, new developments of *case a schiera*, townhouses, are being built, but most Italians prefer to invest their savings not by moving to a bigger property but by buying another property at the seaside or in the mountains, which they call *la seconda casa*, their second home.

Unit 1 › Lesson 1: *Looking for an apartment*

1.1

Video Dialog

Michele goes to meet Ugo to help him find an apartment.

Watch the video dialog online at
Active Italian: Level 4 > Unit 1 > Lesson 1 > Video dialog

Michele: *Ciao, Ugo.*

Ugo: *Oh, ciao, Michele, come stai?*

Michele: *Bene, grazie, e tu?*

Ugo: *Benissimo, grazie. In che cosa posso esserti utile?*

Michele: *Cerco un appartamento e Giulia mi ha detto che magari potresti aiutarmi.*

Ugo: *Certo, senz'altro. Che cosa cerchi?*

Michele: *Qualcosa di non troppo caro.*

Ugo: *A Roma! Non è facile!*

Michele: *Non deve essere grande.*

Ugo: *Ora guardo che cosa abbiamo.*

Michele: *Grazie, sei molto gentile.*

Ugo: *C'è un appartamento libero nello stabile dove abito io, è un miniappartamento al quinto piano.*

Michele: *Potrebbe andare.*

Ugo: *Non è molto caro perché l'edificio è vecchio e l'ascensore è sempre guasto!*

Michele: *Le scale fanno bene alla salute!*

1.1 Livemocha™ Active Italian *Level 4*

Michele:	Hello, Ugo.
Ugo:	Oh, hello, Michele, how are you?
Michele:	Fine, thanks, and you?
Ugo:	Very well, thank you. What can I do for you?
Michele:	I'm looking for an apartment, and Giulia told me that you might be able to help me.
Ugo:	Certainly, what are you looking for?
Michele:	Something not too expensive.
Ugo:	In Rome? That's not easy!
Michele:	It doesn't have to be big.
Ugo:	I will see what we have.
Michele:	Thanks, you're very kind.
Ugo:	There's an empty apartment in the building where I live. It's a small apartment on the 5th floor.
Michele:	It could be OK.
Ugo:	It isn't very expensive because the building is old and the elevator is always out of order.
Michele:	Stairs are good for you!

Grammar

In this section we go over some of the grammar points introduced in the dialog.

 Go to Active Italian: Level 4 > Unit 1 > Lesson 1 > Grammar to listen to these explanations and to access some interactive practice activities.

1 > **On the first floor**

Primo means "first."
To say on which floor something is, use *al*.

Unit 1 › Lesson 1: *Looking for an apartment* **1.1**

al primo piano
on the first floor

Abito al primo piano.
I live on the first floor.

2 › **After the tenth...**

Here is a quick recap of the first 10 ordinal numbers (remember that ordinal numbers are ones that put things in order):

primo/a	1st
secondo/a	2nd
terzo/a	3rd
quarto/a	4th
quinto/a	5th
sesto/a	6th
settimo/a	7th
ottavo/a	8th
nono/a	9th
decimo/a	10th

From 11th onwards, they end in -*esimo/a*. Just take the number, remove the final letter and add -*esimo/a* to get the ordinal.

> 11 *undici* becomes *undicesimo/a* 11th
> 12 *dodici* becomes *dodicesimo/a* 12th
> 13 *tredici* becomes *tredicesimo/a* 13th
> 21 *ventuno* becomes *ventunesimo/a* 21st
> 22 *ventidue* becomes *ventiduesimo/a* 22nd

These are adjectives so they must agree with the noun they refer to:

| *il primo giorno* | the first day |
| *la prima volta* | the first time |

Watch out with dates: in Italian, apart from the first (*il primo*), they are expressed using cardinal numbers: *il sei aprile, il ventotto maggio*.

3 › Old or elderly?

Ugo says about the building where his apartment is:

> *L'edificio è vecchio.*
> The building is old.

Vecchio (old) belongs to a small group of words that can change meaning depending on whether they go before or after the noun.

un vecchio amico is an old friend.

un amico vecchio means that the friend is elderly.

4 › More adjectives that change meaning

Other words that change their meaning include:
Grande means "great" when it comes before the noun but "big" when it comes after. In front of a noun, it often shortens to *gran*.

un grande pittore	a great painter
un grande attore.	a great actor
una casa grande.	a big house

Caro means "dear" when it comes before the noun but "expensive" when it comes after.

una cara amica
a dear friend

un vestito caro
an expensive dress

Stesso means "same" when it comes before the noun but "itself" when it comes after.

> *lo stesso giorno*
> the same day
>
> *il giorno stesso*
> the day itself, that very day

5 › Perhaps

The use of *forse* (perhaps) softens a request, making it less direct.

> *Forse potresti aiutarmi.*
> Perhaps you could help me.
>
> *Forse potrei venire con voi?*
> Perhaps I could come with you?

6 › A free apartment

Ugo says that there is an apartment available in his building: *un appartamento libero*.

Be careful with the word *libero*: it doesn't mean something is free, but that it is available. You may see a sign saying *camere libere*, which means that there are vacancies. In parking lots *libero* means there are spaces.

If there were no rooms or car parking spaces available, you would see or hear the word *completo*, meaning "full."

Unit 1 › Lesson 1: *Looking for an apartment*

Vocabulary

In this section you will learn some useful words and expressions from the dialog.

Go to Active Italian: Level 4 > Unit 1 > Lesson 1 > Vocabulary to listen to each of the words being pronounced and to access some interactive practice activities.

la stanza
room

Le stanze dell'appartamento sono grandi?
Are the rooms in the apartment big?

il monolocale
studio apartment

A che piano è il monolocale?
What floor is the studio apartment on?

la sala da pranzo
dining room

La sala da pranzo è accanto alla cucina?
Is the dining room next to the kitchen?

la camera da letto
bedroom

Nella camera da letto ci sono armadi a muro?
Are there built-in closets in the bedroom?

1.1 Livemocha™ Active Italian *Level 4*

la cucina
kitchen

In cucina c'è spazio per un tavolo?
Is there room in the kitchen for a table?

il salotto
sitting room

C'è una finestra che dà sul giardino nel salotto?
Is there a window in the sitting room that looks out onto the garden?

il soggiorno
living room

C'è spazio per un divano-letto nel soggiorno?
Is there room for a sofa bed in the living room?

il bagno
bathroom

Nel bagno c'è la doccia o la vasca da bagno?
Is there a shower or bathtub in the bathroom?

le scale
stairs

Chi pulisce le scale?
Who cleans the stairs?

Unit 1 › Lesson 1: *Looking for an apartment*

1.1

un edificio
a building

È un edificio moderno con l'ascensore.
It is a modern building with an elevator.

lo stabile
apartment building

L'appartamento è al terzo piano di uno stabile in periferia.
The apartment is on the third floor in an apartment building in the suburbs.

compreso nel prezzo
included in the price

Il costo del riscaldamento è compreso nel prezzo dell'affitto?
Is the cost of heating included in the rental price?

disponibile
available

Quando sarà disponibile l'appartamento?
When will the apartment be available?

andare a piedi al lavoro
to walk to work

Vorrei un appartamento vicino al centro per poter andare a piedi al lavoro.
I'd like an apartment near the center so that I can walk to work.

in affitto
for rent

Avete appartamenti in affitto o solo in vendita?
Do you have apartments for rent or only for sale?

Culture note

Most cities and towns in Italy comprise a *centro storico*, a historic center, which is usually home to the older buildings and places of interest, and surrounding *quartieri residenziali*, the suburbs. Traffic  within *centro storico* is often heavily restricted, and in some cities either completely prohibited or impossible (streets can be extremely narrow in medieval areas). For this reason, parking can be very difficult and many people choose to live in the suburbs where there is ample space for roads and parking lots alike. Another common solution to this problem is to use a *moto* (a scooter), since it can zip between the traffic and requires much less space for parking.

Unit 1 › Lesson 2: *Looking around the apartment*

UNIT 1 › LESSON 2
Looking around the apartment

Culture note

In Italy most people refer to the size of their apartment by stating how many square meters it occupies, then by saying how many rooms other than the kitchen and washroom it has.

Un mini-appartamento or *monolocale* is a studio with kitchen facilities. *Un divano-letto* is a sofa bed.

Video Dialog

Ugo may have found just what Michele has been looking for.

 Active Italian: Level 4 > Unit 1 > Lesson 2 > Video dialog

Ugo: *Ecco l'ingresso e l'angolo-cottura. C'è posto per un piccolo tavolo e una sedia. La cucina è ben attrezzata: lavello, forno, lavastoviglie, frigorifero, e forno a microonde. È piccola, ma c'è tutto il necessario. E qui c'è il salotto con il divano-letto. Qui c'è il bagno: doccia, lavabo, bidet, e WC. Qui c'è lo scaldabagno elettrico per l'acqua calda.*

Michele: *C'è il riscaldamento centrale?*

Ugo: *Sì. E l'appartamento è abbastanza luminoso.*

Michele: *Non c'è la lavatrice?*

Ugo: *No, ma c'è una lavanderia a due passi.*

Michele: *E quanto costa?*

Ugo: *620 euro al mese più le spese. Ma siccome il proprietario ha fretta di trovare un inquilino, forse puoi trattare.*

Ugo: Here's the entrance and the kitchenette. There's space for a small table and a chair. The kitchen is well equipped: sink, oven, dishwasher, fridge, and microwave. It's small but there is everything you need. And here there is the living room with a sofa

Unit 1 › Lesson 2: *Looking around the apartment*

	bed. Here is the bathroom: shower, wash basin, bidet, and toilet. Here's the electric boiler for the hot water.
Michele:	Is there central heating?
Ugo:	Yes. And the apartment is quite bright.
Michele:	Isn't there a washing machine?
Ugo:	No, but there is a Laundromat very close by.
Michele:	And how much is it?
Ugo:	620 euros a month plus charges. But as the owner is in a hurry to find a tenant you might be able to negotiate.

Grammar

....

 Active Italian: Level 4 > Unit 1 > Lesson 2 > Grammar

1 › **How much is it per month?**

Michele asks Ugo how much the apartment is per month. Ugo says: *620 euro al mese più le spese*. 620 euros a month plus charges.

To say "per month," Italian uses *a*. Remember that this is one of the words that combines with the article *il, la*, etc.

al mese	per month
alla settimana	per week
all'anno	per year
al giorno	per day
all'ora	per hour

The euro

Italy is part of the Eurozone. The word euro is an invented word, even though it does look and sound Italian. As with other non-native Italian words, it doesn't change in the plural: *venti euro*.

One euro breaks down into 100 cents. Officially the word is *cent*, but Italians prefer to use *centesimo* instead. Therefore it does have a plural, *centesimi*.

Writing down prices

When writing prices, Italians tend to put the euro symbol after the figure: 620 €.

When writing a figure in thousands, Italians use a period (*punto*): 10.000 (diecimila).

A comma (*virgola*) is used for decimal points: 6,5 (*sei virgola cinque*) and with prices 5,50 € (*cinque euro e cinquanta*).

Unit 1 › Lesson 2: *Looking around the apartment*

4 › **To be in a hurry**

In Italian "to be in a hurry" is *avere fretta*.

> *Il proprietario ha fretta.*
> The owner is in a hurry.

If you are in a hurry to do something, then add *di* followed by the infinitive.

> *Non ho fretta di sposarmi.*
> I'm not in a hurry to get married.

Other expressions using *avere* and *di* include:

avere paura di	to be scared of
avere bisogno di	to be in need of, to need
avere tempo di	to have time to
avere voglia di	to feel like

Ho paura di cadere.	I am scared of falling.
Ho bisogno di un idraulico.	I need a plumber.
Non ho tempo di scriverti.	I don't have time to write to you.
Ho voglia di mangiare una pizza.	I feel like eating a pizza.

5 › There is room for…

Ugo says that there is room for a small table: *C'è posto per un piccolo tavolo.*

Posto is a useful word with a number of meanings. The meaning will be obvious from the context.

> *C'è posto per la macchina?*
> Is there a space for a car?

This means is there somewhere to park the car.

> *Mi dispiace, non c'è posto.*
> Sorry, there is no space.

Posto can also mean a seat on a train or in a theater.

> *Un posto vicino al finestrino.*
> A seat next to the window.

Essere a posto means to be fine.

> *Sono a posto.*
> I am fine.

Mettere a posto means to clean up.

> *Devo mettere a posto la casa.*
> I have to clean up the house.

6 › Check the endings

A clue to the gender of a noun (whether it is masculine or feminine) is often found in its ending.

Nouns ending in -*o* are mainly masculine (*il letto*, *il posto*).
Nouns ending in -*a* are mainly feminine (*la birra*, *la pizza*).
Nouns ending in -*e* can be either (*il mese*, *la notte*).

7 › Feminine noun endings

Remember, nouns ending in -*a* are mainly feminine (*la birra*, *la pizza*).

Other feminine endings include:

-ice: *la lavatrice*	washing machine
-ione: *la stazione*	station
-à: *la città*	city
-udine: *l'abitudine*	habit
-essa: *la professoressa*	teacher

Masculine noun endings

Remember, nouns ending in *-o* are mainly masculine (*il letto*, *il posto*).

Other masculine endings include:

-ore: *il colore*	color
-ale: *il canale*	canal, channel
-ma: *il programma*	program
-è, -ì, -ù: *il caffè, il tassì, il tiramisù*	coffee, taxi, tiramisu

Culture note

The format for writing an Italian address is as follows:

Name
Road name followed by house number
Postal code followed by city

e.g.

Giuseppe Sartori
Via Cavour, 16
00184 Roma

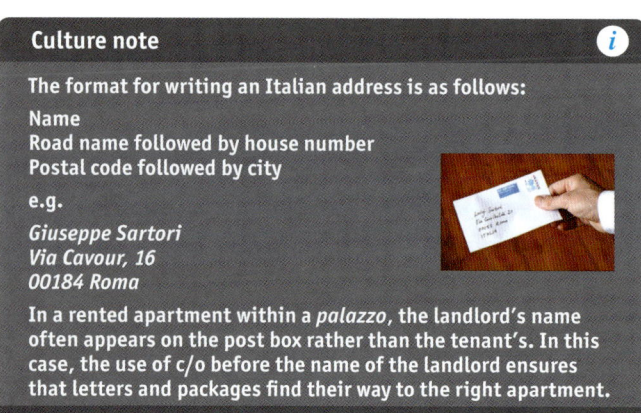

In a rented apartment within a *palazzo*, the landlord's name often appears on the post box rather than the tenant's. In this case, the use of c/o before the name of the landlord ensures that letters and packages find their way to the right apartment.

Unit 1 › Lesson 2: *Looking around the apartment*

1.2

Vocabulary

 Active Italian: Level 4 > Unit 1 > Lesson 2 > Vocabulary

la porta d'entrata
front door

La porta d'entrata ha la serratura elettrica.
The front door has an electric lock.

il tavolo
table

È un vecchio tavolo di legno.
It is an old wooden table.

la sedia
chair

Non ci sono sedie nell'appartamento, dovrebbero arrivare domani.
There are no chairs in the apartment, they should arrive tomorrow.

il lavello
sink

Il lavello in cucina è di marmo.
The sink in the kitchen is marble.

il forno
oven

La cucina ha solo il forno a gas.
There is only a gas oven in the kitchen.

il frigo, il frigorifero
fridge

Il frigo non è molto grande ma ha anche il congelatore.
The fridge isn't very big but it has a freezer.

la lavastoviglie
dishwasher

Abbiamo comprato la lavastoviglie due anni fa.
We bought the dishwasher two years ago.

il forno a microonde
microwave

C'è il forno a microonde in cucina?
Is there a microwave in the kitchen?

il divano-letto
sofa bed

Vorremmo mettere un divano-letto nel soggiorno.
We want to put a sofa bed in the living room.

Unit 1 › Lesson 2: *Looking around the apartment*

la doccia
shower

La doccia non funziona bene.
The shower isn't working properly.

il lavabo
bathroom sink

Il lavabo si è otturato. Mi mandi l'idraulico.
The bathroom sink is blocked. Please send me a plumber.

la vasca da bagno
bathtub

Non c'è la vasca da bagno ma la doccia.
There isn't a bathtub but a shower.

il bagno
toilet, bathroom

Il bagno è in fondo al corridoio.
The toilet is at the end of the corridor.

Active Italian *Level 4*

2

Lesson 1: What will the weather be like?

» How to talk about the weather in the present, future, and past.
» Different parts of the country: *Italia settentrionale* and *Italia meridionale*.
» The future of *essere*.
» The ending *-ata*: *la mattinata*, *la giornata*.

Lesson 2: Making plans

» How to make suggestions.
» The difference in use between *giocare* (to play a sport) and *suonare* (to play an instrument).
» How to say "no" and use the negative.
» How *bello/a* behaves before a noun.

Collins | **Livemocha™**

UNIT 2 › LESSON 1
What will the weather be like?

Culture note

Italy is divided into 20 regions: 8 in northern Italy, 4 in the central part and 8 in the south. The southern regions include the two islands of Sicily (*Sicilia*) and Sardinia (*Sardegna*). The largely hilly region of Tuscany (*Toscana*) is home to Florence and Pisa, Venice is the capital of the northeastern Veneto region, and the capital city, Rome, is located in Lazio, in west central Italy. Italy also has two independent states – San Marino (*la Repubblica di San Marino*) and the Vatican (*lo Stato del Vaticano*), the latter of which is in Rome. Italy's biggest region is Sicily and the smallest is Val D'Aosta (*Valle D'Aosta*), in the northwest.

Unit 2 › Lesson 1: *What will the weather be like?*

Video Dialog

Giulia and Michele make plans around the weather.

 Active Italian: Level 4 › Unit 2 › Lesson 1 › Video dialog

Michele:	*Venerdì è festa. Si potrebbe fare una gita.*
Giulia:	*Dipenderà un po' dal tempo.*
Michele:	*Be', allora vediamo il meteo... Ecco qui... Oggi è mercoledì, pioggia.*
Giulia:	*Non è mica vero, non sta piovendo.*
Michele:	*Giovedì farà bello: ci sarà il sole e farà caldo.*
Giulia:	*Non è mica in questa zona. Stai guardando le previsioni per il Nord d'Italia.*
Michele:	*Oh, scusami... il centro... Ecco: domani, giovedì, farà bello tutto il giorno.*
Giulia:	*E venerdì... sole, ci saranno 22 gradi.*

....

Michele:	Friday is a holiday. We could go on an outing.
Giulia:	It will depend a bit on the weather.
Michele:	OK. let's look at the weather forecast... Here it is... today is Wednesday, rain.
Giulia:	That's not true, it's not raining.
Michele:	Thursday is going to be nice, it will be sunny and hot.
Giulia:	That's not in this area. You're looking at the forecast for northern Italy.
Michele:	Oh sorry... the center... Here we are: tomorrow, Thursday, it's going to be nice all day.
Giulia:	And Friday... sunshine. It will be 22 degrees.

Grammar

 Active Italian: Level 4 > Unit 2 > Lesson 1 > Grammar

1 › **Talking about the weather**

Many weather expressions use *essere* (to be) or *fare* (to make):

C'è il sole.	It's sunny.
C'è la nebbia.	It's foggy.

And with *fare*:

Fa freddo.	It's cold.
Fa caldo.	It's hot.

To ask what the weather is like, say *Com'è il tempo?* or *Che tempo fa?*

2 › **The weather today**

Note that when you are talking about the weather you use the same verb ending as for he/she/it.

Unit 2 › Lesson 1: *What will the weather be like?*

To say what the weather is like today, you use *è* or *c'è* if the expression uses *essere* and *fa* if it uses *fare*.

C'è vento.	It's windy.
È nuvoloso.	It's cloudy.

Fa bel tempo.	It's nice weather.
Fa brutto tempo.	It's horrible weather.

3 › **The weather tomorrow**

To say what the weather will be like, you use the future: *sarà* if the expression uses *essere* and *farà* if it uses *fare*.

> *Ci sarà vento domani?*
> Will it be windy tomorrow?
>
> *Che tempo farà domani?*
> What will the weather be like tomorrow?
>
> *Farà caldo tutto il giorno.*
> It will be hot all day.

To ask what the weather will be like tomorrow, you can also say: *Come sarà il tempo domani?* What will the weather be like tomorrow?

4 › What the weather could be like

The future of *potere* (can) is also used to indicate what the weather might be like:

> *La sera ci potranno essere dei temporali.*
> There could be some thunderstorms in the evening.
>
> *Potrà piovere domani.*
> It might rain tomorrow.

5 › The weather yesterday

To describe what the weather was like, you can use the imperfect tense or the past perfect (with *avere/essere* and past participle):

> *C'era molto vento ieri.*
> It was very windy yesterday.
>
> *Che tempo c'era ieri?*
> What was the weather like yesterday?
>
> *Faceva caldo la settimana scorsa.* or *Ha fatto caldo la settimana scorsa.*
> It was hot last week.

Unit 2 › Lesson 1: *What will the weather be like?*

6 › The future of *essere* (to be)

As you have seen, *essere* is an irregular verb. Here is the future tense.

sarò	I will be
sarai	you (familiar) will be
sarà	he/she/it will be, you (formal) will be
saremo	we will be
sarete	you (plural) will be
saranno	they will be

7 › The ending *-ata*

Morning is *la mattina*. *La mattinata* also means morning but the addition of the ending *-ata* emphasizes the actual span of time rather than the unit of time.

We have met something similar in the expressions

Buona giornata!	Have a good day!
Buona serata!	Have a good evening!

8 › North, south, east, and west

north	*il nord*
south	*il sud*
east	*l'est*
west	*l'ovest*

When talking about the north of Italy, *settentrionale* is often used: *Italia settentrionale* – northern Italy.

Meridionale is used when referring to the south of Italy: *Italia meridionale* – southern Italy.

Western is *occidentale*.

Eastern is *orientale*.

Unit 2 › Lesson 1: *What will the weather be like?*

2.1

Vocabulary

 Active Italian: Level 4 > Unit 2 > Lesson 1 > Vocabulary

il tempo
weather

Ha fatto bel tempo durante il nostro soggiorno a Roma.
We had good weather during our stay in Rome.

le previsioni del tempo
weather forecast

Le previsioni del tempo per domani e per tutta la settimana.
The weather forecast for tomorrow and the whole week.

piovere
to rain

Penso che domani pioverà.
I think it will rain tomorrow.

la neve
snow

Siamo andati a sciare ma c'era poca neve.
We went skiing but there was little snow.

bello/a
nice, lovely

Tempo bello sulle regioni del sud e del centro.
Nice weather in the southern and central regions.

brutto/a
awful, bad

Che brutta giornata!
What an awful day!

cielo coperto
overcast

Cielo coperto su tutte le regioni del nord est.
Overcast in all the regions of the northeast.

il vento
wind

In tutta Italia i venti saranno moderati.
The winds will diminish over the whole of Italy.

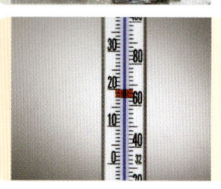

il grado
degree

Ventisei gradi a Roma.
26 degrees in Rome.

variabile
changeable

Tempo variabile su tutte le regioni.
Changeable weather in all the regions.

il temporale
storm

Il temporale ci ha sorpresi mentre camminavamo in campagna.
The storm took us by surprise while we were walking in the country.

Unit 2 › Lesson 1: *What will the weather be like?*

spaventarsi
to be scared

Si è spaventato molto vedendo la pistola.
He was very scared when he saw the gun.

Culture note

Italy is predominantly a mountainous and hilly country. The two main mountain ranges are the Alps (*le Alpi*) in the north, which create a natural frontier with neighboring countries, and the Apenines (*gli Appennini*) that run from north to south, like a backbone. As in other mountainous countries, the weather is very variable from region to region and season to season. In the winter months it can be very cold, especially in the northern and central regions, with temperatures often below freezing. The temperatures tend to get milder the further south you go, but most of Italy enjoys a hot, dry summer. You can always check the weather forecast on the internet. Enter *il meteo* on www.google.it, or go to www.meteo.it and you will find a map of Italy that clearly shows the forecast for the different regions.

UNIT 2 › LESSON 2
Making plans

Culture note

Italians spend their free time in a huge variety of ways. Given the usually warm summer months many people flock to the seaside resorts where they sunbathe, swim, play beach volleyball, windsurf, and waterski. Others seek the cooler mountain air and either go hiking or for picnics. Open-air concerts and movies are also a common sight in most towns throughout the summer. The *piazza* (city square) is a very popular meeting place for people of all ages. Children play here while many of the more elderly citizens gather at local bars that often line such *piazze* to play cards. In the winter skiing is, of course, high on the list of priorities for many Italians. During the soccer season the local bar is a popular place to have a drink and watch your team on television.

Unit 2 › Lesson 2: *Making plans*

Video Dialog

Michele and Giulia make some plans for their day out together.

Active Italian: Level 4 > Unit 2 > Lesson 2 > Video dialog

Michele:	*Allora, venerdì farà bello... che cosa facciamo?*
Giulia:	*Una gita in bicicletta ai Castelli?*
Michele:	*No, la mia bicicletta è a Genova.*
Giulia:	*Dove ti piacerebbe andare?*
Michele:	*Si potrebbe andare a Tivoli.*
Giulia:	*Che bella idea! Non ci sono mai andata. Ma è lontano?*
Michele:	*Non troppo. Ci possiamo andare in macchina.*
Giulia:	*A che ora apre?*
Michele:	*Non lo so. Guardiamo su Internet... alle 8 e mezza...*
Giulia:	*Allora, andiamo verso le dieci. Possiamo visitare la villa la mattina e dopo pranzo fare una passeggiata nei giardini.*
Michele:	*Fantastico!*

Michele:	So on Friday it's going to be nice... what shall we do?
Giulia:	Go for a bike ride to the Castles area?
Michele:	No, my bike is in Genoa.
Giulia:	Where would you like to go?

Michele:	We could go to Tivoli.
Giulia:	What a great idea! I've never been there. But is it far?
Michele:	Not too far. We can go by car.
Giulia:	What time does it open?
Michele:	I don't know. Let's have a look on the Internet... at 8:30.
Giulia:	Well then, let's go at about 10. We can visit the villa in the morning and after lunch go for a walk in the gardens.
Michele:	Fantastic!

Grammar

Active Italian: Level 4 > Unit 2 > Lesson 2 > Grammar

1 › **Suggestions**

The easiest way of making a suggestion is by using the *noi* form of a verb.

> *Facciamo un giro in macchina.*
> Let's go for a drive in the car.
>
> *Andiamo a fare una gita in pullman.*
> Let's go for a bus trip.

Another way is by using *Si potrebbe* (literally "one could"). This is followed by the infinitive:

> *Si potrebbe andare al mare.*
> We could go to the seaside.
>
> *Si potrebbe fare un picnic.*
> We could have a picnic.

Unit 2 › Lesson 2: *Making plans*

2 › Playing – *giocare* a sport, *suonare* an instrument

If you're talking about playing a sport you use *giocare a*:

Giochiamo a tennis.	Let's play tennis.
Giochiamo a golf.	Let's play golf.
Si potrebbe giocare a pallavolo.	We could play volleyball.
Si potrebbe giocare a carte.	We could play cards.

If you're talking about playing an instrument you use *suonare*:

Suono la chitarra.
I play the guitar.

Mio fratello suona il pianoforte.
My brother plays the piano.

3 › Saying no in Italian

"No" in Italian is *no*: "not" is *non*. If you are replying in the negative to a question, you usually use both words.

> *Vuoi giocare?*
> Do you want to play?
>
> ***No**, **non** voglio giocare adesso.*
> No I don't want to play now.

If you are saying no and doing something else, than you would just need *no*.

> *Hai telefonato a Sara? No, le ho scritto.*
> Did you phone Sara? No, I wrote to her.

4 › Negative pair words

There are also several other negative pair words in Italian. We have already met *non* and *mai* meaning "never" or "not... ever."

Giulia says

> ***Non** ci sono **mai** andata.*
> I have never been there.

Non and *niente* mean "nothing" or "not... anything":

> **Non** ho mangiato **niente** ieri.
> I ate nothing yesterday, I didn't eat anything yesterday.

Non and *nulla* also mean "nothing" or "not... anything."

> **Non** ho visto **nulla**.
> I saw nothing, I didn't see anything.

Non and *nessuno* mean "no one" or "nobody."

> **Non** c'è **nessuno** in casa.
> There is no one at home, There is nobody at home.

The *non* and pair word (*mai*, *niente*, etc.) go around the main verb (or the auxiliary verb):

Non bevo mai la birra.	I never drink beer.
Non ho mai bevuto la birra.	I have never drunk beer.

5 › Never, nothing, nobody

Mai (never), *niente* (nothing), *nulla* (nothing), and *nessuno* (nobody) can be used on their own in response to a question.

Sei stato a Tivoli?	Have you been to Tivoli?
Mai.	Never.

Che cos'hai fatto oggi?	What did you do today?
Niente.	Nothing.

Chi hai visto al mercato?	Who did you see at the market?
Nessuno.	Nobody.

6 › About *bello/a* – lovely

Giulia says

> *Che bella idea!*
> What a great idea!

Bello/a meaning nice, beautiful, or good-looking, is one of a number of adjectives that go in front of the noun. By going in front of the noun *bello* behaves like the definite article (*il*, *la*, etc.) and *quello* (that).

Before a masculine noun it is *bel*: *un bel giorno* (a nice day).

Before a masculine noun beginning with a vowel, it is *bell'*: *un bell'uomo* (a good-looking man).

Before a noun that takes the *lo* article, it is *bello*: *un bello stadio* (a great stadium).

Before a feminine noun, it is *bella*: *la bella ragazza* (the lovely girl)

Before a feminine noun beginning with a vowel, it is generally *bella* although you might sometimes see *bell'*: *la bella attrice* (the beautiful actress).

In the plural, it is *bei* with masculine nouns (*i bei giorni*) or *begli* with masculine nouns beginning with a vowel or taking the *lo* article (*i begli uomini, i begli stadi*).

For plural feminine nouns it is *belle* (*le belle ragazze*).

Vocabulary

Active Italian: Level 4 > Unit 2 > Lesson 2 > Vocabulary

fare un picnic
to have a picnic

Siamo andati a fare un bel picnic in campagna.
We went for a nice picnic in the country.

andare in piscina
to go to the (swimming) pool

Ieri siamo andati in piscina a nuotare.
Yesterday we went to the pool to swim.

il campo da tennis
tennis court

Prenotiamo il campo da tennis per domani mattina?
Shall we book the tennis court for tomorrow morning?

il lunapark
carnival (with rides, amusements, etc.)

Al lunapark c'era troppa gente.
There were too many people at the carnival.

smettere di fare
to stop doing

Dovresti smettere di fumare.
You should stop smoking.

fare un giro
to go for an outing, to go for a stroll

Facciamo un giro in centro?
Shall we go for a stroll downtown?

fra poco
in a short time, shortly

Fra poco pioverà.
It will rain shortly.

odiare
to hate

Odio le giornate piovose.
I hate rainy days.

riparare
to repair, fix

Per fortuna eravamo vicini a un'officina dove ci hanno riparato la gomma in poco tempo.
Luckily we were near a garage where they fixed the tire for us in a short time.

Unit 2 › Lesson 2: *Making plans*

in diretta
live

Tutte le partite sono trasmesse in diretta per televisione.
All the games are broadcast live on television.

Culture note

A *passeggiata* is usually an evening stroll around town before or after dinner, and an important Italian social convention. For many people, a *passeggiata* is an opportunity to put on nice clothes and *fare bella figura*, to make a good impression on those who see you out and about. For others, the stroll helps work up an appetite, or burn off some of the calories of a big evening meal. Above all, though, the *passeggiata* is a great way of enjoying a city or a town in Italy and a great way to get a taste for the social side of the country.

Active Italian *Level 4*

3

Lesson 1: How do you like living here?

- » How to say you miss something or someone: *mi manca...*
- » How to use indirect pronouns: *mi*, *ti*, *le*, *gli*, *vi*, etc.
- » Irregular commands for common verbs: *da'/dai*, *fa'/fai*, etc.
- » How to use *essere di* and *venire da*.
- » How to use *molto*, *troppo*, *tanto*, etc. with *da*.
- » How to use the impersonal *si*.

Lesson 2: Making new friends

- » How to get someone to do something using *fare* plus the infinitive.
- » How to use *che* and *cui*.
- » How to make a past infinitive: *averti conosciuto*.
- » About adjectives that go in front of the noun: *nuovo/a*, *bello/a*, *buono/a*, etc.
- » About adding an "s" to a word: *fortunato/a*, *sfortunato/a*.

Collins | **Livemocha™**

UNIT 3 › LESSON 1

How do you like living here?

Culture note

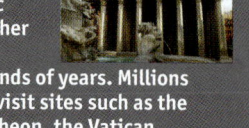

Rome has been the capital city of Italy since 1871 and is one of the most visited cities in the world. The city's history and artistic output has been a great influence on other cities across the Italian peninsula and, indeed, the rest of the world for thousands of years. Millions of tourists come to Rome every year to visit sites such as the Colosseum, the Roman Forum, the Pantheon, the Vatican museums, and the Vatican City, a center of pilgrimage for many Catholics.

The city's character has been formed by a range of historical and artistic periods. Ancient Roman monuments are dotted about the city with many more undiscovered ruins lying below street level. Roman architects were the pioneers of two major architectural structures that are key to later styles of building: the freestanding dome, as can be seen above the Pantheon (which was the largest dome in the world until Brunelleschi's cathedral was built in 1436), and the standing arch, a common structure used in everything from aqueducts, to the Colosseum, to the many triumphal arches that punctuate the city.

Unit 3 › Lesson 1: *How do you like living here?*

3.1

Video Dialog

Giulia tells her new friends about where she is from and compares her hometown to Rome.

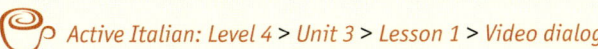
Active Italian: Level 4 > Unit 3 > Lesson 1 > Video dialog

Ugo:	*Allora, Giulia, ti stai abituando a vivere a Roma?*
Giulia:	*Sì, ma mi mancano un po' la mia famiglia e i miei amici.*
Ugo:	*È normale... Dimmi, di dove sei esattamente?*
Giulia:	*Di Lugano. È una città abbastanza piccola.*
Ugo:	*È una bella città?*
Giulia:	*Sì, è molto carina.*
Michele:	*Allora preferisci Roma o Lugano?*
Giulia:	*È difficile... A Roma non c'è molto verde. Sono abituata a passeggiare lungo il lago e a fare escursioni in montagna. D'altra parte, Roma è una città fantastica. Ci sono tante cose da vedere e da fare, non ci si annoia mai.*

....

Ugo:	So, Giulia, are you getting used to living in Rome?
Giulia:	Yes, but I miss my family and my friends a bit.
Ugo:	That's normal... Tell me, where exactly do you come from?
Giulia:	From Lugano. It's quite a small city.
Ugo:	Is it a beautiful city?

Giulia:	Yes, it is very pretty.
Michele:	So do you prefer Rome or Lugano?
Giulia:	That's difficult... There isn't much greenery in Rome. I'm used to walking along the lakeside and going hiking in the mountains. On the other hand, Rome is a fantastic city. There are so many things to see and do, you never get bored.

Grammar

 Active Italian: Level 4 > Unit 3 > Lesson 1 > Grammar

1 › *Mancare* "to miss"

Mancare (to miss) works in a similar way to *piacere* (to like).

> *Mi manca il mio cane.*
> I miss my dog. (Literally, "My dog is missing to me.")

> *Mi mancano i miei amici.*
> I miss my friends. (Literally, "My friends are missing to me.")

So just as with *piacere*, if you are missing one thing, you use *Mi manca*. If you are missing more than one thing, you use *Mi mancano*.

> *Mi piace Roma ma mi manca la mia famiglia.*
> I like Rome, but I miss my family.

> *Mi piacciono questi posti ma mi mancano le montagne.*
> I like these places, but I miss the mountains.

Unit 3 › Lesson 1: *How do you like living here?*

2 › Pronouns to use with *mancare*

The verbs *mancare* and *piacere* are followed by *a*, which means that something is missing or pleasing *to* you (or to him, to her, etc.).

The pronoun that replaces *a me* (to me) is *mi*.

a te is *ti*.	*a lui* is *gli*.
a lei is *le*.	*a noi* is *ci*.
a voi is *vi*.	*a loro* is *gli* (or occasionally *loro* when it goes after the verb).

Perché sei triste? Ti manca la mamma?
Why are you sad? Are you missing your mom?

Ci manca il nostro gatto.
We miss our cat.

Non vi mancano i vostri genitori?
Don't you miss your parents?

3 › Telling someone what to do

Some verbs that are commonly used for telling someone what to do (known as commands) are irregular in the *tu* form.

andare: *va'* or *vai* (go)

> *Vai via!*
> Go away!

dare: *da'* or *dai* (give)

> *Dai l'ombrello a Luca.*
> Give the umbrella to Luca.

dire: *di'* (say)

> *Di' quella parolaccia un'altra volta e...!*
> Say that swear word again and...!

fare: *fa'* or *fai* (do)

> *Fai subito questi compiti!*
> Do this homework right away!

stare: *sta'* or *stai* (keep, stay)

> *Stai zitto!*
> Keep quiet! (usually translated as Shut up!)

Unit 3 › Lesson 1: *How do you like living here?*

4 › **More on commands**

When you use *va'*, *da'*, *di'*, *fa'*, or *sta'* with an object pronoun, the first letter of the pronoun is doubled and you lose the apostrophe:

Dammi l'indirizzo.
Give me the address.

Dille a che ora partiamo.
Tell her what time we are leaving.

Fallo entrare.
Let him in.

Stammi vicino.
Stay close to me.

The doubling of the first letter doesn't happen with *gli* (to him or to them).

Digli di aspettarmi.
Tell him to wait for me.

5 › **Where are you from?**

You normally use *da* to mean "from" in Italian but with *essere* you use *di* (literally "of"). To ask someone where they are from you begin your question *Di dove...?*

Italian is quite fluid in its word order. You can either say

> *Di dove sono i tuoi amici?* or
> *I tuoi amici di dove sono?*
>
> Where are your friends from?

You use *di* with a town or city:

> *di Roma, di New York, di Tokyo, di Firenze*

You can also use *venire da* (to come from) if you are referring to your roots.

| *Da dove vieni?* | Where do you come from? |
| *Vengo dal nord d'Italia.* | I come from the north of Italy. |

Remember that *da* combines with the article (*il*, *la*, etc).

> *Vengo dalla Scozia.*
>
> I come from Scotland.

If you were asking where someone has just come from, you would use *arrivare*. *Da dove arrivi?*

Unit 3 › Lesson 1: *How do you like living here?*

6 › So much to see

To say "so much to" you use *tanto da* followed by the infinitive:

> *A Roma c'è tanto da vedere.*
> In Rome there is so much to see.

You can also follow it with a noun such as *cose* (things), *musei* (museums), etc.

| *A Roma ci sono tante cose da fare.* | In Rome there are so many things to do. |
| *A Roma ci sono tanti musei da visitare.* | In Rome there are so many museums to visit. |

7 › Too much, too little, too few...

Da is also used with *troppo* (too much, too many), *molto* (a lot, much, many), *poco* (little, few), *parecchio* (quite a lot, several), *qualcosa* (something), *niente* (nothing):

> *Ci sono troppi musei da visitare.*
> There are too many museums to visit.
>
> *Hanno poco da dire.*
> They have little to say.

Hanno molto da mangiare.
They have lots to eat.

Ci sono parecchi piatti da lavare.
There are quite a lot of plates to wash.

Avete qualcosa da dire?
Do you have something to say?

Non c'è niente da pagare.
There's nothing to pay.

8 › Impersonal *si* (one)

Si meaning "one," "you," or "we" (depending on which sounds best) is an impersonal pronoun.

Si può parcheggiare qui?
Can we park here?

Come si scrive?
How do you spell it?

Whenever you use *si* with a reflexive verb the first *si* becomes *ci*:

Non ci si annoia mai.
One never gets bored.

Unit 3 › Lesson 1: *How do you like living here?*

You'll come across it with *abituarsi a* (to get used to)

| *Prima o poi ci si abitua al clima.* | Sooner or later one gets used to the climate. |
| *Ci si abitua a vivere a Roma.* | You get used to living in Rome. |

Culture note

The Renaissance and Baroque periods were also fundamental in the development of Rome's character. While fifteenth-century Florence witnessed the early development of Renaissance art and architecture, in many ways it was Rome that reaped the rewards. The columns, arches, and domes of Ancient Rome were given a new lease on life in the sixteenth century, when, in a wave of artistic activity, many new palaces and churches were built across the city in an architectural style that deliberately compared itself to that of the Roman Empire.

Culture note

In the later sixteenth and seventeenth centuries, Rome itself was once again home to a new style of art and architecture, the Baroque. Baroque artists and architects employed many of the same methods as their Renaissance forbearers, yet they injected a much-needed theatrical element into the mix, creating a style that was still in many ways classical, harking back to Ancient Rome, yet exciting, vivid, and human. The wobbly facades and ornate domes of Baroque churches, along with a veritable army of dramatic Baroque statues and golden frescoes, can still be seen all over the city.

Livemocha™ Active Italian *Level 4*

Vocabulary

🍵 *Active Italian: Level 4 > Unit 3 > Lesson 1 > Vocabulary*

allontanarsi da
to distance oneself from, to get away from

A Venezia è difficile allontanarsi dalla gente.
In Venice it is difficult to get away from people.

tranquillo/a
quiet, peaceful

Cerchiamo una spiaggia tranquilla.
We are looking for a quiet beach.

un'isola
an island

Non sono mai stato sull'isola d'Elba.
I have never been to the island of Elba.

sembrare
to seem

Mi sembra molto caro.
It seems very expensive to me.

l'inizio
beginning, start

Mi è piaciuto fin dall'inizio.
I liked it right from the start.

Unit 3 › Lesson 1: *How do you like living here?*

3.1

la fine
end

Non sei ancora arrivato alla fine del libro?
Haven't you gotten to the end of the book yet?

annoiarsi
to get bored

Ci siamo annoiati a messa.
We got bored at mass.

immaginarsi
to picture oneself

Non riesco ad immaginarmi a Londra.
I can't picture myself in London.

il fatto
fact

Il fatto che sono italiano non cambia niente.
The fact that I'm Italian doesn't change anything.

altrove
elsewhere, anywhere else

Non vorrei vivere altrove.
I wouldn't want to live anywhere else.

la gente
people

Iera sera c'era molta gente in piazza.
Last night there were lots of people in the square.

UNIT 3 › LESSON 2
Making new friends

Culture note

The education system in Italy can generally be divided into five stages: *scuola materna* (kindergarten), *scuola elementare* (elementary school), *scuola media* (middle school), *scuola superiore* (high school), and *università* (university). School is compulsory and state funded from the age of 6 to 15 or 16, though there are also many privately funded institutions.

Specialization begins at *scuola superiore*, and there are many different types of school at this level that teach different subjects. A *liceo* offers an academic curriculum of arts and sciences, whereas an *istituto technico* (literally "technical institute") offers more practical subjects like business and computer science. An *istituto professionale* (literally "professional institute") offers more vocational subjects and aims to give students the skills they need to find a job directly after finishing a course.

Students generally begin university at around 19 years of age, and typical courses last for three years. A *liceo* education is usually a prerequisite for entry into a university.

Unit 3 › Lesson 2: *Making new friends*

3.2

Video Dialog

Ugo, Michele, and Giulia discuss their plans for the summer.

 Active Italian: Level 4 > Unit 3 > Lesson 2 > Video dialog

Michele:	*E poi qui non sei sola: ci siamo noi che ti facciamo divertire, no?*
Giulia:	*È vero, sono fortunata ad avervi conosciuto! È bellissimo avere dei nuovi amici.*
Ugo:	*Che cosa farai quest'estate quando finirai lo stage?*
Giulia:	*Penso che andrò in vacanza, ho voglia di fare un viaggio.*
Ugo:	*Ah, che bello essere studenti. Mi ricordo quando avevo la tua età…*
Giulia:	*Ma smettila, non sei mica così vecchio!*
Michele:	*Dove ti piacerebbe andare?*
Giulia:	*Mi piacerebbe andare negli Stati Uniti.*
Michele:	*Perché?*
Giulia:	*È un paese affascinante. Ci sono così tante città e paesaggi diversi. Vorrei vedere New York, il Grand Canyon, San Francisco, New Orleans…*
Ugo:	*Dovranno essere delle vacanze lunghe!*

Michele:	And you're not on your own here. We make sure you enjoy yourself, don't we?
Giulia:	That's true, I'm lucky to have met you! It's really great to have new friends.
Ugo:	What are you going to do in the summer after you've finished your internship?
Giulia:	I think I'm going to go on vacation. I feel like going on a trip.
Ugo:	Ah, it's great being a student. I remember when I was your age...
Giulia:	Oh come off it, you're not that old!
Michele:	Where would you like to go?
Giulia:	I'd like to go to the States.
Michele:	Why?
Giulia:	It's a fascinating country. There are so many different cities and landscapes. I'd like to see New York, the Grand Canyon, San Francisco, New Orleans...
Ugo:	It will have to be a long vacation!

Grammar

 Active Italian: Level 4 > Unit 3 > Lesson 2 > Grammar

1 › **To get someone to do something**

Ugo says to Giulia *Ti facciamo divertire* (literally "We make you enjoy yourself") using *fare* (to do, to make) followed by the infinitive.

You can use this when you want to get someone to do something.

> *Ti faccio vedere la casa.*
> I will let you see the house.
>
> *Ti faccio mangiare la specialità della zona.*
> I will get you to eat the local specialty.

2 › Che meaning who or whom

Ugo says to Giulia *Ci siamo noi che ti facciamo divertire, no?* (literally "It is us who make you enjoy yourself, isn't it?")

As well as meaning "how" as in *Che bello!* (How beautiful!) or "what" as in *Che succede?* (What's happening?), *che* can also mean "who," "whom," "which," or "that."

> *il bambino che piange*
> the baby who is crying
>
> *l'uomo che sta arrivando*
> the man who is arriving
>
> *la casa che ho visto ieri*
> the house that I saw yesterday
>
> *i ragazzi che sono a scuola*
> the children who are at school

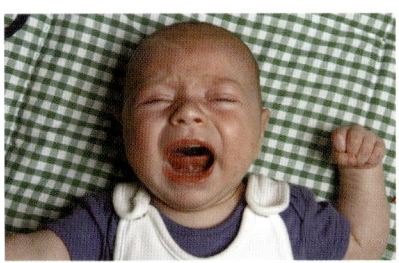

3 › Cui rather than che

After *a* (to), *con* (with), *per* (for), *di* (of), or *da* (from), you use *cui* instead of *che*.

> *L'uomo con cui ti ho visto è qui.*
> The man whom I saw you with is here.

Ecco il dottore a cui ho telefonato.
There's the doctor whom I phoned.

4 › Lucky to have met you

Giulia says *Sono fortunata ad avervi conosciuto.* (I am lucky to have met you.)

Conoscere is the present infinitive. You can also make a past infinitive using *avere* (or *essere*) and the past participle *conosciuto*. However, the final *-e* of *avere* is usually left off.

A past infinitive is often used with *dopo* (after):

Siamo partiti dopo aver mangiato.
We left after having eaten.

È arrivato dopo aver parcheggiato la macchina.
He arrived after parking the car.

5 › New friends – *dei nuovi amici*

Nuovo/a meaning "new" belongs to a group of common adjectives that tend to go in front of the noun rather than after it.

Others include:

bello/a beautiful, nice, good-looking

> *una bella giornata*
> a lovely day

brutto/a ugly, awful

> *una brutta giornata*
> an awful day

buono/a good, tasty

> *una buona pizza*
> a tasty pizza

cattivo/a bad, nasty

> *un cattivo odore*
> a nasty smell

breve short, brief

> *un breve film*
> a short movie

lungo/a long

> *una lunga giornata*
> a long day

piccolo/a small

> *una piccola casa*
> a small house

6 › Stop it – *Smettila*

Giulia says to Ugo *Smettila!* (literally "Stop it!")

Adding an "s" to a verb or adjective in Italian often turns it into its opposite.

> *fortunato/a* is lucky, *sfortunato/a* is unlucky.
> *congelare* is to freeze, *scongelare* is to defrost.
> *montare* is to put up, to assemble, *smontare* is to take down, to dismantle.
> *allacciare* is to fasten, *slacciare* is to unfasten.
> *coprire* is to cover, *scoprire* is to uncover, to discover.
> *caricare* is to upload, *scaricare* is to download.

Culture note

Italy witnessed a century of mass emigration, known as the Italian Diaspora, that began around the time of the country's unification in 1861, and ended in the 1960s during a period of economic growth.

The main reason for this mass emigration was poverty, and Italians looked to other countries for better work opportunities and standards of living.

Today, as a result of Italian emigration, there are millions of people of Italian descent all around the world, with the largest number of people with Italian ancestry found in Brazil, Argentina, and the United States.

Unit 3 › Lesson 2: *Making new friends*

Vocabulary

 Active Italian: Level 4 > Unit 3 > Lesson 2 > Vocabulary

Beato/a te!
Lucky you!

Beati voi che andate in California!
Lucky you going to California!

indovinare
to guess

Indovina chi è arrivato?
Guess who has arrived?

sperare di
to hope to

Spero di andare in Italia l'anno prossimo.
I hope to go to Italy next year.

il padrino
godfather

Non conosco il mio padrino.
I don't know my godfather.

la madrina
godmother

La sua madrina è un'amica di sua madre.
Her godmother is a friend of her mother's.

il patrigno
stepfather

Chi è il patrigno di Alex?
Who is Alex's stepfather?

la matrigna
stepmother

La matrigna di Cenerentola era cattiva.
Cinderella's stepmother was wicked.

due anni fa
two years ago

Due anni fa mi sono sposato per la seconda volta.
Two years ago I got married for the second time.

meraviglioso/a
wonderful

Ieri sera ho conosciuto una ragazza meravigliosa.
Last night I met a wonderful girl.

Unit 3 › Lesson 2: *Making new friends*

piacevole
pleasant

La serata di ieri è stata molto piacevole.
Yesterday evening was very pleasant.

Active Italian *Level 4*

4

Lesson 1: At the tourist office

- » Different meanings of *per*.
- » How to say how long something takes using *durare*.
- » Different expressions using *volere*: *volerci*, *voler bene*, etc.
- » How to use *fare* in addition, multiplication, subtraction, and division.

Lesson 2: Sorting out travel documents

- » What the subjunctive is and how and when to use it.
- » The subjunctive form of *-are*, *-ere*, and *-ire* verbs.
- » How to see how similar words are connected: *sicuro/a*, *assicurato/a*, *assicurare*.

○ Collins | Livemocha™

UNIT 4 › LESSON 1
At the tourist office

Culture note

There are approximately 30 main airports in Italy. The two principal ones are Milan Malpensa and Leonardo da Vinci International in Rome, which deal with the bulk of long-haul flight destinations. Both are well connected with their respective city centers along with the rest of the country (both have attached train stations).

Domestic flights are offered between a variety of Italian airports, and as Italy is almost 750 miles long, air travel is sometimes the fastest and most convenient form of travel within the country. There are a number of low-cost airlines that operate in Italy and offer domestic flights along with cheap flights to other destinations around Europe.

Unit 4 › Lesson 1: *At the tourist office*

Video Dialog

At the travel agent's, Michele plans his trip.

Active Italian: Level 4 > Unit 4 > Lesson 1 > Video dialog

Michele:	*Buongiorno.*
Sig.ra Duranti:	*Buongiorno.*
Michele:	*Devo andare a New York la prossima settimana.*
Sig.ra Duranti:	*Per quanti giorni?*
Michele:	*Due o tre giorni soltanto. Vorrei partire lunedì.*
Sig.ra Duranti:	*C'è un volo Alitalia alle 8.25 che arriva a New York alle 10.35.*
Michele:	*Quanto dura il volo?*
Sig.ra Duranti:	*Dura… attenda… 6 ore e 10 minuti.*
Michele:	*E quanto costa?*
Sig.ra Duranti:	*Volo AZ 022… 771 euro.*
Michele:	*E per il ritorno?*
Sig.ra Duranti:	*Preferisce partire alle 16.50 o alle 23.35?*
Michele:	*A che ora arriva il volo delle 23.35?*
Sig.ra Duranti:	*Il giorno dopo alle 12.30.*
Michele:	*E quanto costa in tutto?*
Sig.ra Duranti:	*In tutto fanno… 1,542 euro.*

Michele:	Good morning.
Mrs. Duranti:	Good morning.
Michele:	I have to go to New York next week.
Mrs. Duranti:	For how many days?
Michele:	Just for two or three days. I'd like to leave on Monday.
Mrs. Duranti:	There's an Alitalia flight at 8:25 that gets to New York at 10:35.
Michele:	How long is the flight?
Mrs. Duranti:	It takes...wait... 6 hours and 10 minutes.
Michele:	And how much is it?
Mrs. Duranti:	AZ flight 022... 771 euros.
Michele:	And the flight back?
Mrs. Duranti:	Do you prefer to leave at 16:50 or 23:35?
Michele:	What time does the 23:35 flight arrive?
Mrs. Duranti:	The next day at 12:30.
Michele:	How does that make in total?
Mrs. Duranti:	In total that makes... 1,542 euros.

Grammar

 Active Italian: Level 4 > Unit 4 > Lesson 1 > Grammar

1 › **For how many days?**

The travel agent asks *Per quanti giorni?* (For how many days?).

Per translates as "for":

> *Per tre giorni.*
> For three days.

> *Devo essere a casa per le nove.*
> I have to be home for 9 o'clock.

Ho comprato un regalo per Luisa.
I bought a present for Luisa.

Per also means "in order to":

Ho preso l'autobus per andare dal dottore.
I took the bus in order to go to the doctor.

It is also used to indicate where something is headed.

Il treno per Roma.
The train to Rome.

Il volo per New York.
The flight to New York.

2 › More meanings of *per*

When you are translating from Italian, be aware that one word can have a variety of meanings depending on the context. Always check the words around it.

Per can also mean "through" or "via."

Il treno passa per Lucca.
The train goes through Lucca.

> *I ladri sono passati per la finestra.*
> The thieves got in through the window.

Per strada means "in the street."

> *L'ho trovato per strada.*
> I found it in the street.

3 › *Per* in polite expressions

Per is used in a number of polite expressions, all essentially meaning please:

> *per favore*
> *per piacere*
> *per cortesia* (slightly more formal)

4 › How long does it take?

Michele asks how long the journey takes, *Quanto dura il viaggio?*, using the verb *durare* (to last).

> *Il volo* is a flight.
> *La traversata* is a crossing (over water).
> *Il viaggio* is a journey or trip.

Quanto dura il volo?	How long is the flight?
Quanto dura la traversata?	How long is the crossing?
Quanto dura il viaggio?	How long is the journey?

Unit 4 › Lesson 1: *At the tourist office*

5 › Another way of saying how long something takes

If you ask how long something takes, you might get the reply.

Ci vuole un'ora.
It takes one hour.

Volerci (to take) can be used for time.

| *Quanto ci vuole per cuocere la pasta?* | How long does it take to cook the pasta? |
| *Ci vogliono venti minuti.* | It takes 20 minutes. |

Note how you need the plural verb – *vogliono* – because *minuti* (minutes) is plural.

*Ci **vuole** un giorno.*
It takes one day.

but:

*Ci **vogliono** tre giorni.*
It takes three days.

Volerci can also mean "to be needed."

| *Quanta farina ci vuole per fare questa torta?* | How much flour is needed to make this cake? |
| *Ci vogliono 300 grammi di farina.* | You need 300 grams of flour. |

6 › Other expressions using *volere*

Voler dire means "to mean."

Che cosa vuol dire "chiocciola"?
What does "chiocciola" mean?

Voler bene a means "to love" or "to be very fond of." You are more likely to use *voler bene a* with a boyfriend or girlfriend than *amare* (to love).

Ti voglio bene.	I love you.
Mi vuoi bene?	Do you love me?
Si vogliono bene.	They love each other.

7 › Making in total

The travel agent says

> *In tutto fanno... 1542 euro.*
> In total that makes... 1,542 euros.

Fare is used when adding up numbers.
2 + 2 = 4 translates as *due più due fa quattro*.

In multiplication *per* means "times."
2 × 3 = 6 translates as *due per tre fa sei*.

In subtraction *meno* means "minus."
8 – 1 = 7 translates as *otto meno uno fa sette*.

In division *diviso* means "divided by."
10 ÷ 2 = 5 translates as *10 diviso due fa cinque*.

Unit 4 > Lesson 1: *At the tourist office* **4.1**

Vocabulary

 Active Italian: Level 4 > Unit 4 > Lesson 1 > Vocabulary

il visto
visa

Per andare in vacanza in America non c'è bisogno del visto.
To go on vacation to America you don't need a visa.

la dogana
customs

Devo dichiarare questi souvenir alla dogana?
Do I need to declare these souvenirs to customs?

il volo
flight

Il volo per Londra partirà con 20 minuti di ritardo.
The flight to London will leave 20 minutes late.

l'uscita
gate (in an airport)

I passeggeri in partenza per New York con il volo Alitalia AZ25 sono pregati di presentarsi all'uscita numero 6 per l'imbarco.
Passengers departing for New York on flight Alitalia AZ25 are requested to go to gate number 6 for boarding.

4.1 Livemocha™ Active Italian *Level 4*

il biglietto dell'aereo
airplane ticket

Ti sei ricordata di portare i biglietti dell'aereo?
Did you remember to bring the airplane tickets?

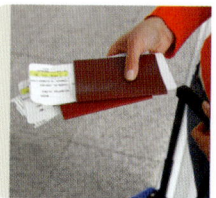

la carta d'imbarco
boarding card

Non dimenticarti la carta d'imbarco come ha fatto tua madre.
Don't forget the boarding card like your mother did.

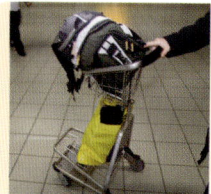

il bagaglio a mano
hand luggage

Il bagaglio a mano non deve superare i dieci chili.
Hand luggage shouldn't weigh more than 10 kilos.

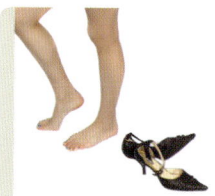

togliere le scarpe
to take off one's shoes

Quando sarò seduto nell'aereo mi toglierò le scarpe.
When I am sitting in the plane I will take my shoes off.

perdere il volo
to miss the flight

Il treno era in ritardo e abbiamo rischiato di perdere il volo per Parigi.
The train was late and we nearly missed our flight to Paris.

Unit 4 › Lesson 1: *At the tourist office*

4.1

il decollo
takeoff

L'aereo è in pista pronto per il decollo.
The plane is on the runway ready for takeoff.

atterrare
to land

Allacciate le cinture di sicurezza: stiamo per atterrare.
Fasten your seatbelts: we are about to land.

Culture note

There are many ports and harbors in Italy that accommodate both trade and tourism. From Italian ports, it is possible to travel by boat to many destinations around the Mediterranean sea. Enormous cruise ships  are a common sight at the port of Venice, dwarfing even the largest buildings as they travel between the island of La Giudecca and Saint Mark's Square.

The biggest port is in Genoa (*Genova*), which was once a powerful, independent seafaring nation. Along with Venice, Amalfi, and Pisa, three of the other most important seafaring powers of the past, Genoa competes in the annual Regatta of the Ancient Maritime Republics. Held in a different city each year, participants, and spectators alike dress in traditional clothing for a procession through the streets of the host city before the start of the race.

UNIT 4 › LESSON 2
Sorting out travel documents

Culture note

Italy lies in a single time zone, or *fuso orario*, one hour ahead of Greenwich Mean Time (GMT+1). If you travel east from New York to Rome, for example, then the time difference is 6 hours. If you travel on long-distance flights from east to west then you will be turning your watch back on arrival. You can always find out the time difference between your area and other world cities by checking a world clock online.

Unit 4 › Lesson 2: *Sorting out travel documents*

Video Dialog

Mrs. Duranti, the travel agent, helps Michele with the organization of his trip to New York.

 Active Italian: Level 4 > Unit 4 > Lesson 2 > Video dialog

Sig.ra Duranti:	*Vuole che le prenoti questo volo?*
Michele:	*Sì, grazie.*
Sig.ra Duranti:	*Ha un passaporto a lettura ottica?*
Michele:	*Non sono sicuro. Perché?*
Sig.ra Duranti:	*Perchè se il passaporto non è a lettura ottica, bisogna richiedere un visto... Questo va bene. È a lettura ottica. Non ha bisogno del visto. Deve solo compilare il modulo ESTA su Internet. Vedrà, è molto facile... Allora... Cognome e nome?*
Michele:	*Berti, Michele.*
Sig.ra Duranti:	*Come vuole pagare?*
Michele:	*Con la carta di credito.*
Sig.ra Duranti:	*Benissimo, grazie.*

Mrs. Duranti:	Do you want me to book this flight for you?
Michele:	Yes, please.
Mrs. Duranti:	Do you have a biometric passport?
Michele:	I'm not sure. Why?
Mrs. Duranti:	Because if it's not biometric you will need to apply for a visa... This one is OK. It's biometric.

	You don't need a visa. You just need to fill in an ESTA form on the Internet. You'll see, it's very easy... So... Last name and first name.
Michele:	Berti, Michele.
Mrs. Duranti:	How do you want to pay?
Michele:	By credit card.
Mrs. Duranti:	Very good, thank you.

Grammar

 Active Italian: Level 4 > Unit 4 > Lesson 2 > Grammar

1 › **The subjunctive**

The travel agent asks Michele:

> *Vuole che le prenoti questo volo?*
> Do you want me to book this flight for you?

Let's take a closer look at this sentence and translate it literally. *Vuole che* (Do you want that), *le prenoti* (I should book for you), *questo volo* (this flight).

Prenoti is in the subjunctive mood. So far we have been dealing with the indicative mood, which is the one that deals with certainty and fact.

The subjunctive mood is one that expresses doubt, fear, wishes, and possibility. The subjunctive is very common in Italian. Here it is used because the travel agent cannot be certain that Michele wants her to book his ticket so there is an element of doubt.

The subjunctive is often used after *che* (*Vuole **che** le prenoti questo volo?*).

Unit 4 › Lesson 2: *Sorting out travel documents*

2 › The present subjunctive of -*are* verbs

To form the subjunctive of nearly all verbs, take the first person form (*io*) and add the following endings.

For -*are* verbs (*lavorare* to work)

*lavor****i***	I may work
*lavor****i***	you (*familiar*) may work
*lavor****i***	he / she / it may work
*lavor****i***	you (*formal*) may work
*lavor****iamo***	we may work
*lavor****iate***	you (*plural*) may work
*lavor****ino***	they may work

3 › The present subjunctive of -*ere* verbs

To form the subjunctive of nearly all verbs, take the first person form (*io*) and add the following endings.

For *-ere* verbs (*vendere* to sell)

*vend**a***	I may sell
*vend**a***	you (*familiar*) may sell
*vend**a***	he / she / it may sell
*vend**a***	you (*formal*) may sell
*vend**iamo***	we may sell
*vend**iate***	you (*plural*) may sell
*vend**ano***	they may sell

4 › The present subjunctive of *-ire* verbs

To form the subjunctive of nearly all verbs, take the first person form (*io*) and add the following endings.

For *-ire* verbs (*dormire* to sleep)

*dorm**a***	I may sleep
*dorm**a***	you (*familiar*) may sleep
*dorm**a***	he / she / it may sleep
*dorm**a***	you (*formal*) may sleep
*dorm**iamo***	we may sleep
*dorm**iate***	you (*plural*) may sleep
*dorm**ano***	they may sleep

finire to finish

finis**ca**	I may finish
finis**ca**	you (*familiar*) may finish
finis**ca**	he / she / it may finish
finis**ca**	you (*formal*) may finish
fin**iamo**	we may finish
fin**iate**	you (*plural*) may finish
finis**cano**	they may finish

5 › When to use the subjunctive

The subjunctive is often introduced by *che* as in *vuole che...* (do you want...) and is used with:

Uncertainty:

> *Vuole che le prenoti il volo?*
> Do you want me to book the flight for you?

Possibility:

> *È possibile che Luca non dorma stanotte.*
> It is possible that Luca may not sleep tonight.

Fear:

> *Ho paura che non troviate la chiave.*
> I'm afraid that you may not find the key.

Hope:

> *Spero che veniate a trovarci a Roma.*
> I hope that you come and see us in Rome.

Desire:

> *Voglio che Laura ritorni presto.*
> I want Laura to come back soon.

6 › The subjunctive after set expressions

The subjunctive is also used after set expressions such as *È difficile che* (It is unlikely that, literally It is difficult that), *È necessario che* (It is necessary that).

> *È difficile che Tom ritorni a casa prima delle due.*
> It is unlikely that Tom will get home before 2 o'clock.
>
> *È necessario che dormiate bene stanotte.*
> You have to sleep well tonight. (literally It is necessary that you sleep well tonight)

The subjunctive is also used after words such as *perché* and *affinché* (both meaning "in order that", "so that"):

> *Te lo dico perché Maria non si spaventi.*
> I am telling you this so that Maria doesn't get scared.

7 › Let's use the subjunctive

The subjunctive is also used to make suggestions. For example:

> *Andiamo a mangiare la pizza.*
> Let's go and eat a pizza.

Note that the *noi* form of the subjunctive is the same as the *noi* form of the present tense.

8 › More on the subjunctive

Because the *io*, *tu*, *lui*, and *lei* forms of the subjunctive all have the same ending, the subject pronouns (*io*, *tu*, *lui*, etc.) are used more frequently to avoid any confusion.

> *È possibile che **lui** mi chiami.*
> It is possible that he may call me.
>
> *Ha paura che **tu** non trovi la casa.*
> She's afraid that you might not find the house.

9 › To be sure – *essere sicuro*

Michele says *Non sono sicuro* (I'm not sure).

Sicuro/a also means "safe" or "secure."

> *È in un posto sicuro?*
> Is it in a safe place?

> *Assicurare* means to insure.
> *Assicurato/a* means insured.
> *L'assicurazione* means insurance.

Note how one word can often lead you to a number of other associated words.

Unit 4 › Lesson 2: *Sorting out travel documents*

Vocabulary

 Active Italian: Level 4 > Unit 4 > Lesson 2 > Vocabulary

compilare il modulo
to fill out a form

Compili questo modulo e poi si presenti allo sportello 5.
Please fill out this form and then go to counter 5.

firmare
to sign

Deve firmare in fondo al modulo.
You have to sign at the bottom of the form.

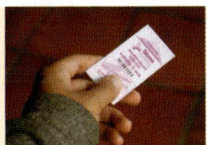

valido/a
valid

Il biglietto è valido solo per tre giorni.
The ticket is only valid for three days.

scaduto/a
out of date, expired

Mi dispiace ma il suo passaporto è scaduto due mesi fa.
I am sorry but your passport is two months out of date.

in stampatello
in capital letters

La prego di compilare questo modulo in stampatello.
Please fill out this form in capital letters.

a b c d e f g h i l m n o p q r s t u v z

lettere minuscole
lowercase letters

I nomi dei mesi si scrivono con l'iniziale minuscola.
The months of the year are written with a lowercase initial letter.

l'inchiostro nero
black ink

Il modulo va compilato con una penna a inchiostro nero.
The form should be filled out using black ink.

Culture note

All main Italian airports are well connected with the city center. The cheapest option when making your way into town is either by bus (*pullman*) or train (*treno*), although not all airports are connected to a train station. Most shuttlebus services will drop you in a central location, usually costing between €5 and €15, depending on the city. Trains run frequently and will take you to the city's main train station, along with a variety of other destinations. Alternatively, taxis are also readily available outside the arrivals terminal, but though they are often a much faster option, they can be quite expensive.

Venice Marco Polo Airport probably boasts the most interesting form of transportation to the city center, offering both water-taxis (*motoscafi*) and water-buses (*vaporetti*) that leave from a dock outside the main terminal and operate all across the Venetian lagoon.

Unit 4 › Lesson 2: *Sorting out travel documents* **4.2**

la matita
pencil

Potresti scrivere a matita il tuo numero di telefono?
Could you write your telephone number in pencil?

la penna
pen

Posso compilare il modulo a penna? O dev'essere battuto a macchina?
Can I fill this form out in pen? Or does it need to be typed?

fare un errore
to make a mistake

Scusi, ho fatto un errore, mi può dare un altro modulo?
Sorry, I've made a mistake, can you give me another form?

correggere
to correct

Il conto è sbagliato, potrebbe correggerlo?
The check is wrong, could you correct it?

Active Italian *Level 4*

5

Lesson 1: Booking a hotel in Rome

» The future tense of *avere* (to have): *avrò*, *avrai*, etc.
» Irregular futures of other verbs: *andrò*, *saprò*, *berrò*, etc.
» About Italian spelling.
» How vowels affect the pronunciation of letters.
» About the letter *k* and the *ch* sound in Italian.
» The subjunctive of *essere*.

Lesson 2: Getting a hotel room in New York

» More on the difference between *sapere* and *conoscere*.
» How to use *fra* and *tra* meaning "between" and "in... time."
» How to use *servire*.
» About adding the suffix *ri-* to a word.
» How to use the pronoun *ciò*.
» The subjunctive of *avere*: *abbia*, etc.

Collins | **Livemocha™**

5.1

Livemocha™ Active Italian *Level 4*

UNIT 5 › LESSON 1
Booking a hotel in Rome

Culture note

Hotels in Italy are rated in the same way as in many other countries: *una stella* (one star) is the lowest, cheapest category and *cinque stelle* (five star) the highest and most expensive. *Pensioni* are usually smaller, often family-run and don't usually offer all the comforts and facilities of a hotel. *Agriturismi* have become more and more popular over the last twenty years or so, but they are usually located outside cities and can sometimes be difficult to access without the use of a car.

Unit 5 › Lesson 1: *Booking a hotel in Rome*

Video Dialog

Michele goes over his flight details and almost everything seems to fit into place.

 Active Italian: Level 4 > Unit 5 > Lesson 1 > Video dialog

Sig.ra Duranti: *Dovrà arrivare all'aeroporto di Fiumicino alle 5.30 del mattino. Vuole che le prenoti una camera in un albergo vicino all'aeroporto?*

Michele: *Sì, buona idea.*

Sig.ra Duranti: *C'è un albergo proprio di fronte al Terminale 3. È molto pratico. Una camera singola?*

Michele: *Sì. Mi può prenotare anche un posto macchina nel parcheggio, per favore?*

Sig.ra Duranti: *Sì, certo, ecco fatto. Una camera singola per la notte del 25 aprile e il volo Roma Fiumicino–New York il 26 aprile con il ritorno il 29 aprile alle 23.35, con l'arrivo a Roma il 30 aprile alle 12.30. Avrà anche tempo di visitare la città e di fare un giro per i negozi.*

Michele: *Perfetto, grazie.*

Mrs. Duranti: You'll have to be at Fiumicino airport at 5:30 in the morning. Do you want me to get you a room in a hotel near the airport?

Michele:	Yes, good idea.
Mrs. Duranti:	There's a hotel right across from Terminal 3. It's very handy. A single room?
Michele:	Yes. Can you reserve me a space in the parking lot, too, please?
Mrs. Duranti:	Yes, certainly, that's it done. A single room for the night of April 25th and the flight Rome Fiumicino–New York on April 26th returning on April 29th at 23:35, getting into Rome on April 30th at 12:30. You will even have time to visit the city and to go around the stores.
Michele:	Perfect, thanks.

Grammar

 Active Italian: Level 4 > Unit 5 > Lesson 1 > Grammar

1 › **Future of *avere* (to have)**

The travel agent tells Michele *Avrà anche tempo di visitare la città* (You will even have time to visit the city). *Avrà* comes from the future tense of *avere* (to have).

Here is the full future tense:

avrò	I will have
avrai	you (*familiar*) will have
avrà	he / she / it will have
avrà	you (*formal*) will have
avremo	we will have
avrete	you (*plural*) will have
avranno	they will have

Unit 5 › Lesson 1: *Booking a hotel in Rome*

2 › **More on futures**

The future endings for all verbs are the same. For *-are* and *-ere* verbs, drop the *-are* and *-ere* endings and add *-erò, -erai, -erà, -eremo, -erete, -eranno*.

For *-ire* verbs, drop the *-ire* ending and add *-irò, -irai, -irà, -iremo, -irete, -iranno*.

There are a few variations on this rule:

For *essere* the stem for the endings is *sar-*: *sarò, sarai* and so on.

For *dare* (to give), *stare* (to be) and *fare* (to do), drop the final "e" and add the future endings: *darò, starò, farò*.

For *andare* (to go), *vedere* (to see), *potere* (to be able to), and *sapere* (to know), drop the *-are* or *-ere* ending: *andrò, vedrò, potrò, saprò*

A final group of verbs drop the final "e" and double the "r": *bere* (to drink) *berrò*, *volere* (to want) *vorrò*, *venire* (to come) *verrò*.

You will find that many of the irregularities in Italian occur because they help to make words flow better in speech.

3 › **Main spelling variations**

Italian is a very regular language with clear rules for both spelling and pronunciation. Most changes occur to word endings. As this can affect how that word is then pronounced, Italian has a number of techniques to ensure that the pronunciation of those words remains the same.

We know that to make nouns ending in -o or -e plural, you generally replace the final letter with an -i: *bambino* becomes *bambini*, *mese* becomes *mesi*.

And with nouns ending in -a, the final -a is replaced with an -e in the plural: *bambina* becomes *bambine*.

In Italian the vowels (a, e, i, o, u) can be split into ones that have a hard effect (*a, o* and *u*) and ones that have a softening effect (*e* and *i*).

4 › Hard vowels: *a, o* and *u*

Problems occur when c and g are involved. Followed by a, o, and u, both c and g have a hard sound: *lago* (lake), *parco* (park), *fungo* (mushroom).

To make these words plural in Italian the endings change to i. However, c followed by i is pronounced *tchee* and g followed by i is pronounced *djee*. To keep the hard sound in the plural, the letter h is inserted: *laghi, parchi, funghi*.

This doesn't just happen at the ends of words; it also occurs in the middle of verbs where endings have been added.

Unit 5 › Lesson 1: *Booking a hotel in Rome*

With *cercare* (to look for), an h has to be inserted with *cerchi* (you look for) and *cerchiamo* (we look for) to keep the hard sound. This occurs throughout the tenses where required.

The same occurs with *pagare* (to pay for); an h is inserted to give *paghi* (you pay for) and *paghiamo* (we pay for). Again, this occurs throughout the tenses where required.

5 › Soft vowels: *e* and *i*

The Italian vowels e and i soften the letters g and c as in *Genova*, *Perugia*, *centro* and *cinema*.
Feminine words ending in *-a* change to *-e* in the plural. If the ending is *-ca* or *-ga*, an h is inserted in the plural to keep the hard sound: *banca* becomes *banche* (banks), *paga* becomes *paghe* (wages).

Note the different pronunciations of *gu* and *giu*:

gusto	taste
giusto	just

Wherever you see spelling changes occur in Italian, try to work out why they occur. In the majority of cases it will be to facilitate the flow of speech and to keep the pronunciation of words uniform.

6 › The letter *k*

The letter *k* does not exist in the Italian alphabet. It is used only to spell foreign words.

The *k* sound in Italian is made by the letter combination *ch*. This is why "kilo" and "kilometer" begin with *ch* in Italian: *un chilo*, *un chilometro*. However, on road signs the k spelling is used for the abbreviation of kilometer (*km*).

In text messages you find that *ki* stands for *chi* and *ke* stands for *che*.

7 › Subjunctive of *essere* (to be)

As *essere* is one of the main irregular verbs, it is worth spending some time learning all its forms.

The subjunctive of *essere* is commonly used in Italian.

sia	I may be
sia	you (*familiar*) may be
sia	he / she / it may be
sia	you (*formal*) may be
siamo	we may be
siate	you (*plural*) may be
siano	they may be

È possibile che il treno sia in ritardo.
It is possible that the train may be late.

Spero che voi siate più fortunate di noi.
I hope that you may be more fortunate than us.

Note that we use "may" in the English above just to show more clearly that the subjunctive tense is being used. It may not be appropriate to always translate it as such.

Unit 5 › Lesson 1: *Booking a hotel in Rome*

Vocabulary

 Active Italian: Level 4 > Unit 5 > Lesson 1 > Vocabulary

una camera singola
a single room

Avete una camera singola con bagno per domani sera?
Do you have a single room with a bathroom for tomorrow night?

una camera doppia
a double room

Avete una camera doppia per tre notti?
Do you have a double room for three nights?

il letto matrimoniale
double bed

Vorremmo una camera con un letto matrimoniale.
We'd like a room with a double bed.

un asciugamano
a towel

Abbiamo bisogno di un altro asciugamano.
We need another towel.

la doccia
shower

La doccia non funziona e l'acqua è fredda.
The shower doesn't work and the water is cold.

la saponetta
bar of soap

Non ci sono saponette in bagno e manca la carta igienica.
There are no soaps in the bathroom nor is there any toilet paper.

sporco/a
dirty

Scusi, può mandare qualcuno a pulire il bagno? È sporco!
Excuse me, can you send someone to clean the bathroom. It's dirty!

pulire
to clean

La camera non è stata pulita oggi.
The room hasn't been cleaned today.

il rumore
noise

C'è molto rumore e non riesco a dormire!
There is a lot of noise and I can't sleep!

compreso/a
included

Scusi, la prima colazione è compresa?
Excuse me, is breakfast included?

Unit 5 › Lesson 1: *Booking a hotel in Rome*

Culture note

Hotel breakfasts in Italy are usually continental buffets, offering a range of cereals, bread, pastries, fruit, and yogurts, along with hot beverages and fruit juice. However, some hotels also offer cooked
breakfasts, including eggs, bacon, and sausages. Many hotels have a self-service drinks machine that automatically prepares the hot beverages, but often if you ask one of the hotel staff on hand, they will be able to prepare you a more traditional drink at the bar, such as an *espresso* or a *cappuccino*.

Alternatively, there are always many bars that cater to the locals where you can enjoy a great, relatively cheap breakfast of coffee and pastries if you don't mind standing up (many bars will charge extra if you choose to sit down). Perhaps the best place to try a traditional Italian breakfast is at a *pasticceria* (a pastry bakery), where all the local pastries are prepared fresh on a daily basis.

UNIT 5 › LESSON 2
Getting a hotel room in New York

Culture note

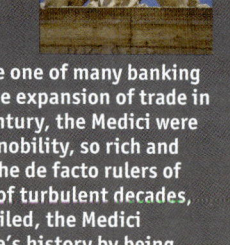

Italy is home to some of the oldest banks in the world, and cities like Florence and Siena are famous for their banking histories. Perhaps the most famous bankers of Italy's past are those of the Florentine Medici family. The Medici were one of many banking families in the city who capitalized on the expansion of trade in the late Middle Ages. By the fifteenth century, the Medici were no longer mere bankers but had become nobility, so rich and powerful that they managed to become the de facto rulers of the Florentine Republic. After a number of turbulent decades, with numerous family members being exiled, the Medici managed to secure their place in Florence's history by being made hereditary Dukes of Florence, remaining in power until well into the eighteenth century.

Unit 5 › Lesson 2: *Getting a hotel room in New York*

Video Dialog

Michele realises that he can't leave the travel agent just yet!

 Active Italian: Level 4 > Unit 5 > Lesson 2 > Video dialog

Sig.ra Duranti:	*Ha prenotato un albergo a New York?*
Michele:	*… No, accidenti…*
Sig.ra Duranti:	*Dove vuole stare a New York?*
Michele:	*Non lo so, non conosco New York.*
Sig.ra Duranti:	*Dov'è il suo appuntamento?*
Michele:	*Vicino a Central Park.*
Sig.ra Duranti:	*Allora, a Manhattan. C'è l'Hotel On The Park… a tre stelle. Completamente rinnovato, vicino a tutte le attrazioni principali, centrale, di fronte a Central Park. Ristorante nelle vicinanze, camere per non-fumatori, 68,70 dollari a notte.*
Michele:	*Non è caro per niente. Qual è la differenza di fuso orario?*
Sig.ra Duranti:	*Sei ore tra Roma e New York.*
Michele:	*Adesso sono le 11, vuol dire che a New York sono le 5 di mattina?*
Sig.ra Duranti:	*Sì. Vuole acquistare dei dollari?*
Michele:	*Quant'è il cambio?*

Sig.ra Duranti:	*1 euro vale 1,41 dollari.*
Michele:	*Mi dia 200 euro in dollari, per favore.*
Sig.ra Duranti:	*Ecco... i biglietti dell'aereo, l'albergo a Fiumicino, il parcheggio, l'albergo a New York, i dollari... È tutto ciò che le serve. Le auguro buon viaggio.*
Michele:	*Grazie, arrivederci.*
Sig.ra Duranti:	*Arriverderci.*

Mrs. Duranti:	Have you booked a hotel in New York?
Michele:	... No, oh darn it...
Mrs. Duranti:	Where do you want to stay in New York?
Michele:	I don't know, I don't know New York.
Mrs. Duranti:	Where is your meeting?
Michele:	Near Central Park.
Mrs. Duranti:	Manhattan then. There's the Hotel On The Park... three stars. Completely renovated, near all the main attractions, centrally situated, facing Central Park. Restaurants nearby, non smoking rooms, $68.70 per night.
Michele:	It's not at all expensive. What is the time difference?
Mrs. Duranti:	Six hours between Rome and New York.
Michele:	It's 11 now, that means in New York it's 5 in the morning.
Mrs. Duranti:	Yes. Do you want to buy some dollars?
Michele:	What is the exchange rate?
Mrs. Duranti:	1.41 dollars to the euro.
Michele:	Give me 200 euros in dollars, please.
Mrs. Duranti:	Here we are... plane tickets, hotel at Fiumicino, parking, hotel in New York, dollars... That's everything you need. Have a good trip.

Michele:	Thank you, goodbye.
Mrs. Duranti:	Goodbye.

Grammar

....

 Active Italian: Level 4 > Unit 5 > Lesson 2 > Grammar

1 › Knowing things and places

Michele says *Non lo so, non conosco New York* (I don't know, I don't know New York).

Do you remember the difference between the two verbs meaning "to know," *sapere* and *conoscere?*

Sapere is to know facts and how to do things:

> *È sposata? Non lo sapevo.*
> Is she married? I didn't know.
>
> *Non so nuotare.*
> I don't know how to swim. / I can't swim.

Conoscere is to know people and places or to be familiar with a book, movie, song, etc:

> *Non consosco Piero. Chi è?*
> I don't know Piero. Who is he?

> *Io abito a Roma. La conosci?*
> I live in Rome. Do you know it?

> *Non conosco La Traviata.*
> I'm not familiar with La Traviata.

2 › **Between places**

In Italian there are two words for "between" – *tra* and *fra* – and they are interchangeable.

Michele asks what the time difference is *tra Roma e New York* (between Rome and New York).

> *Quale preferisci fra limone e cioccolato?*
> Which do you prefer between chocolate and lemon?

Unit 5 › Lesson 2: *Getting a hotel room in New York*

Fra and *tra* can also mean "in" as in "in two days' time": *tra due giorni* or *fra due giorni*.

> *Partiamo fra una settimana.*
> We are leaving in a week's time.

> *Arriva tra un'ora.*
> He is arriving in an hour.

3 › To be of use – *servire*

The tourist officer says *È tutto ciò che le serve* (That's everything you need).

Servire is a useful verb that can be used impersonally to tell someone what you require. If it is just one thing you need, use *serve*. If it is more than one, use *servono*.

Mi serve un coltello.	I need a knife.
Mi servono delle scarpe da ginnastica.	I need some sneakers.
Ci serve una macchina piccola.	We need a small car.

4 › ### The pronoun *ciò*

The pronoun *ciò* means "this" or "that" in general terms, rather than to replace a specific noun. The tourist officer has just handed Michele a whole bunch of items and not one particular thing: *È tutto ciò che le serve* (That's everything you need).

It can also apply to situations or ideas.

> *Tutto ciò è difficile da capire.*
> All that is difficult to understand.

5 › ### The suffix *ri-*

Adding *ri-* to a word implies redoing something or repeating the action.

ridipingere	to repaint
ritelefonare	to phone back
ristampare	to reprint
riscrivere	to rewrite
rileggere	to reread
rivedere	to see again

Unit 5 › Lesson 2: *Getting a hotel room in New York*

6 › Subjunctive of *avere* (to have)

Avere is a verb worth learning in all its forms. This is the subjunctive.

abbia	I may have
abbia	you (*familiar*) may have
abbia	he / she / it may have
abbia	you (*formal*) may have
abbiamo	we may have
abbiate	you (*plural*) may have
abbiano	they may have

È possibile che il tuo cane abbia fame?
Is it possible that your dog may be hungry?

Speriamo che Carla non abbia ragione.
Let's hope that Carla may not be right.

Culture note

Today the euro is the currency used in Italy, having officially replaced the lira in 2002. The symbol used for the euro is €, and is divided into *centesimi*, cents, indicated by a c. The € and c symbols usually follows the numerical value of an item like this: 10.00€ or 99c. Coins are available in 2€, 1€, 50c, 20c, 10c, 5c, 2c and 1c denominations, whereas notes are available in 500€, 200€, 100€, 50€, 20€, 10€ and 5€ denominations.

The 1€ and 2€ coins' colors and size are the same across Europe. However, every country that uses the Euro has an individual design on one side of the coin that usually represents an aspect of the respective country's culture. In Italy, the 1€ coin shows the image of da Vinci's "Vitruvian Man", whereaas the 2€ coin has the profile of Dante Alighieri embossed upon it.

Vocabulary

 Active Italian: Level 4 > Unit 5 > Lesson 2 > Vocabulary

il bancomat
ATM, cash machine

Scusi, c'è un bancomat qui vicino?
Excuse me, is there an ATM nearby?

lo sportello
counter, desk

C'è una lunga fila a questo sportello.
There is a long line at this desk.

il cambio
exchange rate

A quant'è il cambio con il dollaro oggi?
What is the exchange rate for dollars today?

in contanti
in cash

Se pago in contanti posso avere uno sconto?
If I pay in cash can I get a discount?

un assegno
a check

A chi intesto l'assegno?
Who do I make the check payable to?

Unit 5 › Lesson 2: *Getting a hotel room in New York*

il codice segreto
PIN (number)

La prego di digitare il codice segreto.
Please key in your PIN.

selezionare
to select

Selezioni quello che desidera.
Select the one that you want.

fuori servizio
out of order

Il distributore di benzina è fuori servizio.
The gas pump is out of order.

l'importo
amount

La prego di accreditare l'importo che mi deve sul mio conto corrente.
Please credit the amount that you owe me to my checking account.

lo scontrino
receipt

Vada al banco con lo scontrino per il suo caffè.
Go to the counter with your receipt to get your coffee.

l'IVA
sales tax

Scusi, l'IVA è compresa nel conto?
Excuse me, is sales tax included in the bill?

Active Italian *Level 4*

6

Lesson 1: Saying farewell

- » Key points about agreement.
- » About all the different meanings of short words.
- » The past tense of reflexive verbs.
- » The past tense of impersonal verbs.

Lesson 2: Have a good trip, Michele!

- » How to give your e-mail address.
- » About Italian text messages.
- » About object pronouns and where they are placed.
- » Combining object pronouns: *glielo*, *gliela*, etc.
- » Verbs that take *essere*: *andare*, *venire*, etc.

Collins | **Livemocha™**

UNIT 6 › LESSON 1
Saying farewell

Culture note

Most people in Italy now own a cell phone. There are various network operators that can sell you a pay-as-you-go SIM card if you need an Italian phone number, and top-up cards for pay-as-you-go phones are sold in most *tabacchi* shops. A top-up card is called *una ricarica*, and they are usually sold with values between €5 and €50.

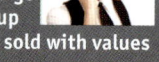

Bear in mind that in order to use an Italian SIM card, you will need an "unlocked" handset, meaning that the cell phone is not tied to any one operator. Handsets in Italy are usually sold "unlocked," however, and simple models can be bought relatively cheaply.

Unit 6 › Lesson 1: *Saying farewell*

Video Dialog

While they wait for Giulia to join them, Lucia, Ugo, and Michele chat about Michele's trip to New York.

 Active Italian: Level 4 > Unit 6 > Lesson 1 > Video dialog

Lucia:	*Buona sera, Michele.*
Michele:	*Ciao, Lucia, buona sera, Ugo.*
Ugo:	*Buona sera.*
Michele:	*Non c'è ancora Giulia?*
Lucia:	*No, mi ha mandato un sms, ha perso l'autobus.*
Ugo:	*E allora tu vai negli Stati Uniti?*
Michele:	*Sì. Tu ci sei mai stato?*
Ugo:	*Sì, ci sono andato due anni fa.*
Michele:	*E tu, Lucia?*
Lucia:	*Non ci sono mai stata ma mi piacerebbe molto andarci.*
Ugo:	*Quando parti?*
Michele:	*Domani.*
Lucia:	*Hai preparato la valigia?*
Michele:	*Sì, penso di aver fatto tutto…*

Lucia: Good evening, Michele.

6.1 Livemocha™ Active Italian *Level 4*

Michele:	Hi, Lucia. Good evening, Ugo.
Ugo:	Good evening.
Michele:	Isn't Giulia here yet?
Lucia:	No, she texted me, she missed the bus.
Ugo:	So you're off to the States?
Michele:	Yes. Have you ever been?
Ugo:	Yes. I went two years ago.
Michele:	And you, Lucia?
Lucia:	I've never been but I would love to go.
Ugo:	When are you off?
Michele:	Tomorrow.
Lucia:	Have you packed?
Michele:	Yes, I think I have done everything…

Grammar

  Active Italian: Level 4 > Unit 6 > Lesson 1 > Grammar

1 › **Agreement of adjectives: Key points**

Wherever the verb *essere* is used there is agreement:

> *Luisa è content**a**.*
> *I genitori di Max sono gentil**i**.*
> *Noi siamo molto stanch**i**.*

Unit 6 › Lesson 1: *Saying farewell*

Whenever there is a mix of genders (whether among people or things), the masculine ending is always used.

> *Pietro e Sara sono i miei cugini italiani e sono simpaticissimi.*

2 › **Don't jump to conclusions**

Gli zii may not just mean uncles. It is just as likely to be an aunt and an uncle. The same is true for *i nonni* (grandparents).

> *Quanti fratelli hai?*
> How many brothers and sisters do you have?

Tre figli doesn't necessarily mean there are only three sons. It may include a daughter or two.

There are a few nouns that are always feminine even when referring to a man:

| *la vittima* | victim |
| *la persona* | person |

3 › ### The past tense of impersonal verbs

Most impersonal verbs form the past tense with *essere*. These include:

Piacere *(piaciuto)* to please

> *Mi è piaciuta tanto la visita a New York.*
> I really liked my visit to New York.

Succedere *(successo)* to happen

> *Cos'è successo durante il viaggio?*
> What happened during the trip?

Costare *(costato)* to cost

> *Il biglietto d'aereo mi è costato parecchio.*
> The plane ticket cost me quite a lot.

Volerci *(voluto)* to take, to be needed

> *Ci sono voluti due giorni per arrivarci.*
> It took two days to get there.

Unit 6 › Lesson 1: *Saying farewell*

4 › The past tense of reflexive verbs

All reflexive verbs form the perfect tense with *essere*.

Fermarsi (to stop, to stay)

mi sono fermato/a	I stayed
ti sei fermato/a	you (*familiar*) stayed
si è fermato/a	he / she / it stayed
si è fermato/a	you (*formal*) stayed
ci siamo fermati(e)	we stayed
vi siete fermati(e)	you (*plural*) stayed
si sono fermati(e)	they stayed

Per quanto tempo ti sei fermato a New York?	How long did you stay in New York?
Quanto tempo ti sei fermato?	How long did you stay?

When using the *lei* form, the past participle agrees with the gender of the person you are addressing.

> *Signor Bianchi, per quanto tempo si è fermato a Lugano?*
>
> Mr. Bianchi, how long did you stay in Lugano?

6.1 Livemocha™ Active Italian Level 4

5 › **Beware short words with different meanings**

Remember that short words can often have many meanings. Let's look at the word *le*.

le

1. plural of the article *la*: **le** *bambine* the girls
2. to her: *Dov'è Tina?* **Le** *devo dare un libro.* Where is Tina? I have to give her a book.
3. to you (when referring to formal *lei*): *Posso dar**le** una mano?* Can I give you a hand?
4. them: *Che belle scarpe! Posso provar**le**?* What nice shoes! Can I try them on?

Now take a word like *gli* and see how many different meanings you can find for it.

Vocabulary

Active Italian: Level 4 > Unit 6 > Lesson 1 > Vocabulary

voler bene a
to love

John vuole veramente bene a Luciana.
John loves Luciana very much.

beneducato/a
polite

È piacevole incontrare dei ragazzi beneducati.
It is pleasant to meet polite young people.

Unit 6 › Lesson 1: *Saying farewell* **6.1**

innamorarsi
to fall in love

Mario è un tipo che s'innamora facilmente.
Mario is the type of person who falls in love easily.

lasciarsi
to break up

Silvio e Maria si sono lasciati all'improvviso.
Silvio and Maria broke up suddenly.

il fidanzato/la fidanzata
fiancé/fiancée

Il fidanzato di Elena è veramente un ragazzo in gamba.
Elena's fiancé is a very capable young man.

uscire con
to go out with

Mary esce con Lucio da anni, si vogliono proprio bene.
Mary has been going out with Lucio for years. They really love each other.

baciare
to kiss

Quando ci incontriamo ci baciamo e abbracciamo.
When we meet we kiss and hug.

salutare
to say hello to

Quando vedi i tuoi salutameli.
When you see your parents, say hello to them for me.

un appuntamento
a date

Domani ho un appuntamento con Elena.
Tomorrow I have a date with Elena.

litigare
to quarrel, to have a disagreement

Matteo e Alessia hanno litigato, non si frequentano più.
Matteo and Alessia have quarreled. They aren't seeing each other any more.

UNIT 6 › LESSON 2
Have a good trip, Michele!

Culture note

Here are a few set phrases that are used in various social situations in Italy:

Buon viaggio! Have a good trip!
Buon appetito! Enjoy your meal!
Cin cin/Salute! Cheers! (when toasting your drink)
In bocca al lupo! Good luck (to which you should respond *Crepi!*)
Tanti auguri! Happy birthday!
Buon anniversario! Happy anniversary!
Auguri! Congratulations!
Buon Natale! Merry Christmas!
Buona Pasqua Happy Easter
Buon finesettimana! Have a good weekend!
Buona serata! Have a nice evening!

Livemocha™ Active Italian Level 4

Video Dialog

The friends exchange contact details, order drinks, and enjoy each other's company.

Active Italian: Level 4 > Unit 6 > Lesson 2 > Video dialog

Giulia:	*Scusate il ritardo... ho perso l'autobus.*
Ugo:	*Non fa niente.*
Lucia:	*Mi devi mandare una cartolina con la Statua della Libertà.*
Michele:	*Dammi il tuo indirizzo.*
Ugo:	*Qual è il tuo numero di cellulare?*
Michele:	*È 347*
Ugo:	*347*
Michele:	*653*
Ugo:	*653*
Michele:	*12*
Ugo:	*12*
Michele:	*34.*
Ugo:	*34.*
Michele:	*E ti do anche il mio indirzzo e-mail: Michele18photos@libero.it*
Ugo:	*Allora, buon viaggio, Michele!*
Giulia:	*Buon viaggio!*
Lucia:	*Salute!*

Unit 6 › Lesson 2: *Have a good trip, Michele!*

Michele:	*Salute!*
Giulia:	*Salute!*

....

Giulia:	Sorry I'm late… I missed the bus.
Ugo:	It doesn't matter.
Lucia:	You must send me a postcard of the Statue of Liberty.
Michele:	Give me your address.
Ugo:	What's your cell phone number?
Michele:	It's 347
Ugo:	347
Michele:	653
Ugo:	653
Michele:	12
Ugo:	12
Michele:	34.
Ugo:	34.
Michele:	And I'll give you my email address as well: Michele18photos@libero.it
Ugo:	Well, have a good trip, Michele.
Giulia:	Enjoy your trip!
Lucia:	Cheers!
Michele:	Cheers!
Giulia:	Cheers!

Grammar

....

 Active Italian: Level 4 > Unit 6 > Lesson 2 > Grammar

1 › **Giving your e-mail**

When giving your e-mail address you can begin:
La mia mail è… (My e-mail is…) or *Il mio indirizzo e-mail è…* (My e-mail address is…) followed by the e-mail address.

Key words include:

chiocciola	at (@)
punto	dot (.)
trattino	hyphen (-)
trattino basso	underscore (_)

So an address could be *marco punto bianchi chiocciola libero punto it* (marco.bianchi@libero.it)

2 › Texting

It is also worth learning some of the most common abbreviations used in Italian texting. The list below provides some of these abbreviations, along with the words they correspond to.

a dp = *a dopo*	c u later
cm = *come*	how, as
cn = *con*	with
cs = *cosa*	what
xk = *perché*	why, because
xò = *però*	however

x = per	for
xsn = persona	person
ki = chi	who
ke = che	what, that
bn = bene	well
tnt = tanto	so, so much
nn = non	not
nnt = niente	nothing
qnd = quando	when
qst = questo	this
qll = quello	that
sn = sono	I am, they are
6 = sei	you are
qlcs = qualcosa	something
dv = dove	where
grz = grazie	thanks
tvttb = ti voglio tanto tanto bene	I like / love you very much
+ = più	more
− = meno	less

3 › ### Give me – *Dammi*

In Italian, nouns are very frequently replaced with pronouns to avoid clumsy repetition.

In many cases the pronoun is attached to a part of the verb. Michele says *Dammi il tuo indirizzo* (Give me your address). *Da'* is the verb and *mi* has been attached. Note how an extra letter m has been inserted, making it easier to say.

Often the pronoun is attached to the infinitive.

> *Puoi darmi il tuo indirizzo?*
> Can you give me your address?

Let's see what happens if we go on to ask the same thing using just pronouns.

> *Puoi darmelo?*
> Can you give it to me?

Note how *mi* has changed to *me*.

Unit 6 › Lesson 2: *Have a good trip, Michele!*

4 › Indirect object pronouns

Direct object pronouns are

me	me
te	you
la	you using the *lei* form
lo	him / it
la	her / it
ci	us
vi	you *plural*
li	them *masculine*
le	them *feminine*

Indirect object pronouns are:

mi	to me	**me** before an object pronoun
ti	to you	**te** before an object pronoun
le	to you: using *lei*	**glie-** before an object pronoun
gli	to him / it	**glie-** before an object pronoun
le	to her / it	**glie-** before an object pronoun
ci	to us	**ce** before an object pronoun
vi	to you *plural*	**ve** before an object pronoun
gli / loro	to them	**glie-** before an object pronoun

If the two types of pronoun appear together in a sentence, then the indirect pronoun (to me, to you, etc.) goes first and changes spelling.

Me lo dai?	Will you give it to me?
Perché non **glielo** dai?	Why don't you give it to him (or to her, or to you, or to them).
La mail? **Ce la** mandate domani?	The e-mail? Will you send it to us tomorrow?

5 › Verbs that take *essere*

Remember that the following verbs usually take *essere* as the auxiliary verb and therefore the past participle must agree with the subject of the verb.

andare (andato)	to go
arrivare (arrivato)	to arrive
cadere (caduto)	to fall
entrare (entrato)	to enter
essere (stato)	to be
morire (morto)	to die
crescere (cresciuto)	to grow up
diventare (diventato)	to become
nascere (nato)	to be born

Unit 6 › Lesson 2: *Have a good trip, Michele!*

6 › More verbs that take *essere*

Note how many of the verbs that take *essere* are to do with movement, either of oneself or a vehicle:

partire (partito)	to leave
restare (restato)	to stay, to remain
rimanere (rimasto)	to stay, to remain
salire (salito)	to go up, to get on (a bus)
scendere (sceso)	to go down
stare (stato)	to be, to stay
tornare (tornato)	to return
uscire (uscito)	to go out
venire (venuto)	to come

7 › More on the subjunctive

Normally the subjunctive is used after expressions of doubt and fear. However, look at the following sentence:

*Ho paura di **perdere** il volo.*
I am afraid of missing my flight.

Livemocha™ Active Italian *Level 4*

Did you notice that the infinitive of the verb is used, not the subjunctive? This is because the person who is afraid is the same person who would miss the flight: that is, the subject of each part of the sentence is the same.

If you were afraid on someone's behalf, the subjunctive and *che* (rather than *di*) would be used.

*Ho paura **che tu perda** il volo.*	I am afraid that you may miss your flight.
*Max ha paura **di perdere** il treno.*	Max is afraid of missing the train.
*Max ha paura **che sua madre perda** il treno.*	Max is afraid that his mother may miss the train.

Vocabulary

Active Italian: Level 4 > Unit 6 > Lesson 2 > Vocabulary

mandare
to send

Mandami un sms appena puoi.
Send me a text as soon as you can.

un sms
a text

Non è facile capire i suoi sms!
It's not easy to understand his texts!

Unit 6 › Lesson 2: *Have a good trip, Michele!*

una scheda telefonica
a phonecard

Ha schede telefoniche?
Do you have any phonecards?

il francobollo
stamp

Ho bisogno di un francobollo per questa lettera.
I need a stamp for this letter.

tenersi in contatto
to keep in touch

Mi raccomando, teniamoci in contatto.
Let's be sure to keep in touch.

via email
by e-mail

Ti manderò notizie via email.
I will send you news by e-mail.

l'indirizzo di casa
home address

Mi fai sapere il tuo nuovo indirizzo di casa?
Can you let me know your new home address?

scrivere
to write

Non dimenticare di scrivermi una lettera.
Don't forget to write me a letter.

ritornare
to return, to come / go back

Quando ritorni in Italia?
When are you coming back to Italy?

farsi molti amici
to make lots of friends

Quando ero a Firenze mi sono fatta molti amici.
When I was in Florence I made lots of friends.

un buon ricordo
happy memories

Ho un buon ricordo delle vacanze trascorse ad Ischia.
I have happy memories of the vacations I spent at Ischia.

Buon viaggio!
Have a good trip!

Ti auguro buon viaggio.
I wish you a good trip.